Italian

THE COLLOQUIAL SERIES
Series Adviser: Gary King

The following languages are available in the Colloquial series:

Afrikaans	French	Portuguese of Brazil
Albanian	German	Romanian
Amharic	Greek	Russian
Arabic (Levantine)	Gujarati	Scottish Gaelic
Arabic of Egypt	Hebrew	Serbian
Arabic of the Gulf and	Hindi	Slovak
Saudi Arabia	Hungarian	Slovene
Basque	Icelandic	Somali
Breton	Indonesian	Spanish
Bulgarian	Irish (forthcoming)	Spanish of Latin
Cambodian	Italian	America
Cantonese	Japanese	Swahili
Catalan	Korean	Swedish
Chinese	Latvian	Tamil
Croatian	Lithuanian	Thai
Czech	Malay	Turkish
Danish	Mongolian	Ukrainian
Dutch	Norwegian	Urdu
English	Panjabi	Vietnamese
Estonian	Persian	Welsh
Filipino	Polish	Yoruba (forthcoming)
Finnish	Portuguese	

COLLOQUIAL 2s series: *The Next Step in Language Learning*

Chinese	German (forthcoming)	Spanish
Dutch	Italian	Spanish of Latin
French	Russian	America

All these Colloquials are available in book & CD packs, or separately. You can order them through your bookseller or via our website www.routledge.com.

Colloquial
Italian

The Complete Course for Beginners

Sylvia Lymbery

 Routledge
Taylor & Francis Group

LONDON AND NEW YORK

First published 1996 by Routledge
Reprinted 1998, 1999 (twice), 2000, 2001

Second edition published 2005
by Routledge
2 Park Square, Milton Park, Abingdon Oxon OX14 4RN

Simultaneously published in the USA and Canada
by Routledge
270 Madison Ave, New York, NY 10016

Reprinted 2007

*Routledge is an imprint of the Taylor & Francis Group,
an informa business*

© 2005 Sylvia Lymbery

Typeset in Times by
Florence Production Ltd, Stoodleigh, Devon
Printed and bound in Great Britain by
TJ International Ltd, Padstow, Cornwall

British Library Cataloguing in Publication Data
A catalogue record for this book is available from the
British Library

Library of Congress Cataloging in Publication Data
Lymbery, Sylvia.
   Colloquial Italian: the complete course for beginners/
Sylvia Lymbery. – 2nd edn.
       p. cm – (The colloquial series)
    Includes index.
      1. Italian language – Conversation and phrase books –
English. 2. Italian language – Textbooks for foreign
speakers – English.   3. Italian language – Spoken Italian.
   I. Title. II. Series
     PC1121.L95   2005
     458.3'421 – dc22   2004024087

ISBN 978–0–415–36271–9 (pack)
ISBN 978–0–415–36268–9 (book)
ISBN 978–0–415–36270–2 (CD)

This book is dedicated to
Charlotte

Contents

Acknowledgments

I would like to offer my warmest thanks to the many friends who helped me when I was writing *Colloquial Italian*. In particular, to Angioletta Viviani, whose hospitality and advice helped me start to prepare this new edition, and to Sandra Silipo for help and advice. Others too numerous to list have helped in various ways, and their support is very much appreciated. Thanks must also go to Antonio Ravarino for his plan and architectural drawings.

I am also grateful to: the Editor of *La Stampa*, Torino, for permission to reproduce a weather forecast; to *La Stampa* and Lietta Tornabuoni for permission to use parts of her article, *Italia 1945–1995 Con gli occhi aperti*; the Editor and editorial staff of *Vera* magazine for permission to reproduce parts of the article *Per le vie dei borghi doc* from the March 2003 issue; Bernardo Cioni and Lorenzo Enriques of Zanichelli Editore for permission to reproduce Dott. Cioni's email; the Mayor of Apricale for permission to reproduce the photo of Apricale from the town's website: www.apricale.org; Bologna Turismo – Redazione IAT for permission to reproduce the photos of the Palazzo del Podestà in Piazza Maggiore and of the fruit and vegetable shop in the Mercato Antico; the IAT of Perugia for permission to reproduce the photo of the Palazzo dei Priori and the Fontana Maggiore; the Azienda di Promozione Turistica di Roma for permission to reproduce the photos of the Campidoglio and of the Vittoriano; Suzanne Cousin for the photograph of Santa Maria Novella, Florence; the Servizi Turistico-Ricreativi department of the Province of Verona for permission to reproduce the photo of the Roman Arena; the Comando Generale dell'Arma dei Carabinieri for permission to reproduce the photo of a carabiniere at work.

And finally my thanks go to Sophie Oliver and her helpful team at Routledge.

Permission to use the extract 'Il mio primo computer: Il pc ideale per un bambino?' from *Anna* magazine was sought but no reply received.

Italy: regions and regional capitals

About this book

So you are thinking of learning Italian? Or perhaps you are already learning and want another approach to help you on your way? Read on and you will see why *Colloquial Italian* could be just what you are looking for.

Why Italian?

Italian is the language of Italy and it is also one of the four official languages of Switzerland. With a population of some 58 million and an area of 301,323 sq km, Italy is a small country; but for more than two thousand years its inhabitants have had significant effects on civilization, while the land of Italy has for centuries been a source of pleasure and interest to travellers. Today it continues to offer the tourist many and varied delights: scenery, artistic treasures, music, good food and wine, snow, sun and sea. The Italian Republic is one of the founder members of the European Union and for businesses Italy offers both opportunities and challenges.

There *are* problems of a political, economic and environmental nature that may frustrate and annoy the traveller but overall Italy is a very welcoming country and a fascinating subject of study.

The language is arguably the easiest European language for English speakers to learn. The pronunciation seems easier than French for English speakers, the grammar less tricky than that of German or Russian. Furthermore, the spelling of the language reflects the way words are said and the meanings of many of the words are guessable.

Italian has its origins in Latin, the language spoken in Ancient Rome. For anyone who has studied Latin or one of the Romance languages (languages derived closely from Latin such as Spanish, French or Portuguese), it is particularly approachable, for not only will many more words be guessable but the structure too will be similar to that of the language they know. This is not to say it is trouble free, but you, the learner, can feel optimistic as you start the task.

As a nation-state Italy is young. It was united between 1860 and 1870 after centuries of division into a number of smaller states. At the time of unification Italian was essentially a written language used by poets, playwrights and other writers. Only a small percentage of the population spoke it. Most communicated in their local dialect. Today universal education, military service, population mobility and television and radio mean that most Italians speak and understand Italian although many also continue to speak their local dialect.

Colloquial Italian

The aim has been to write a book in which the learner, who may not have experience of learning foreign languages, is helped with the difficulties, particularly in the early and potentially confusing stages. At the same time we have tried not to insult the learner's intelligence. As has been said, many Italian words are guessable and we have deliberately challenged the learner by introducing a wide vocabulary, confident that he/she will find it manageable. We have tried, too, to entertain and stimulate.

As a language learner you need to be aware that different people learn languages in different ways. Try to find the way that works for you. There are few people who can sit down with a grammar book, read the rules, do some exercises and start speaking the language. Many people find it helpful to become familiar with chunks of language, for instance the dialogues and texts in *Colloquial Italian.* Listen to the recordings and try to get to know them well; go back over them after a break, too, brushing up your memory. Why not listen to the recordings in your car while you sit in a traffic jam? Or while you are doing something that does not engage your mind? Gradually you will find you can start to express yourself in Italian. You can also try talking to yourself in Italian, again in idle moments. It doesn't matter that you may not always get it right. It is the *practice* in trying to find a way of saying what you want to in Italian that helps.

Learning a language takes patience and determination. You will have your ups and downs, your moments of frustration but moments of satisfaction too. We recommend you try a 'little and often' routine: work at your Italian regularly but not necessarily for long periods of time.

Many people find it helpful to back up their learning in every way available to them: exchanging a few words with a friendly waiter in an Italian restaurant, or watching Italian films. Treat yourself to an Italian magazine or newspaper occasionally. The biggest aid of all is a trip to Italy. Don't, however, expect too much from the first visit. Much will depend on the extent to which you are able to be with Italians and 'have a go'. 'Having a go' is probably the key to success. But beware: you will always understand more than you can say. Make the most of each opportunity and above all don't worry about making mistakes. Italians are usually delighted when foreigners try to speak their language. We can almost guarantee they won't laugh at you.

Getting started

You almost certainly already know a number of Italian words. Stop reading and write down those that come into your mind. Add to your list the names of places in Italy or of famous Italians that come to mind.

Did your list include greetings such as **ciao, arrivederci**? Or perhaps words relating to food and drink such as: **pasta, spaghetti, pesto, pizza, ciabatta, gelato, vino, cappuccino, gorgonzola, Chianti, Asti spumante.** You know words related to music such as: **orchestra, cello, piccolo, pianoforte, solo, soprano, aria.** Or words such as: **chiaroscuro, fresco, ghetto, piazza, viva voce.***

How about the names of people and places? Did you have **Armani, Dolce e Gabbana, Gucci, Versace**? Or **Giotto, Botticelli, Piero della Francesca**? Or maybe **Vivaldi, Puccini, Verdi, Palestrina.** Or again **Maserati, Ferrari, Lamborghini, Fiat, Lancia,** or **Romano Prodi, Roberto Benigni, Andrea Bocelli, Cecilia Bartoli,** ... Oh, we nearly forgot **Luciano Pavarotti**! Or perhaps you had some other words or names. It all depends on your own personal interests. Place names are often anglicized: Rome, Venice, Milan, Florence, Tuscany, Sicily ... but you may know **Palermo, Cattolica, Rimini, Como, Garda, Brindisi** ...

---

* See p. xviii for an explanation of the use of underlining in this book to indicate stress.

So you see you already have an idea of how Italian looks and sounds. One immediately noticeable feature is that words mostly end with vowels. You will gradually learn that these final vowels often carry meaning. Italian is an *inflected* language. This means the endings of words vary to express grammatical information. To a certain extent this happens in English: 'book/books', where the 's' expresses the plural. It is more developed in Italian but you, the learner, should not worry too much: in the heat of a conversation, if you are unsure, your meaning will usually be clear even if you slur the word ending to cover your uncertainty. Gradually, with practice, this aspect of the language slots into place.

So, you're ready to go.

Good luck! **In bocca al lupo!**

The sounds
of Italian 🎧

What follows does not pretend to be a full treatment of Italian pronunciation but rather a practical guide to help the foreign learner speak in a way that is reasonably comprehensible and acceptable. It should also be viewed as a reference section, which will be difficult to absorb in one reading but can be returned to from time to time. There is also help in the matching section of the recording that accompanies *Colloquial Italian*.

Italian spelling reflects the sounds of the Italian language on a more direct basis than English spelling does for English. There are however some cases where the spelling conventions of Italian conflict with those of English and it is important that students get these clear in their mind from the start.

Two consecutive vowels

Two vowels next to each other are each pronounced, rather than run into each other as in English. For example, the Italian unit of currency is **un *euro***, in which, in contrast to English, the 'eu' is pronounced as two separate sounds. Similarly:

p*au*ra b*uo*no p*ae*se *ae*reo l*ui* l*ei*

Double consonants

When a word is spelled with a double consonant, it is because the sound is different from the same consonant written as a single letter. It takes practice to get this right but it is important. Try to linger on the double consonant or pause before it. The preceding vowel becomes shorter: Listen to the difference:

**pena/penna steso/stesso fata/fatta
eco/ecco**

Here are some more words with double consonants:

> **freddo   bello   mamma   anno   cappuccino**
> **terra   stesso   pazzo   nonno**

'r' in Italian

The Italian **r** is rolled with the tongue. There is no real English equivalent. The letter appears only when the r is pronounced: **porta**, **arte**. Note the difference between **cane** 'dog' and **carne** 'meat'. Some Italians make their **r** in their throats but it is always audible and more prominent than in standard English.

And when there is double **rr** in the spelling, there are two **r**s in the sound. Try these:

at the beginning of a word:	**riso**	**Roma**	**Rialto**	**ragazzo**
between two vowels:	**ora**	**caro**	**durare**	**Torino**
double r:	**birra**	**ferro**	**terra**	**burro**
after another consonant:	**prima**	**crollo**	**dramma**	
before another consonant:	**arte**	**porta**	**ormai**	**urlo**

So far, so good. The remaining sounds are, however, those where the spelling conventions of English and Italian differ significantly and learners should pay particular attention to them. Using the recordings and imitating them throughout the course will also help you avoid errors.

The spellings gn, gli

These spellings represent sounds that are a little difficult to pronounce:

> **gn**   is similar to the sound in the middle of o*n*ion
>
> **giu*gn*o**   **ba*gn*o**   **a*gn*ello**
>
> **gl(i)**   is a little like the sound in the middle of mi*ll*ion:
>
> **lu*gl*io**   **fi*gl*io**   **ma*gl*ia**   ***gl*i**

The sounds k and g (as in 'come' and 'go') and ch and j (as in 'church' and 'judge')

With the sounds **k** (as in 'come' in English) and **g** (as in 'go') there is no pronunciation problem, but the spelling *depends on which vowel follows*. The vowels divide into two groups:

1 If the vowel following **k** or **g** is **a, o, u**:

    k is written 'c'   **cane, campo, caffè, casa, cosa, costa, come, Como, curioso, cuore, cultura**

    g is written 'g'   **galleria, gamba, gallese, Garda, gondola, gorgonzola, Goldoni, Gonzaga, guidare, guardare, Gubbio, Guttuso**

2 If the vowel following **k** or **g** is **e, i**:

    k is written 'ch'   **che, orchestra, bruschetta, chi, chilo, Cherubino, Michelangelo, Chianti, Chiusi, Chioggia**

    g is written 'gh'   **ghetto, spaghetti, Ghirlandaio, Lamborghini**

The same grouping of vowels is also important in the spelling conventions for the sound pairs **ch** (as in 'church') and **j** (as in 'judge')

1 If the vowel following **ch** or **j** is **a, o, u**:

    ch is written 'ci'   **ciao, ciò, Luciano, Lancia**

    j is written 'gi'   **giapponese, giallo, giorno, giovedì, giù, giusto, Giulia, Giuseppe**

2 If the vowel following **ch** or **j** is **e, i**:

    ch is written 'c'   **cento, cena, certo, violoncello, San Francesco, Botticelli, cibo, cinema, cappuccino, Puccini**

    j is written 'g'   **gente, generalmente, gelato, geografia, gita, girare, Gino, Gilda**

The sound sh

Finally the spelling of the sound **sh** (as in 'shoe'):

1 followed by **a, o, u** it is written 'sci':

    sciarpa, sciopero, sciupare

2 followed by **e** or **i** it is written just 'sc':

    scendere, pesce, sci, Gramsci

Stress

The most common place for an Italian word to be stressed is on the syllable before the last (the *penultimate* syllable, as underlined):

itali̱ano   aeropo̱rto   interessa̱nte   il mo̱ndo mode̱rno
la stazio̱ne de̱lla ferrovi̱a

Some words are stressed on the *final* vowel. In that case the vowel is written with an accent:

cittа̱   possibilitа̱   perciо̱   tivὺ

The most problematic words for the foreign learner are those where the *antepenultimate* (the third from the end) syllable is stressed:

sa̱bato   dome̱nica   a̱lbero   ci̱nema   chilo̱metro   le̱ttera
li̱bero   ma̱cchina   me̱dico   tele̱fono

There is no rule for this. Certain types of words, e.g. adjectives ending in **-a̱tico** (**simpa̱tico**, **democra̱tico**) or in **-a̱bile** (**proba̱bile**, **ama̱bile**) always have the stress on the antepenultimate syllable.

Occasionally, for instance, the stress may fall on the *fourth* syllable from the end: this occurs in the third person plural of some verbs, e.g. **tele̱fonano**.

Dictionaries give help with stress and so does our 'Italian–English glossary' (pp. 303–36), where underlining shows unusual stress. Stress is also indicated in this way in the pronunciation section of the book and in verb tables, etc. But in print or in writing, it is not normally indicated. The best you can do is *listen* to Italians speaking and try to build up a sound memory. However, stress *is* important. The wrong stress is more likely to obscure your meaning than a generally not very Italian-sounding accent.

Related to stress is *intonation*, the 'tune of the phrase'. This is also best acquired by imitation and should not constitute a big problem.

The Italian alphabet

The Italian language uses an alphabet of twenty-one letters. The other letters of our familiar twenty-six-letter alphabet are used in writing foreign words. When spelling something out for someone, especially over the telephone, it is usual to use the names of towns to make the letter clear (as shown in the following list). Below is a list of letters, with their pronunciations and the town name usually used:

a	*a*	Ancona	m	*emme*	Milano
b	*bi*	Bologna/Bari	n	*enne*	Napoli
c	*ci*	Como	o	*o*	Otranto
d	*di*	Domodossola	p	*pi*	Pisa
e	*e*	Empoli	q	*cu*	cu
f	*effe*	Firenze	r	*erre*	Roma
g	*gi*	Genova	s	*esse*	Savona
h	*acca*	hotel	t	*ti*	Torino
i	*i*	Imola	u	*u*	Udine
l	*elle*	Livorno	v	*vi/vu*	Venezia
			z	*zeta*	Zara

The following are not considered Italian letters and are used mainly in foreign words:

j	*i lungo/a*		x	*ics*
k	*cappa*		y	*i greco/a, ipsilon*
w	*vi/vu doppio/a*			

Examples of how a name can be spelt out, especially over the telephone:

Roma, Otranto, Savona, Savona, Imola = *Rossi*

Savona, Milano, Imola, Torino, hotel = *Smith*

Livorno, i greco, Milano, Bologna, Empoli, Roma, i greco
= *Lymbery*

The letters are considered either masculine or feminine: some people will say **i greca** rather than **i greco**. They are not usually made plural, so **ss** is **due esse**; also **doppio esse** or **doppia esse**.

Accents

An accent is used to indicate the stress when it falls on the final vowel of a word. There is some discussion in Italy about using acute (´) or grave (`) accents, particularly over the letter **e**, where some people like to show an open **e**/closed **e** distinction. In practice, when writing, Italians write something that could be either: ⌣. You are advised to do the same.

In a very few cases an accent is used to distinguish one word from another:

e	and	**è**	is
da	from	**dà**	gives
ne	of it, of them etc.	**nè**	neither, nor
si	oneself	**sì**	yes
se	if	**sè**	oneself, himself, herself (reflexive pronoun, strong form)
la	the (also a pronoun)	**là**	there
li	(pronoun)	**lì**	there

Did you find all this difficult to absorb? Of course you did. Don't worry, it will gradually make sense. And don't forget to use the 'Sounds of Italian' section on the recording.

1 Buongiorno, un caffè per favore

Good morning, a coffee please

In this unit you will learn about:

- Ordering a drink or a snack
- Greetings and simple courtesies
- Introducing Italian nouns, with indefinite articles, e.g. 'a coffee', 'an orangeade'; nouns ending in **-o** and **-a**
- Prices
- Numbers 1–10, 20–100, 200 etc.; 1,000, 2,000 etc.
- Singular personal pronouns, e.g. 'I, she' etc.
- The verbs 'to be' and 'to have' in the singular, e.g. 'am'

Cultural point

First things first, let's get a drink. In Italy the bar (**bar** or **caffè**) is a popular meeting place as well as being a place to drop in for a coffee, a glass of water on a hot day, a snack or an ice cream. Many bars have terraces where, in the summer, people sit outside chatting, reading the newspaper or watching everyone else go by. Of course there are bars of all sorts, from the very elegant to the simple and down to earth. Popular drinks are:

caffè a small very strong black coffee, also called **espresso**
cappuccino a small, very strong, black coffee with frothy milk added, often sprinkled with powdered chocolate
vino, bianco o rosso wine, white or red
acqua minerale, naturale o gassata (bottled) mineral water, still or fizzy

tè, con latte o con limone   tea, with milk or with lemon
tè freddo   iced tea, a refreshing drink in hot weather
birra   beer
succo di frutta   fruit juice
succo di pera, di mela, di arancia   pear, apple, orange juice
spremuta di arancia, limone, pompelmo   juice of a freshly
     squeezed orange, lemon or grapefruit

You can also order **un panino**, a bread roll with a filling, for example
ham, egg or mozzarella and tomato; **un toast**, a toasted ham and
cheese sandwich; or, for the sweet-toothed, **una pasta** 'a pastry', or
una brioche 'a brioche' or **un gelato** 'an ice cream'.

Dialogue 1 🎧

If you have the recording, for this and all dialogues, see if you can
understand without looking at the book. Good practice for real life
situations! Answer the question below. You may need to listen
more than once but persevere.

Al bar

A group of friends order drinks.

- **Among the drinks ordered are some not explained above. Can
  you pick them out and guess what they are?**

CAMERIERE:	Buongiorno. Prego.
PAOLO:	Una birra, per favore.
ANNA:	Per me, un caffè.
TOMMASO:	Un vino bianco.
MARISA:	Un'aranciata.
FILIPPO:	Una Coca-Cola.
CAMERIERE:	Una birra, un caffè, un vino bianco, un'aranciata e una Coca-Cola. Va bene.

The drinks not explained were **un'aranciata** 'an orangeade (fizzy)'
and **una Coca-Cola**. No prizes for guessing that! You will find
answers to questions and exercises in the 'Key to exercises' at the
back of the book.

Vocabulary notes

prego   lit. 'I pray, I beg'. Here an invitation to order. **Prego** is also used
   to reply when someone thanks you for something: 'don't mention it,
   not at all, you're welcome'.
per favore   'please'
per me   'for me'
va bene   'fine, OK'. **Va bene** is used not just in casual speech, like OK.
   It is acceptable in a formal context too.

Language point

Introducing Italian nouns and indefinite articles

Italian nouns are either *masculine* or *feminine*. This is sometimes
related to sex, in the cases of people or animals for example, but
not always. The word for 'a, an' is **un** with a masculine noun and
una with a feminine noun.

	Masculine		Feminine
un	vino caffè gelato succo di frutta panino tè toast	una	birra aranciata spremuta pasta brioche Coca-Cola

Note: When **una** comes before a noun beginning with a vowel, such
as **acqua**, it is usual to drop the **a** of **una** and just say **un'**. When
speaking, it comes naturally to run one vowel into another. When
writing this, you put an apostrophe (') to show something has been
left out: **un'aranciata, un'acqua minerale**.

   un, una also mean 'one'. When the word 'one' is not used with
a noun, the masculine form is **uno**. See below, p. 6.

   Many masculine Italian nouns end in **-o**, and many feminine
nouns end in **-a**. This makes it easy to guess the gender of a noun

in very many cases. In the above list there are some foreign words adopted by Italian which do not fit this pattern: **caffè**, **Coca-Cola**, **tè**, **toast** and **brioche**. Mostly foreign words adopted into Italian are masculine. **Brioche** and **Coca-Cola**, which are feminine, are exceptions. Try to learn the *gender* of a noun at the same time as learning the noun.

Cultural point

Many Italians like to breakfast in a bar on their way to work. This is not just to save time, but they will tell you they prefer the coffee from the espresso machines in the bar. In most bars, particularly in cities, you go to the cash desk first and say what you want. You pay and are given a receipt (**scontrino**), which you then give to the barman, repeating your order. It is usual to stand at the bar with your drink. If you sit down, you get service at the table and pay extra – sometimes double. So think whether you want to sit and relax for some time, or whether in fact you just want a quick drink.

Dialogue 2 🎧

Prima colazione

It's the early morning rush hour in a busy bar. Maria and Piera pop in for breakfast. Maria first goes to the cash desk to pay.

1 What do Piera and Maria order to eat?
2 Do they each have the same drink?

CASSIERE:	Desidera?
MARIA:	Per me un cappuccino e una brioche.
PIERA:	E per me un caffè e una pasta.
CASSIERE:	4 euro.
MARIA:	Ecco.
CASSIERE:	Ecco lo scontrino.

Maria and Piera go to the bar.

MARIA:	Scusi!
BARISTA:	Sì, signorina. Mi dica.
MARIA:	Un cappuccino e una brioche, per favore.

BARISTA: (*to her friend*) E Lei?
PIERA: Per me un caffè e una pasta.
BARISTA: Un cappuccino e un caffè. Va bene.

*Maria and Piera help themselves to the **brioche** and the **pasta** in the display case on the counter.*

Vocabulary notes

prima colazione 'breakfast'
desidera? lit. 'you desire?'. The cashier is asking what Maria wants.
ecco 'here you are'; also 'here is/here are, there is/there are' (pointing something out)
scusi 'excuse me'. In a busy bar, use **scusi** or **mi scusi** to catch the barman's attention; another way is **senta**, literally 'listen'.
mi dica (often just **dica**) lit. 'tell me'. The barman is indicating that he is ready to listen to the order. Compare with **desidera** and in the previous conversation **prego**.
Lei 'you' (formal)
una pasta 'a pastry'. **pasta** is also, of course, the generic word for all the various types of **spaghetti**, **macaroni** etc.

Language points

Prices

Italy adopted the **euro**, the European Union common currency, from the start. It is divided into 100 **centesimi**. The euro symbol is €. Note: **euro** does not change in the plural. So we have:

1 **euro**, 2 **euro** etc.

but

1 **centesimo**, 2 **centesimi** etc.

Numbers 🎧

To deal with prices you will need numbers, **i numeri**.

1	**uno, una**	**6**	**sei**
2	**due**	**7**	**sette**
3	**tre**	**8**	**otto**
4	**quattro**	**9**	**nove**
5	**cinque**	**10**	**dieci**

From these it is easy to move to the hundreds and thousands:

100	**cento**	**200**	**duecento**	**300**	**trecento**
1.000	**mille**	**2.000**	**duemila**	**3.000**	**tremila**

Note: **mille** has a plural form **mila** but **cento** does not change in the plural. You will notice that the thousands are marked by a full stop as in **10.000** and not by a comma (English '10,000'). A comma is used where English uses the decimal point: **virgola** = 'comma', so **2,5** is said **due virgola cinque** '2.5, two point five'.

For prices you will need the numbers between 20 and 99, which are plain sailing:

20	**venti**	**60**	**sessanta**
30	**trenta**	**70**	**settanta**
40	**quaranta**	**80**	**ottanta**
50	**cinquanta**	**90**	**novanta**

And the following should serve to show the pattern of the numbers in between:

21	**ventuno**	**31**	**trentuno**
22	**ventidue**	**32**	**trentadue**

23	ventitrè	33	trentatrè
24	ventiquattro	34	trentaquattro
25	venticinque	35	trentacinque
26	ventisei	36	trentasei
27	ventisette	37	trentasette
28	ventotto	38	trentotto
29	ventinove	39	trentanove

Note: The final vowel is **i** for **venti** and **a** for **trenta** and all the others; it is dropped when the word is combined with **uno** and **otto**, e.g. **settantuno**.

Reminder: This applies only to the numbers 21 to 98. It does not apply to **cento**, **centouno** etc.

The accent on **ventitrè** etc. is to indicate the stress.

More about indefinite articles

Can you guess whether the word **scontrino** is masculine or feminine? Like most nouns ending in **-o** it is masculine. However, 'a till receipt' is *uno* scontrino. As you will perhaps know from listening to Italians speaking English, the Italian language avoids clusters of consonants and Italians find them difficult in English. The combination **n + s + c** is avoided by inserting an **o**: **un*o* scontrino**.

This applies to other masculine words beginning with **s** + another consonant. For example the English word 'sport' has been adopted into Italian. Like most foreign words used in Italian it is . . .? Yes, masculine. So you say **uno sport**.

The problem does not arise with feminine nouns because there is already the vowel **-a** in **un*a***; e.g. **una spremuta**.

Exercise 1

You are a waiter with a long list of drinks to get for a large group at a table on the terrace outside in the square. Here is the list, but the word for 'a' has been left out. Recite the list to the barman, using the appropriate word for 'a'.

____ vino rosso ____ gelato ____ birra ____ caffè
____ acqua minerale ____ spremuta ____ succo di frutta
____ tè ____ vino bianco ____ aranciata

When you have checked your answers, say the words out loud to get used to the sound. It will also be helpful in memorizing them.

Exercise 2

You are an Englishman who is on holiday in Italy with your family. They decide that, since you have been learning Italian, you ought to do the ordering for them. So, be the interpreter to the barman in this bar. This means you have to put the words in italics into Italian in the spaces provided.

BARISTA:	**Buongiorno. Prego.**
YOU:	(to your wife) What would you like, darling?
YOUR WIFE:	(1) *A white coffee.*
YOU:	(to the barman) _____.
	(to your daughter) And you, Jane?
JANE:	(2) *An orangeade.*
YOU:	(to the barman) _____.
	(to your son) Mark?
MARK:	(3) *A fresh orange drink.*
YOU:	(to the barman) _____.
BARISTA:	**E per Lei, signore?**
YOU:	(for yourself order (4) *a beer*; you deserve it after all that) _____.

Exercise 3

Read the following numbers out loud and then write them out as numerals.

1	sette	2	nove
3	quattrocento	4	ottocentotre
5	duemilacinquecento	6	milletrecento
7	diecimila	8	seimilacento
9	cinquantacinque	10	settantanove

Exercise 4

Here are some travel tickets and receipts. Write down the price in words and say it to yourself.

1 Train ticket: Firenze – Pisa Centrale.
2 Bus ticket.
3 Books at the airport bookshop (Berretta SRL).
4 The hat bought at Lorenzini in Cortona?

5 Two coffees at the Bar la Posta. How much was each?
6 Meat at the Macelleria Jacomoni.

You may have noticed that the butcher's receipt also shows the total in lire and gives the value of a euro. Doubtless the till was programmed to help customers at the time of the changeover.

Greetings and courtesies (1)

As in English, the greeting you use depends on the time of day and who you are talking to. **buongiorno** is the equivalent of both 'good morning' and 'good afternoon'. It is used in any formal situation: in a shop, a hotel, in a bank, greeting someone you do not know well, greeting colleagues in the morning etc.

Dialogue 3

Un appuntamento con il signor Rossi

Angela Smith has an appointment to see signor Rossi. She goes into the outer office, where the secretary greets her.

1   **What does the secretary invite Mrs Smith to do?**
2   **What words does Mr Rossi use to invite Mrs Smith to sit down?**

SEGRETARIA:	Buongiorno, signora. Mi dica.
SMITH:	Buongiorno, signorina. Sono Angela Smith.
SEGRETARIA:	Ah, signora Smith, buongiorno. Un attimo, prego. Si accomodi.

(*The secretary disappears into the inner office and a moment later Mr Rossi comes out to Mrs Smith.*)

ROSSI:	Buongiorno, signora Smith. Venga, venga. (*He motions to Mrs Smith to go into his office.*)
SMITH:	Buongiorno, signor Rossi.
ROSSI:	S'accomodi, prego. (*He indicates a chair for Mrs Smith.*) Come va?
SMITH:	Bene, grazie. E Lei?

Vocabulary

sono	I am
un attimo	just a moment
s'accomodi, si accomodi	sit down, make yourself comfortable
prego	here please, do (sit down)
venga	come this way (lit. come)
come va?	how are you?
bene grazie, e Lei?	well thanks, and you?
signor (abbr. to **sig.**)	Mr
signora (abbr. to **sig.ra**)	Mrs
signorina (abbr. to **sig.na**)	Miss

It is usual *not* to capitalize these titles. As yet, there is no Italian equivalent to 'Ms'. Italian women continue officially to use their maiden name after marriage, although socially they may use their husband's name.

When you do not know a person's name, it is usual to refer to them as:

signore
signora
signorina

e.g. **Scusi, signora ...**

Note that the word **signore** has an **-e** on the end when it is used without the name, i.e. it becomes three syllables. In practice, too, the choice of **signora** or **signorina** depends partly on the age of the lady although **signorina** is not used a great deal. **signora** is preferred.

Dialogue 4

Un incontro per la strada

Mrs Martini meets her son's school teacher in the street. Her son, Marco, is at home with a cold.

- **Why is the conversation a rather short one?**

INSEGNANTE:	Buongiorno, signora. Come va?
SIG.RA MARTINI:	Buongiorno, professore. Bene grazie, e Lei?
INSEGNANTE:	Bene grazie. E Marco?
SIG.RA MARTINI:	Marco sta male. Ha un raffreddore.
INSEGNANTE:	Mi dispiace, signora. E Suo marito?
SIG.RA MARTINI:	Sta bene, grazie. Lavora molto.
INSEGNANTE:	Mi scusi, devo andare. ArrivederLa a presto. Auguri a Marco e saluti a Suo marito.
SIG.RA MARTINI:	ArrivederLa, professore. Buongiorno.

Vocabulary

insegnante	teacher
Lei	you (formal form)
Marco sta male	Marco is ill

ha un raffreddore	he has a cold
mi dispiace	I am sorry, lit. 'it displeases me'. Expressing regret about something unpleasant or unfortunate. It is slightly different from **mi scusi** (see below).
e Suo marito?	and your husband?
sta bene	he's well
grazie	thank you
lavora molto	he is working hard (**molto** = a lot)
mi scusi	I am sorry, I apologize, excuse me (**mi** is often omitted)
devo andare	I have to go
a presto	see you soon
auguri	best wishes
saluti	greetings, say 'hello' to

Greetings and courtesies (2)

arrivederLa is a very formal way of saying 'goodbye'. It is often used by shopkeepers, bank clerks etc. Less formal is **arrivederci**. It is also very common, when saying goodbye in formal conversations, to add **buongiorno** too, as Mrs Martini does. After mid-afternoon, people often use **buonasera** (lit. 'good evening') both to open the conversation and to close it. **buonanotte** means 'good-night' and is used to say goodbye at night, really wishing someone a good night's sleep.

Mrs Martini's relationship with her son's teacher is formal so she calls him **professore** ('teacher'). It is usual to use titles like this when talking to professional people (e.g. **avvocato, dottore, ingegnere**).

Look at Dialogue 5 to find out what you say when you are greeting friends.

Dialogue 5 🎧

Ciao, Gianni

PAOLO:	Ciao, Gianni. Come va?
GIANNI:	Oh, ciao Paolo.
PAOLO:	Tutto bene?
GIANNI:	Sì, grazie, e tu?

PAOLO: Sì, tutto bene. Mi dispiace, devo scappare. Ciao. A presto.

GIANNI: Ciao.

Vocabulary

tutto bene?   Is everything all right? (lit. 'all well?')

scappare   to run away (**devo scappare** is often used colloquially instead of **devo andare**)

Greetings and courtesies (3)

You say **ciao** both when you meet a friend and to say goodbye to him/her. You don't say **Lei** to a friend, you use **tu**. You also use **tu** when talking to children, family and colleagues. These days, Italians on the whole prefer to use **tu** once they get to know you or if they are working with you. It is similar to using first names.

Language point

Personal pronouns and verbs

You have now met the word **Lei** several times. By convention it is written with a capital **L** although this convention is not always observed nowadays. It should be used in formal letter-writing. You have also met **tu**. 'I' is **io**. You may have noticed that after **per** (a preposition) you have a different form.

Pronoun subject with verb		Pronoun after preposition				
io	I			**me**		me
tu	you (familiar)	**per**	{	**te**	for	you
Lei	you (formal)			**Lei**		you

Personal pronouns as subjects of a verb ('I, you, he, we' etc.) are usually not expressed in Italian as it is generally clear from the form of the verb who or what the subject of the verb is. For example, Angela Smith said **Sono Angela Smith**. She would only have said **Io sono Angela Smith** if she had been wanting to stress the 'I'.

The verb **essere** 'to be' is irregular in Italian. Here are the forms for the singular:

(io) sono	I am
(tu) sei	you are (familiar)
(Lei) è	you are (formal)

Since the forms are different from each other, the subject pronoun is unnecessary, which is why it is given in brackets.

The present singular of **avere** 'to have' is:

(io) ho	I have
(tu) hai	you have (familiar)
(Lei) ha	you have (formal)

Note: The **h** is silent. This verb provides the only cases in Italian of an initial **h**.

Exercise 5

Rewrite this short conversation between two friends as an exchange between two people whose relationship is formal, Sig. Rossi and Avv. Bruni.

GIORGIO:	Ciao, Marco, come va?
MARCO:	Bene, grazie. E tu?
GIORGIO:	Bene. Devo andare. Ciao.
MARCO:	Ciao.

Exercise 6

Look back over the dialogues and pick out the verbs used without subject pronouns. (*Note*: **scusi** and **mi dica** are verbs in the command (imperative) form and would never have a pronoun with them. You are looking for other verbs.) Consult the 'Key to exercises' to see if you found them successfully.

Reading 🎧

Bar famosi

Read the passage and try to answer the questions. It is not necessary to understand every word. (*Warning*: These bars are expensive!)

1 **When did Florian's open?**
2 **What are the ingredients of the aperitif that is the speciality of Harry's Bar?**
3 **If you were hungry would it be a good place to go?**
4 **What is the name of its owner?**

In Piazza San Marco a Venezia c'è un bar antico e famoso: il Florian. Esiste dal 1720. All'interno, c'è un senso di intimità nelle sale di stile '700. Fuori ci sono numerosi tavolini proprio in Piazza San Marco, con un'orchestrina che suona per i clienti. E' bello sedersi lì e guardare la piazza famosa e la gente che passa.

Un altro bar famoso a Venezia è l'Harry's Bar. E' un bar molto elegante. Offre naturalmente caffè, vino, whisky e così via, ma anche un aperitivo famoso, 'il Bellini', vino bianco frizzante con succo di pesca. Harry's è un bar ma è anche un ristorante molto buono. L'Harry's Bar era il locale preferito di Hemingway e ancora oggi è frequentato da persone famose, attori, scrittori e così via. Il proprietario, Arrigo Cipriani, è anche lui un personaggio famoso a Venezia.

Vocabulary notes

stile '700 'eighteenth-century style', the style of the years from 1700 to 1799. It is usual in Italian to refer to a century this way. The twentieth century is the '900 – **Il novecento** (an abbreviation for **millenovecento**); as yet nothing similar has developed for the twenty-first century.

la gente 'people'. **La gente** is singular, even though it refers to an idea that seems plural.

frizzante 'sparkling' (of wine)

pesca 'peach'

Exercise 7

As a revision exercise, go over the unit again and make a list of all the words used as greetings and courtesies in the various dialogues. Make sure you understand them and try to learn them.

It is wise to revise when learning. To do Exercise 7 you have to read this unit again. This will help you remember it. It would also be helpful to listen to the recording again. And, very importantly, do this again after each unit. Gradually things, which at first seemed difficult or strange, fall into place and become simple. **Auguri!**

2 Mi chiamo Harry, sono americano, e Lei?

My name's Harry, I'm American, and you?

In this unit you will learn about:

- Giving information about yourself
- Asking others for information about themselves
- Adjectives, singular
- More about nouns, those ending in **-e**
- Verbs in the present tense, singular, first group (infinitive ending in **-are**)
- Saying you like something/like doing something: **mi piace**
- Saying you have to do something: **dovere**
- Saying what you do for a living
- Talking about other people; **lui**, **lei**; and the form for formal 'you', **Lei**

Dialogue 1 ⏵

Sono americano, e Lei?

An American businessman is reading the 'International Herald Tribune' as he breakfasts in a hotel in Bologna. An Italian, sitting at the next table, is watching him and eventually leans over.

1 **Where is the American's home?**
2 **And the Italian's?**
3 **What explanation does the American give for his good Italian?**

4 What seems to be the reason for the Italian's interest in the US?

5 Is the Italian pleased to be in Bologna?

ITALIANO: Mi scusi, signore. Buongiorno. Lei è americano?

AMERICANO: Buongiorno. Sì, sono americano. Mi chiamo Harry McNamara. Abito a Boston. E Lei?

ITALIANO: Io sono italiano. Mi chiamo Pietro Mussi. Sono romano, di Roma. Lei parla molto bene l'italiano.

AMERICANO: Grazie. Mia madre è italiana. E' siciliana. E' di Siracusa.

ITALIANO: Ah, capisco. Mio fratello abita in America. Abita a Los Angeles. Mi piace molto l'America. E' un paese simpatico e interessante. Lei è in Italia in vacanza o per lavoro?

AMERICANO: Sono qui per lavoro. E Lei? E' a Bologna per lavoro?

ITALIANO: Sì, sono qui per lavoro. Vengo spesso a Bologna. Mi piace. E' una città simpatica e interessante. Ora

Bologna: Piazza Maggiore and the Palazzo del Podestà. Courtesy EPT Emilia Romagna.

mi scusi ma devo andare. Arrivederci a stasera, forse?

AMERICANO: Sì, sono qui per una settimana. A stasera.

ITALIANO: Arrivederci. Buona giornata.

Vocabulary

mi chiamo	my name is (lit. 'I call myself')
abito	I live
Lei parla molto bene l'italiano	you speak Italian very well
mia madre	my mother
capisco	I understand
mio fratello	my brother
mi piace	I like
in vacanza	on holiday
per lavoro	for work
vengo spesso	I often come
simpatico	nice, friendly (There is no exact translation. When you say a person or a place is **simpatico** it means you like them.)
a stasera	see you this evening
forse	perhaps
una settimana	a week
buona giornata	have a nice day

Language point

Adjectives

In Italian adjectives 'agree with the noun they qualify'; that is, if the noun is masculine, the adjective must be in the masculine form; if the noun is feminine, the adjective must be in the feminine form. Look back over Dialogue 1. Underline or highlight all the adjectives you can find or write them on a piece of paper.

You probably picked out: americano, italiano, romano, italiana, siciliana, simpatico, interessante.

Look to see which nouns they qualify. You have two men talking who say: **io sono americano; io sono italiano**. But Harry says his mother is **italiana, siciliana**.

You also had adjectives used to qualify the words **paese** (m.) **simpatico**, **interessante** and **città** (f.) **simpatica**, **interessante**.
Adjectives are of two types.

1 The first type ends in **-o/-a**, e.g. **italiano/italiana**, **americano/ americana**. A man is **americano**, a woman is **americana**; i.e. the **-o** is the masculine ending and the **-a** is the feminine ending. Many adjectives for nationality are of this sort. *Note*: They are written with a small letter.

Country	Adjective
Australia	**australiano/a**
Austria	**austriaco/a**
Brasile	**brasiliano/a**
Germania	**tedesco/a**
Gran Bretagna	**britannico/a**
Messico	**messicano/a**
Nigeria	**nigeriano/a**
Spagna	**spagnolo/a**
Svizzera	**svizzero/a**
Sud Africa	**sudafricano/a**

This applies not to only adjectives of nationality, for example: **un paese è simpatico**, **una città è simpatica**.

2 The second group of adjectives in Italian ends in **-e**, for example *interessante*. Many adjectives of nationality, for instance, end in **-e**:

Country	Adjective
Inghilterra	**inglese**
Irlanda	**irlandese**
Galles	**gallese**
Ghana	**ghanese**
Scozia	**scozzese**
Canada	**canadese**
Nuova Zelanda	**neozelandese**
Francia	**francese**
Giappone	**giapponese**
Olanda	**olandese (Paesi Bassi =** 'the Netherlands')

Note: Many Italians don't understand the difference between British and English. Scots, Welsh and Northern Irish should try not to feel too offended when Italians assume they are English. Americans (and others) should note that America can be **America**, but also **Stati Uniti** 'United States' – see Unit 5. The adjective **statunitense**, derived from **Stati Uniti**, is sometimes heard. The usual word is **americano**.

Now, here's some good news: adjectives that end in an **-e** do not have separate masculine and feminine forms. A man and a woman will both say:

$$\textbf{sono} \left\{ \begin{array}{l} \textbf{inglese} \\ \textbf{francese} \\ \textbf{canadese} \end{array} \right.$$

And you can say:

$$\textbf{è} \left\{ \begin{array}{l} \textbf{un paese} \\ \textbf{una città} \end{array} \right. \quad \textbf{interessante}$$

Talking of the USA:

> **è un paese** (m.) **simpatic*o* e interessant*e***

Talking of Bologna:

> **è una città** (f.) **simpatic*a* e interessant*e***

Note: Adjectives usually follow the noun in Italian.

Exercise 1

Say in Italian what nationality you think the following people might be.

> *Example*: **Luciano Pavarotti.**
> *Answer*: **Luciano Pavarotti è italiano.**

1 Sean Connery
2 Michael Schumacher
3 Kofi Annan
4 Tiger Woods
5 Arnold Schwarzenegger
6 Meryl Streep

Say in Italian which countries you think these cities belong to.

> *Example*: **Los Angeles.**
> *Answer*: **Los Angeles è una città americana.**

7　Roma
8　New York
9　Rio de Janeiro

10　Toronto
11　Sydney
12　Tokyo

Language points

More about nouns: nouns ending in -e

Nouns ending in **-e**, such as **paese, madre**, form the third big group of nouns in Italian. The first two are those that end in **-o** (masculine) and those that end in **-a** (feminine). Some nouns in the third group are masculine and some are feminine. Where they relate to people it is easy to guess which gender they are: **madre** 'mother' is feminine; **padre** 'father' is masculine.

But in most cases you have to learn the gender. For example, **paese** is masculine. It helps to learn the noun with an adjective of the **-o/-a** type (which shows gender), e.g. **un paese simpatico**.

More about verbs

In the text you met the following verbs in the first person singular:

io sono　**mi chiamo**　**abito**　**vengo**　**devo**

io was used when the Italian said **io sono italiano** because the Italian man was contrasting his nationality with the American's. In English we would stress the 'I' using our voice. After the first verb it is no longer necessary for him to use **io** because the ending of the verb tells us who the subject is. Can you tell which verb ending indicates **io**? It is **-o**.

When you look up a verb in the dictionary, you will find the *infinitive form*. For very many Italian verbs the infinitive will end in the letters **-are**. Traditionally verbs are grouped according to their infinitive ending and those ending in **-are** form the first group (group 1 verbs). There are three groups in all. In the text you met some verbs of the first group in the first person, that is to say in the 'I' form:

abitare　　　　**parlare**
abito　　　　**parlo**

Here are some more:

lavorare	studiare	telefonare	fumare	ballare	cantare
lavoro	studio	telefono	fumo	ballo	canto

Note the first person forms all end in **-o**. This is the first person marker. You can possibly guess at the meaning of them. If not, check in the Glossary.

The **tu** form of verbs always end in **-i**:

lavori	studi	telefoni	fumi	balli	canti

For **-are** verbs *only*, the **Lei** form ends in **-a**. So you get:

parlare

(io) parlo	I speak, I am speaking
(tu) parli	you speak, you are speaking (familiar)
(Lei) parla	you speak, you are speaking (formal)

Note: The present tense in Italian can translate both the English simple present ('I speak') and the English present continuous ('I am speaking'). So if the forms seem difficult, console yourself with the knowledge that the one tense will do two jobs for you.

You also met some irregular verbs: **sono**, **vengo**, **devo**, and one of a different pattern from the **-are** type. **capisco**. Their infinitives are:

sono	**essere**	to be
vengo	**venire**	to come
devo	**dovere**	to have to, must
capisco	**capire**	to understand

In Unit 1, you met the forms of **essere**.

There was another verb in Dialogue 1: **mi chiamo**, lit. 'I call myself'. It is used when in English we would say 'my name is ...' or 'I'm called ...'. **chiamare** is also an **-are** verb. For the time being, however, don't worry about **mi chiamo**. **chiamo** by itself means 'I call, I am calling'. We will come back to this later.

Exercise 2

Look at the drawings on the facing page and match each with one of the following verbs.

canta	fuma	lavora	telefona	balla	studia

Lucia

Paolo

Chiara

Marco

Anna

Luigi

Imagine you are doing each of these things. How would you say each one?

Example: **(io) canto**

Exercise 3

Look back at Dialogue 1 and work out how you would say the following in Italian.

1 My name is Charlie Hardcastle.
2 I am South African.
3 I live in Johannesburg.
4 I speak English and French.
5 My mother is French, from Bordeaux.
6 Bordeaux is a nice, friendly city.

mi piace 'I like'

mi piace means, literally, 'it is pleasing to me'; it is the everyday way of saying 'I like':

$$Mi\ piace \begin{cases} \textbf{la pizza} \\ \textbf{Roma} \\ \textbf{la musica} \end{cases} \quad or \quad Mi\ piace \begin{cases} \textbf{parlare italiano} \\ \textbf{ballare} \\ \textbf{studiare} \end{cases}$$

mi piace can be followed by: (1) a noun ('I like pizza'); or (2) the infinitive of a verb ('I like speaking Italian/to speak Italian'). You have also met **mi dispiace**, which literally means 'it is displeasing to me', but we would normally say 'I am sorry'. It is not the opposite of **mi piace**.

dovere 'to have to do something'

dovere is followed by an infinitive, for example: **devo andare**, **devo scappare**.

Exercise 4

How would you say you like the following?

1 working (to work)   4 Rome
2 New York   5 speaking Italian
3 singing   6 Luciano Pavarotti

Exercise 5

How would you say you have to do the following?

1 to telephone   3 to come
2 to work   4 to study

Reading 1 ∩

Mi chiamo Paolo Bianchi

An Italian doctor is talking about himself.

1 **What is the doctor's name?**
2 **Where does he come from?**

3 **Where does he live?**
4 **Where does he work?**
5 **Can you say something about what he looks like?**
6 **Is he married?**
7 **What does he like doing in his leisure time?**

Mi chiamo Paolo Bianchi. Sono italiano. Sono di Milano. Sono alto e biondo. Sono medico e lavoro in un ospedale a Milano. Naturalmente abito a Milano. Sono sposato e ho due figli. Mia moglie si chiama Luisa. E' insegnante. Mi piace giocare a tennis, mi piace anche la musica classica.

Vocabulary

alto	tall, high	**biondo**	fair-haired
sposato	married	**figlio**	son (**figli** (pl.) can mean 'sons'
moglie	wife		or 'sons and daughters')

You probably found you could get quite a lot of the information you were asked for. The answers are printed in the 'Key to exercises'.

Language point

Saying what you do for a living

Paolo says **sono medico**. When you say what your job is, the word for the occupation functions as an adjective and so 'a' is usually omitted. You will also hear: **sono un medico**. Here are some other jobs:

albergatore/trice	hotelier	**avvocato/tessa**	lawyer
casalinga	housewife/ homemaker	**commesso/a**	shop assistant,
dentista	dentist	**cuoco/a**	cook
ingegnere	engineer	**infermiere/a**	nurse
segretario/a	secretary	**insegnante**	teacher
uomo d'affari	businessman	**studente/tessa**	student

Note: Some of these words have a masculine and feminine form as indicated. Nouns ending in **-ista** are masculine or feminine according to the sex of the person described. There are many women lawyers and doctors in Italy but it is not usual to make a feminine form for the words **avvocato** and **medico**. Indeed this is a field in which some women have strong views and feel the feminine form belittles them. As for the feminine for **uomo d'affari**, a businesswoman would call herself ... well, it depends on the precise nature of her work. She might be **una donna-manager**, or simply **manager** (yes, using the English word). If she actually owns a company/companies she could perhaps be **donna d'affari**, but to some people it sounds odd.

Exercise 6

Here is another person's description of himself, but the verbs have been left out. Fill in the gaps using the verbs listed (you may use a verb more than once).

> **abito**   **sono**   **lavoro**

Mi chiamo Silvio, Silvio Mancini. (1) _____ italiano. (2) _____ di Roma. Ma (3) _____ a Firenze. (4) _____ in una banca a Firenze. (5) _____ cassiere. Mi piace il mio lavoro.

Exercise 7

You have just met Giorgio at a reception and he gives you a short portrait of himself. Complete what Giorgio says using the words below (use each word once only).

> **scusi**   **madre**   **devo**   **sportivo**   **lavoro**
>
> **chiamo**   **mi**   **abito**   **ospedale**   **giocare**

Mi _____ Giorgio. Sono italiano. _____ a Napoli. Mia _____ abita a Roma con mio fratello. Sono medico in un _____ a Napoli. Mi piace il mio _____. Sono _____ e mi piace _____ a golf e a tennis. Mi _____; _____ scappare. _____ dispiace. Arrivederci.

In these passages you met some more adjectives: **sposato**, **alto**, **biondo**. You will notice these adjectives all end in **-o**. Keep an eye open to see what happens when Paolo's wife, Luisa, talks about herself. Don't forget to listen to the recordings as you read.

Reading 2

Mi chiamo Luisa Lucchini

Paolo's wife is talking about herself.

1 What does Luisa teach?
2 Does she like sports?
3 Why does she like Milan?

Mi chiamo Luisa, Luisa Lucchini. Sono italiana. Sono bionda, e sono alta. Sono di Bologna ma abito e lavoro a Milano. Sono insegnante. Lavoro in un liceo e insegno storia e geografia. Sono sposata e ho due figli. Mio marito si chiama Paolo. E' medico e lavora in un ospedale qui a Milano. Io sono sportiva. Mi piace giocare a tennis e a golf. Amo la musica lirica e quando ho tempo mi piace andare alla Scala. Mi piace Milano. E' una città grande, vivace, interessante e stimolante.

Vocabulary

un liceo	a high school, upper secondary school
amo	I love
la musica lirica	opera

Notice that Luisa says:

sono $\begin{cases} \textbf{italiana} \\ \textbf{bionda} \\ \textbf{alta} \end{cases}$

Exercise 8

Match the nouns on the left with the adjectives on the right. Take into account sense and gender (some adjectives can go with more than one word). How many reasonable and grammatically correct combinations can you make?

una birra	**vivace**
un signore	**australiana**
un vino	**romana**
una signora	**alto**

un lavoro	americano
un paese	sportivo
una madre	interessante
un marito	simpatico
una città	bionda
una signorina	sposato
un professore	bianco
un fratello	

You have now learned to give other people some simple, basic information about yourself. It is also useful to be able to do the same about other people.

Dialogue 2 🎧

Suo marito, come si chiama?

Luisa Lucchini, the Milanese teacher, is talking to a Canadian tourist in the hotel where they are both spending their holiday. They have talked about themselves. Now they are talking about their husbands.

1 What new piece of information do you learn about Paolo's leisure activities?
2 Is the Canadian woman's husband Canadian too?
3 What is his job?
4 Does he enjoy sports?
5 Where do the couple live?

CANADESE:	E Suo marito, come si chiama?
LUISA:	Si chiama Paolo.
CANADESE:	Che lavoro fa?
LUISA:	E' medico. Lavora in un ospedale a Milano.
CANADESE:	E come passa il suo tempo libero?
LUISA:	E' molto sportivo. Gioca a tennis e ama anche il golf. Gli piace anche la musica classica. Suona il pianoforte. E' molto bravo. Spesso la sera ascolta musica. E Suo marito, come si chiama?
CANADESE:	Si chiama Bill. Non è canadese, è scozzese.
LUISA:	Che lavoro fa?
CANADESE:	Lavora in una banca a Toronto. E' commercialista. La banca è una banca inglese.

LUISA:	E' sportivo, ama lo sport?
CANADESE:	No, non è sportivo. Invece è appassionato per il fai-da-te.
LUISA:	Oh, che bello!
CANADESE:	Dipende!

Vocabulary

che lavoro fa?	what's his job?		
commercialista	accountant, financial adviser (has a degree in economics and business studies)		
ascolta	he listens to	**il fai-da-te**	do-it-yourself
oh, che bello!	oh, how lovely!	**dipende**	it depends

Language points

Talking about other people – third person singular of -are *verbs; and the formal 'you'*

Did you notice the verbs used by Luisa and the Canadian woman to talk about their husbands? They were:

si chiama fa lavora passa è gioca ama suona ascolta

These forms are, as you will realize, the same as those for **Lei**, the formal 'you'. In fact, **lei** is also the word for 'she'. 'He' is **lui** but neither speaker used it. It wasn't necessary, because it was quite clear who they were referring to when they spoke.*

Cultural point

You may be puzzled by the statement that **Lei** is the formal 'you' and **lei** is also 'she'. This use of **Lei** goes back to the days of deference when the people in positions of importance were addressed in the third person rather than directly, for example, 'your excellency's wish is my command'. The initials **SV** or **VS** (for **Signoria Vostra**, **Vostra Signoria** 'your excellency, your lordship') are still

---

* In this book we use **Lei** rather than **lei** to clarify that we are not talking about 'she' or 'it' but 'you' (formal).

occasionally to be found in formal invitations and bureaucratic letters. **Lei** is, however, everyday usage for 'you' to people when the relationship is not one of familiarity and you should use it in preference to **tu** when in doubt. It is better to be too formal than too familiar. It is used to men as well as to women, because of the gender of **Signoria**. The confusion with 'she', often feared by learners, is not the problem it at first seems. The deferential origin of the usage probably also accounts for the practice of writing **Lei**, especially in formal letters, with a capital letter.

Present singular of -are *verbs;* *also* essere

Now we can see the full singular pattern of an **-are** verb:

(io)	**parlo**
(tu)	**parli**
(Lei)	**parla**
(lui)	**parla**
(lei)	**parla**

Il signor Smith parla molto bene l'italiano.

And of **essere**:

(io)	**sono**
(tu)	**sei**
(Lei)	**è**
(lui)	**è**
(lei)	**è**

Exercise 9

Pretend to be the following people and talk about yourself.

1 A woman with the following attributes: you are Australian; tall and blonde; married; and you work in Sydney.
2 You are a Canadian man and you are married. Your wife is English. You live in Milan.
3 You are an Italian man. You are Sicilian, from Palermo. Your name is Salvatore. You live in Bologna. You work in a bank. You are married and your wife is Scottish. She is a teacher.

How would you say the same things about someone else?

4 She is Australian; tall and blonde; married; and she works in Sydney.
5 He is Canadian and he is married; his wife (**sua moglie**) is English; he lives in Milan.
6 He is Italian; Sicilian, from Palermo; his name is Salvatore; he lives in Bologna; and he works in a bank; he is married and his wife is Scottish; she is a teacher.

Exercise 10

Try to describe yourself using the words you have met in this unit. This exercise has no set answer, of course – it depends on you. Also try to describe someone else – a friend or member of your family.

3 In città

In town

In this unit you will learn about:

- Finding your way around the sights
- Asking for and understanding directions to specific places
- The definite article, 'the'
- **questo/a** 'this'
- **dove** 'where'; **dov'è** 'where is . . .'
- Asking questions
- Negative sentences
- Ordinal numbers
- Present tense singular of second group verbs (infinitive ending in **-ere**)

Dialogue 1 ∩

A Perugia

Jack is visiting Perugia, a lively modern city but with roots going back to the Etruscans, whose civilization preceded that of the Romans in Italy. Maria is showing Jack a brochure containing a plan of the city and pictures of some of the sights.

1 Can you guess what the Palazzo Comunale is used for?
2 Where do people like to stroll in the evening?
3 Why might you want to go to the garden at the end of Corso Vannucci?

JACK: Che cos'è questo?

MARIA: Questo è il Palazzo Comunale, il municipio. Si chiama anche il Palazzo dei Priori.

JACK: E' magnifico. E questo?

Palazzo dei Priori and the Fontana Maggiore, Perugia.
Courtesy IAT Perugia.

MARIA: E' la cattedrale.
JACK: (*Pointing to another photo*) Questa è una fontana?
MARIA: Sì. E' la Fontana Maggiore. E' l'opera di Nicola e
          Giovanni Pisano.
JACK: E' molto bella. E la via, come si chiama?
MARIA: E' Corso Vannucci. E' molto importante per la città. La
          sera la gente viene qui a fare la passeggiata. In fondo
          c'è un giardino con un panorama molto bello sulla valle
          e verso Assisi.
JACK: E questo?
MARIA: Questo è l'Arco Etrusco.
JACK: E il museo famoso, dov'è?
MARIA: La Galleria Nazionale? L'entrata è qui, in Corso
          Vannucci.

Vocabulary notes

questo/a 'this'
il municipio 'the town hall'
il Palazzo dei Priori 'the Palace of the Priors'. In the Middle Ages,
    Perugia was a city state; the Priori were the elected officers who
    governed it.

opera 'work' (produced by a creative artist)
la via 'the street'
la sera 'the evening' (here, 'in the evenings')
c'è (ci è) 'there is'
un panorama a view'. A number of nouns ending with **-ma** are
    masculine. *Hint*: Learn it with an adjective that shows gender, e.g.
    un panorama magnifico.
in fondo 'at the far end, at the bottom'
verso 'towards'

Cultural point

fare una passeggiata means 'to go for a walk', but in much of Italy
fare la passeggiata is *not* exercise: it is a social event. You walk up
and down the main street, stopping to chat to friends, looking at
everyone else and generally seeing what is going on. People of all
ages do this, so you will see both groups of young people and also
their parents. It means you will see your friends frequently and
news is passed on quickly!

Language points

The definite article

                il for masculine nouns
                la for feminine nouns

un palazzo	a palace	**un giardino**	a garden
il palazzo	the palace	**il giardino**	the garden
una fontana	a fountain	**una via**	a street
la fontana	the fountain	**la via**	the street

Note: For *both* masculine and feminine nouns beginning with a
vowel we use **l'** for 'the'.

un arco	an arch	**un'acqua minerale**	a water[1]
l'arco	the arch	**l'acqua**	the water

1 You say this when ordering a glass of water; it is usual to order spring/mineral
water rather than ask for it from the tap.

Note also:

uno scontrino	a till receipt	**uno studente**	a student
lo scontrino	the till receipt	**lo studente**	the student

Words that have **uno** for 'a', have **lo** for 'the' (see Unit 1). This also applies to nouns beginning with **z**, pronounced 'ts' or 'ds' e.g. **lo zucchero** ('sugar').

questo/a

This can be a pronoun or an adjective. When it replaces (as a pronoun) or describes (as an adjective) a feminine noun it becomes **questa**.

Asking questions 🎧

Yes/no questions are made simply by using a rising intonation for the last word:

Questa è una fontana.	This is a fountain.
Questa è una fontana?	Is this a fountain?
Harry è americano.	Harry is American.
Harry è americano?	Is Harry American?
Paolo lavora in un ospedale.	Paolo works in a hospital.
Paolo lavora in un ospedale?	Does Paolo work in a hospital?
Giorgio abita a Firenze.	Giorgio lives in Florence.
Giorgio abita a Firenze?	Does Giorgio live in Florence?

You do not need 'do' or 'does' as in English, nor the word order change which English requires with the verb 'to be'. Word order is, however, more flexible in Italian than in English, so you will often hear in everyday speech:

E' una fontana, questa?
E' americano, Harry?
Lavora in un ospedale, Paolo?
Abita a Firenze, Giorgio?

The first form (i.e. statement with voice raised at the end: **Questa è una fontana?**) should be your model. The answer will normally be either **sì** or **no** 'yes' or 'no'.

When asking a question in a way that seems to be expecting confirmation that the information in the question is correct, e.g. 'You do work in a hospital, don't you?', simply tag on to the statement: **vero?** or (sometimes) **non è vero?**:

> **Lavori in un ospedale, vero?**
> **Questa fontana si chiama la Fontana Maggiore, vero?**

Information questions require a question word. The subject, if expressed, follows the verb:

> **Come si chiama il medico?**
> What's the doctor's name?
> (lit. 'How does the doctor call himself?')

> **Che cos'è questo?**
> What's this?

> **Come va Suo marito?**
> How is your husband?

Question words met so far:

Come?	How?
Come va?	How are you?
Che ...?	**Che** + noun means 'which?, what?'
Che lavoro fa?	What is your job?
	(lit. 'What work do you do?')
Che cosa?	What? (often just **cosa?**)

Note: **Una cosa** means 'a thing'; so **che cosa** is lit. 'which, what thing'.

Exercise 1

Look back at the dialogues in Unit 2. Make a list of the questions you find in them.

Exercise 2

On the facing page are pictures of some famous places in Italy. For each one there is a question and the answer. Complete the answer with the correct word for 'the'. If you do not know what the word means, it does not really matter because you can find the correct gender from the **un, una** in the question. Try guessing and then check from the 'Glossary'.

1 The Doges' Palace in Venice.

2 The Ponte Vecchio in Florence.

3 The Basilica of San Pietro in Rome.

4 The Leaning Tower of Pisa.

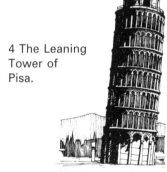

5 The Campanile by Giotto in Florence.

1 Questo è un palazzo?
   Sì, è ＿＿＿ Palazzo Ducale a Venezia.

2 Questo è un ponte?
   Sì, è ＿＿＿ Ponte Vecchio a Firenze.

3 Questa è una basilica?
   Sì, è ＿＿＿ Basilica di San Pietro a Roma.

4 Questa è una torre?
   Sì, è ＿＿＿ Torre Pendente di Pisa.

5 Questo è un campanile?
   Sì, è ＿＿＿ Campanile di Giotto a Firenze.

Cultural point

Technically the Leaning Tower of Pisa is a **campanile**, the bell tower for the cathedral of Pisa, **il duomo di Pisa**. Cathedrals are sometimes called **cattedrale**, more often **duomo**. The famous Leaning Tower is part of a particularly lovely group of buildings, the **duomo**, the **campanile** and the **battistero** (the baptistery of the cathedral), all by Nicola and Giovanni Pisano, who were also responsible for the Fontana Maggiore in Perugia.

Vocabulary

More town vocabulary: the first group is very easy to guess, but use the 'Glossary' to check or if you cannot guess.

aeroporto	**ambasciata**	**banca**
cinema (m.)	**consolato**	**farmacia**
galleria	**pizzeria**	**ristorante** (m.)
stazione (f.)	**supermercato**	**teatro**
ufficio postale		

The following are more difficult to guess:

albergo	hotel
cambio	foreign currency exchange
chiesa	church
mercato	market
fermata dell'autobus	bus stop

Dialogue 2 🎧

C'è una banca qui vicino?

A tourist needs to change some money. He stops a passer-by.

1 **What does the tourist ask for first?**
2 **The passer-by suggests he goes to a foreign exchange bureau. Why?**

TURISTA:	Scusi, c'è una banca qui vicino?
PASSANTE:	Una banca, sì. E' in Piazza Garibaldi.
TURISTA:	Dov'è Piazza Garibaldi? E' lontano?
PASSANTE:	No, è qui vicino. Vede l'albergo Bristol? (*pointing down the road*)
TURISTA:	Sì.
PASSANTE:	Piazza Garibaldi è subito dopo, sulla sinistra.
TURISTA:	Grazie. E' aperta la banca a quest'ora?
PASSANTE:	Penso di no. Lei deve cambiare valuta o travellers cheques?
TURISTA:	Sì, travellers cheques.
PASSANTE:	C'è un ufficio di cambio lì, sulla destra, subito dopo la farmacia.
TURISTA:	Oh, grazie. Buongiorno.
PASSANTE:	Prego. Buongiorno.

Vocabulary

vicino	near
lontano	far
qui	here
qui vicino	near here
vede l'albergo?	do you see the hotel?
lì	there
aperto	open
penso di no	I think not, I don't think so
valuta	currency
subito	immediately, suddenly
dopo	after
sulla sinistra	on the left
sulla destra	on the right

Exercise 3

Make the question you need in the following circumstances, using a sentence on the pattern of: **C'è una banca qui vicino?**

1 You are hungry and want something to eat.
2 You have a headache and want to buy something for it.
3 It's getting late and you realize you are going to have to spend the night in this town.
4 You're tired of walking and want to get a bus to your destination.
5 You need to do some food shopping.

Language point

Using dove *and* dov'è *'where, where is'*

You may need to look for a specific place, not *a* bank but *the* bank you want to use. You will need to ask **dov'è** 'where is'.

Note:

dove	stress the first syllable	where
dov'è (dove è)	stress on the **è**	where is

Dialogue 3 🎧

Scusi, dov'è il consolato americano?

Our tourist has lost his passport and needs the consulate. He stops another passer-by.

- **Where *is* the American Consulate?**

TURISTA:	Mi scusi, Lei sa dov'è il consolato americano?
PASSANTE:	Mi dispiace, non lo so. Ma c'è l'Azienda per il Turismo in Via Mazzini. Provi a chiedere lì.
TURISTA:	E dov'è Via Mazzini?
PASSANTE:	E' la seconda via a destra. L'Azienda per il Turismo è sulla sinistra.
TURISTA:	Grazie. Buongiorno.
PASSANTE:	Prego. Buongiorno.

Vocabulary

Lei sa	do you know?
non lo so	I don't know (lit. 'I don't know it')
provi a chiedere	try asking

Language points

Negative sentences

To make a sentence negative, put **non** before the verb:

Jane è americana.	Jane is American.
Jane non è americana.	Jane isn't American.
Piero abita a Milano.	Piero lives in Milan.
Piero non abita a Milano.	Piero doesn't live in Milan.
Mi piace New York.	I like New York.
Non mi piace New York.	I don't like New York.
Capisco.	I understand.
Non capisco.	I don't understand.

In the last dialogue you met **non lo so**. You can say **non so** but Italians usually say:

lo so	I know (it)	**non lo so**	I don't know (it)

So is from **sapere**, an irregular verb.

Note: Do not confuse **no** (which means 'no') and **non** (which is used with a verb to make a negative sentence).

Exercise 4

Vero o falso? Read the following statements and say whether they are true or false.

1 New York non è in Irlanda.
2 Luciano Pavarotti non è biondo.
3 Roma non è una città interessante e bella.
4 Il Teatro alla Scala non è a Milano.
5 Assisi non è lontano da Perugia.

Which of the following are true for you?

6 Non sono americano/a.
7 Non abito in Italia.
8 Non sono sposato/a.
9 Non parlo francese.
10 Non lavoro in una banca.
11 Non mi piace il fai-da-te.
12 Per me, questo esercizio è molto difficile.

Exercise 5

Someone is pestering you with questions. The answer to them all is 'no'. You feel a bit irritated by the onslaught so answer them, stressing the 'no' answer by giving the full sentence in the negative. You may find it helpful to look back to Unit 2 and check the 'you' and 'I' verb endings.

> *Example*: **Lei fuma?**
> *Answer*:   **No, non fumo.**

1 Lei lavora qui?
2 Abita in questa città?
3 E' qui in vacanza?
4 E' americano/a?
5 Parla francese?

Ordinal numbers

You know the numbers 1 to 10 (Unit 1). Here are the corresponding ordinal numbers. The abbreviated way of writing each is given in brackets.

first	**primo**	(1°)
second	**secondo**	(2°)
third	**terzo**	(3°)
fourth	**quarto**	(4°)
fifth	**quinto**	(5°)
sixth	**sesto**	(6°)
seventh	**settimo**	(7°)
eighth	**ottavo**	(8°)
ninth	**nono**	(9°)
tenth	**decimo**	(10°)

After **decimo**, take off the final vowel from a given number and add: **-esimo**, for example:

twentieth	**ventesimo**	(20°)
thirtieth	**trentesimo**	(30°)
forty-ninth	**quarantanovesimo**	(49°)

Ordinal numbers are adjectives and agree with the noun they refer to:

| **il primo giorno** | the first day |
| **la prima sera** | the first evening |

Directions for finding places

The general word for 'street' is **strada**. However, when streets are named, they are usually called **via**, e.g. **via Cavour**. **Strada Rosero** would be a name used in a rural area and would indicate where the road *leads to*. Streets are often named after important historical figures, events or even dates. **corso** means a particularly important street, **viale** (m.) a wide, tree-lined street. **una piazza** is a square, **un piazzale** a large square.

Question: **Dov'è la Banca Popolare?**

You may be told to take:

Often you will be told what you *have to* do (see Unit 1):

Lei deve prendere la seconda sulla sinistra.
You have to take the second on the left.

Lei deve girare a destra.
You have to turn right.

You may hear:

Prenda la quarta a sinistra.
Take the fourth left.

Giri a destra qui e poi è sempre diritto.
Turn right here and then it's straight on.

These last two forms are 'commands' (imperatives), such as **dica**, **scusi**, **provi**. More about them soon.

Another way of posing a question is: **Per la stazione, per favore?**

If you want *a* supermarket, *a* bank etc., that is *any* one rather than a specific one, you say:

C'è un supermercato/una banca qui vicino?

Vocabulary

Here is a summary of vocabulary for giving directions:

dov'è ...	where is ...
per ...	(roughly) what is the way to ...
a destra/sulla destra	to the right, on the right
a sinistra/sulla sinistra	to the left, on the left
poi	then, next
sempre dritto (or **diritto**)	straight on
in fondo	at the end, at the bottom
dopo (il cinema, il museo ecc.)	after (the cinema, the museum etc.)
prima di (prima della chiesa)	before (before the church)
accanto a (accanto al palazzo)	next to (next to the palace)
dietro	behind
davanti a	in front of
di fronte a	opposite
oltre	beyond
è lontano?	is it far?
vicino	near
è a 100 metri	it's 100 metres (100 yards approx.) away
è a 5 minuti	it's 5 minutes away
a piedi	on foot
in macchina	by car
fino a	as far as
il semaforo	the traffic lights

Hint: When you are given directions, it is a good idea to repeat the main points to the person who gave them, e.g. **seconda a sinistra**, **poi sulla destra**. In this way you can check you have understood and it also helps you to memorize what was said.

More verbs, present tense singular: verbs with an infinitive ending in -ere

You have already met the verbs ending in **-are**. A second group have an infinitive ending in **-ere**:

vedere (to see)	**(io) vedo**
	(tu) vedi
	(lui) vede
	(lei)
prendere (to take)	**(io) prendo**
	(tu) prendi
	(lui) prende
	(lei)
chiedere (to ask)	**(io) chiedo**
	(tu) chiedi
	(lui) chiede
	(lei)

They differ very little from the **-are** verbs, however the third person singular has **-e** where the first group has **-a**. Other verbs you have met that belong to this group are commonly used only in the third person singular:

piacere	**dipendere**
piace	**dipende**

piacere 'to be pleasing' is not a regular verb, but few parts of it are used frequently. **Dovere** 'to have to' is also an irregular verb but it follows the **-ere** pattern for the present tense singular endings, although the stem (the first part) changes:

devo
devi
deve

One further point about **-ere** verbs. Some have the stress on the first **e** of the infinitive, some on the previous syllable: **vedere** but **prendere**. This has no bearing on any other part of the verb. Where stress is on the antepenultimate syllable, this is given in the Glossary. When in doubt, check in a dictionary where the stress should fall.

Exercise 6

A map of the centre of Torino is shown below. You are standing
at the spot marked **X**. Follow the instructions given and work out
where you get to.

1 Prenda Via Po, qui, sulla nostra sinistra. Vada sempre dritto
   sotto i portici, sul lato sinistro, fino alla quarta via sulla sinistra:
   Via Montebello. Ed è lì in Via Montebello, sulla destra, dopo
   il cinema Massimo.
2 Allora, lei deve girare la piazza verso sinistra e prendere Via
   Roma. Vede, è lì, sulla sinistra. Prosegua per Via Roma, sotto
   i portici, e arriva in _____.
3 Lei deve fare il giro della piazza verso destra poi sulla destra
   trova il cortile di Palazzo Reale. Attraversi il cortile diagonal-
   mente, verso sinistra. Passi sotto l'arco; arriva in una via stretta
   ed è lì sulla destra.

Exercise 7

Work out how to explain to an Italian how to get to your home/place of work from the bus stop/railway station/motorway exit (**uscita**).

> *Example:* **L'uscita è 'corso Marconi'. Sempre dritto per 200 metri; al secondo semaforo, a sinistra, e poi la prima sulla destra. La casa è sulla sinistra, il numero 23.**

Exercise 8

Here are some sentences and, shown separately, some verbs. Can you pick the correct verb in the correct form to complete the sentence? Use each verb once only.

> **abito   abita   chiama   chiedo   chiedere   dipende
> lavora   piace   prenda   prendi   vedi   vedo**

1 Io non _____ la banca. Dov'è?
2 Non so se vengo. _____ dal mio lavoro.
3 Devo _____ la strada. Non _____ in questa città e non so dov'è il duomo.
4 _____ la terza sulla sinistra e il museo è lì.
5 Un attimo. _____ a questo signore se la banca è qui vicino.
6 Il mio amico _____ a Milano, proprio in centro.
7 Mi _____ molto la fontana. E' bella.
8 Questo Palazzo si _____ il Palazzo Pubblico. E' molto antico.
9 Carlo _____ al museo di arte moderna. E' un lavoro molto interessante.
10 Ecco il bar Roma. Tu _____ Enzo? Deve essere qui. Ah si. Ciao, Enzo. Cosa _____?

Reading 🎧 ③

A Roma

1 **What is the origin of the name of Palazzo Venezia?**
2 **Why do you think the Museum of Italian Unification is in the Vittoriano?**
3 **Why was the Campidoglio important in Ancient Rome?**
4 **Why do you think the Via dei Fori Imperiali is so called?**
5 **Between which two Piazze does Via del Corso run?**

Siamo a Roma. La piazza in primo piano è Piazza Venezia. Sulla destra c'è Palazzo Venezia, in passato residenza degli ambasciatori di Venezia, oggi un museo. Davanti a noi, c'è il Vittoriano, il monumento al re Vittorio Emanuele II, il primo re d'Italia dopo l'unificazione nel 1861. Qui si trova anche l'Altare della Patria e la tomba del Milite Ignoto. All'interno del Vittoriano c'è il Museo del Risorgimento. Oltre questo monumento si trova il Campidoglio, il centro religioso della Roma antica e ancora oggi il cuore della città.

Alla sinistra del Vittoriano c'è Via dei Fori Imperiali e in fondo il Colosseo. A destra e a sinistra di questa via ci sono i ruderi del Foro Romano. Di fronte al Vittoriano, in primo piano, c'è l'inizio della famosa Via del Corso, la strada principale della città. Lunga più di un chilometro, finisce in Piazza del Popolo.

Piazza Venezia and the Monument to Vittorio Emanuele.
Courtesy APT di Roma.

Vocabulary

il re	the king
il Milite Ignoto	the Unknown Soldier
il Risorgimento	the name given to the nineteenth-century movement for Italian unity
i ruderi	ruins

Cultural point

Vittorio Emanuele II was the first king of the united Italy but the second Victor Emanuel of the kingdom of Sardinia. The kingdom, which orginally included Savoy, encompassed Piedmont as well as the island of Sardinia, and its capital was Turin. It was the prime mover for the unity of the peninsula, through its Prime Minister, Count Cavour, the romantic patriot, Garibaldi, and Victor Emanuel II.

4 In viaggio

Travelling

In this unit you will learn about:

- Travelling – by train, bus, air
- **ogni** 'every'
- Numbers 11 to 19
- Years: how to say, e.g. 1492, 2005
- Telling the time
- Verbs with infinitives in **-ire** (singular), third group
- Relative pronouns (the man who . . ., the book which . . .)
- Using **proprio** 'exactly'; **un po'/poco** 'a little'
- Impersonal/unspecified **si**

Dialogue 1 🎧 ③②

Devo andare a Torino

*While in Milan, Angela Smith needs to go to Turin for a day. She enquires at the Milan Central Station (**Milano–Stazione Centrale**) about the journey.*

1 What sort of train does the Interregionale seem to be?
2 And the Eurostar?
3 How much, in total, does Angela's ticket cost?
4 What would it have cost in first class?

IMPIEGATO:	Buongiorno, dica.
SMITH:	Buongiorno. Devo andare a Torino. Posso fare l'andata e il ritorno in una giornata?
IMPIEGATO:	Certo, signora. C'è un treno quasi ogni ora e ci mette più o meno due ore. A che ora vuole partire?

SMITH:	Verso le otto.
IMPIEGATO:	Allora, c'è un treno che parte alle 8.20. Arriva a Torino alle 10.30.
SMITH:	E' un rapido?
IMPIEGATO:	No, è un Interregionale. C'è l'Eurostar che parte alle 8.15 che arriva a Torino alle 9.33 ma che naturalmente costa di più. Però l'Eurostar ci mette solo 1 ora e 20 minuti.
SMITH:	Benissimo. Prendo quello. E' necessario prenotare per domani?
IMPIEGATO:	Sì, è obbligatorio.
SMITH:	E per tornare? Vorrei essere a Milano prima delle venti.
IMPIEGATO:	C'è un Eurostar ogni ora, alle 14.07, alle 16.15, alle 17.07, e alle 18.15.
SMITH	Perfetto. Prendo quello delle 17.07.
IMPIEGATO:	Quello delle 17.07 ferma a Vercelli e Novara e ci mette 10 minuti in più.
SMITH:	Va bene. Mi dia un'andata e ritorno per domani.
IMPIEGATO:	Prima o seconda classe?
SMITH	Quanto costa?
IMPIEGATO:	In prima classe 20 euro all'andata e in seconda 15 euro. Il ritorno costa lo stesso.
SMITH:	Preferisco la seconda classe.
IMPIEGATO:	Allora, 30 euro in tutto.
SMITH:	Va bene.

Vocabulary

andare	to go
posso ...?	can I ...?
in una giornata	in a day
quasi	almost
più o meno	more or less
a che ora vuole partire?	at what time do you want to leave?
verso	at about
quello	that one
tornare	to come back
domani	tomorrow
vorrei ...	I'd like, I should like ...
ferma a Vercelli ...	it stops at Vercelli ...

Language point

ogni 'every'

ogni	**ora**	every	hour
	giorno		day
	dieci minuti		ten minutes

Ogni quanto c'è un treno per Torino?
How often do the trains for Turin run?
(lit. 'every how much?')

Vocabulary

Il treno

l'orario (dei treni)	the (train) timetable
biglietto (di andata e ritorno)	a (return) ticket
andata	outward journey
ritorno	return
biglietteria	ticket office
fare il biglietto	to buy a ticket
dove devo cambiare?	where do I have to change?
arrivo	arrival
partenza	departure
prenotare, prenotazione	to book a seat, booking (sometimes obligatory on fast trains)
binario	track (the platform trains leave from is given as **binario** ...)
da che binario parte il treno per Verona?	which platform does the train for Verona leave from?
un viaggiatore	a traveller
viaggiare	to travel
il treno è in orario	the train is on time
anticipo	early
ritardo	late
partenza	leaving
arrivo	arriving

Cultural point

Italian Railways are nowadays called Trenitalia, although you will see the old name Ferrovie dello Stato and initials FFSS. It is quite easy now to check train times and book on line (www.trenitalia. com) and a ticket bought that way is called: **ticketless**, using the English term. Eurostar, Intercity, Interregionale are types of train, in ascending order of the number of stops they make and therefore increased journey times.

Numbers 11 to 19

We can't put it off any longer! You need to learn the remaining numbers, 11 to 19. If necessary, remind yourself of the numbers in Unit 1. The numbers 11 to 19 are perhaps the most difficult for the learner. They divide into two groups according to the way they are formed:

11	**undici**
12	**dodici**
13	**tredici**
14	**quattordici**
15	**quindici**
16	**sedici**
17	**diciassette**
18	**diciotto**
19	**diciannove**

You will recognize part of each word as being similar to **dieci** (10) but in the first group that part comes at the end and in the second group at the beginning of the word. Notice too that the stress of the first group falls on the third syllable from the end.

The numbers 11 to 19 can all be turned into ordinals by the addition of **-esimo**, e.g.:

quattordicesimo
diciottesimo

Exercise 1

Here are some addresses. How would you say the house numbers?

Example: **Via Tiziano 11.**
Answer: **Undici.**

1 Corso Vittorio Emanuele 18
2 Via Mazzini 17

3 Via San Francesco 12
4 Piazza della Repubblica 19
5 Corso Cavallotti 16

Exercise 2

Work out how to say these famous dates in history in Italian. *Note*:
In Italian you always say: **millenovecento** ..., i.e. 'one thousand
nine hundred ...' and not 'nineteen hundred ...'

1	1215	2	1492	3	1789	4	1815
5	1848	6	1918	7	1946	8	2005

Telling the time

Che ora è? Che ore sono?

To ask someone 'what's the time?' you can say either **che ora è?**
or **che ore sono?**. **ora** means 'hour', and its plural is **ore**.

E' l'una	It's one o'clock
Sono le due	It's two o'clock
Sono le tre	It's three o'clock
... e così via	... and so on

But at 12 noon and 12 midnight respectively:

E' mezzogiorno
E' mezzanotte

For minutes past, you simply use **e**:

Sono le cinque e	**cinque**	It's five past five
	dieci	ten
	venti	twenty
	venticinque	twenty-five

and for minutes to, **meno**:

Sono le sei meno	**venticinque**	It's twenty-five to six
	venti	twenty
	dieci	ten
	cinque	five

For quarters and halves:

Sono le cinque e un quarto	It's a quarter past five
le cinque e mezzo	half past five
le sei meno un quarto	a quarter to six
E' mezzogiorno e un quarto	It's a quarter past twelve
e mezzo	half past twelve
meno un quarto	a quarter to twelve

When giving the times of trains, flights etc. Italians use the 24-hour clock, which avoids the possibility of misunderstanding:

Il treno parte alle sedici e cinquanta.
The train leaves at 16.50.

Note also that when you are saying 'at 16.50' the **a** ('at') combines with **le** or **l'**:

Parto all'una	I'm leaving at one
alle due	at two

More about this later.

Exercise 3

What times are the clocks showing? Use the conversational way of telling the time.

Example: **Sono le dieci e venticinque.**

1   2   3

4   5

Exercise 4

Say at what time you:

1 get up
2 leave for work
3 have lunch
4 finish work
5 arrive home

Verbs ending in -ire

Angela used **preferisco**. You have already met **capisco**. The third group of verbs in Italian has an infinitive ending in **-ire**. In the present tense, but not in most other tenses, this group of verbs divides into two sub-groups.

(1)	*capire*	*preferire*	*finire*
(io)	capisco	preferisco	finisco
(tu)	capisci	preferisci	finisci
(Lei/lui/lei)	capisce	preferisce	finisce
(2)	*partire*	*dormire*	*sentire*
(io)	parto	dormo	sento
(tu)	parti	dormi	senti
(Lei/lui/lei)	parte	dorme	sente

The second sub-group has the same endings as **-ere** verbs, while the first have an extra syllable: **-isc-**. Try to learn, as you go along, which group each type of **-ire** verb belongs to.

You have now seen the forms for the singular of all regular verbs in Italian. Verb tables often look daunting but study the summary table below carefully and you will see that the differences between the groups are small.

-are	*-ere*	*-ire (1)*	*-ire (2)*
-o	-o	-isco	-o
-i	-i	-isci	-i
-a	-e	-isce	-e

Don't forget, the Italian present can express the meaning of both the English simple present ('I speak') and also the English present continuous ('I am speaking').

Exercise 5

Here are pictures of Carla doing various things. Match each drawing with one of the sentences in the list below.

1	Carla	balla in discoteca	5	Carla	legge il giornale
2		visita un museo	6		scrive una lettera
3		prende un caffè	7		parte per le vacanze
4		guarda la TV	8		dorme

How would you say *you* were doing each of these actions? You need to change the endings of the verbs to the **io** form.

Example: **Ballo in discoteca.**

Exercise 6

Giorgio has been telling you about himself. Tell someone else what he said, i.e. rewrite his words so that you are talking about him, changing the endings of the verbs from the 'I' form to the 'he' form.

Example: **Giorgio è pilota.**

Sono (1) pilota. *Abito* (2) a Verona e *lavoro* (3) per una compagnia privata. Spesso *devo* (4) portare gente a Roma o a Bruxelles. Generalmente *parto* (5) da Verona presto e *arrivo* (6) a Roma per le 9. La sera *torno* (7) a Verona e *finisco* (8) di lavorare alle 18 o alle 19. Se non è possible tornare *dormo* (9) all'albergo, ma *preferisco* (10) tornare a Verona. Ma non *decido* (11) *io*, decide il cliente.

Saying how long something takes

Ci mette is used to say how long it takes:

Il treno ci mette due ore.
The train takes two hours.

Per fare questo, ci metto mezz'ora.
To do this, I take half an hour.

Mettere in other contexts means 'to put' and works like **prendere** in the present tense.

Dialogue 2

Vorrei andare in Piazza Castello

In Torino Angela wants to go to Piazza Castello. It is raining as she gets off the train so she thinks she'll take the bus. She finds a bus information office in the station.

1 **If Angela takes the number 63, does it take her right to Piazza Castello?**
2 **Where does she have to get off?**
3 **Which bus will take her right into Piazza Castello?**

ANGELA: Buongiorno. Vorrei andare in Piazza Castello. Che autobus devo prendere?

IMPIEGATO: Può prendere il 4, il 12 o il 63. Scende in Via XX Settembre dietro il duomo. Trova una piccola via che la porta in Piazza Castello.

ANGELA: Dov'è la fermata?

IMPIEGATO: E' in Via Sacchi, accanto alla stazione.

ANGELA: Non c'è un autobus che mi porti proprio in Piazza Castello?

IMPIEGATO: C'è il 15, che deve prendere in Via XX Settembre. La lascia proprio in Piazza Castello.

ANGELA: Sembra un po' difficile. E piove. Dove posso trovare un taxi?

Vocabulary

può	you can	**scende**	you get off
la lascia	it leaves you	**sembra un po'**	it seems a bit
piove	it's raining	**difficile**	difficult
trovare	find		

Language points

Using che *as an interrogative adjective or pronoun*

The word **che** has a number of uses, one of which is to make a question (*interrogative adjective or pronoun*):

Che autobus devo prendere?   Which bus must I take?
Che ora è?   What time is it?
Che cosa devo fare?   What must I do?

Using che *as a relative pronoun*

Another use is to show the relationship between a noun followed by a phrase and the main part of the sentence (*relative pronoun*):

Trova una piccola via che la porta in Piazza Castello.
You'll find a little street which takes you into Piazza Castello.

As a relative pronoun (e.g. in the last example), **che** can refer to people or things, and be the subject or object of the clause it introduces. In this it differs from, and is easier than, both English and French.

- People as subject:

  L'amica che viene stasera abita proprio in Piazza Castello.
  The friend who is coming this evening lives right in Piazza Castello.

- People as object:

  Giorgio è una persona che conosco bene.
  Giorgio is a person (who) I know well.

- Things as subject:

  Tu vedi il taxi che arriva?
  Do you see (can you see) the taxi that is arriving?
  L'Albergo Londra che è in Via Londra è molto famoso.
  The Hotel Londra which is in Via Londra is very famous.

- Things as object:

  Il libro che cerco è di un amico.
  The book (that) I am looking for belongs to a friend.

Using proprio *'exactly'*

This is an adverb meaning 'exactly, really, indeed, right, just'.

Arrivi proprio al momento giusto.
You are arriving (have come) exactly at the right moment.

Abita proprio in centro.
He lives right in the centre.

Sei proprio gentile.
You really are kind.

Using un po' *'a little'*

un po' is a very commonly used abbreviation for **un poco** 'a little'.

Vuole un po' di vino?
Would you like a little wine?

Parla italiano?
Do you/does he/she speak Italian?

Un po'
A little

poco without **un** can also be an *adverb*:

Legge poco.
He reads little (i.e. he doesn't read very much).

Dorme poco.
He doesn't sleep very much.

E' poco simpatico.
He's not very nice.

It can also be *an adjective*:

poca gente
few people, not very many people

Reading 1 🎧 ３ ５

Come si fa a prendere l'autobus?

1 **Where do you usually buy bus tickets?**
2 **Is the cost related to the distance travelled?**
3 **Why might the foreigner find travelling by bus more pleasant
   than driving?**

Quando si prende l'autobus in Italia, occorre generalmente
acquistare il biglietto prima di salire. Di solito questo si fa dal
tabaccaio, dal giornalaio, al bar o in qualsiasi posto dove si vede
un cartello che annuncia la vendita dei biglietti. Salendo
sull'autobus, occorre obliterare il biglietto con la macchinetta. Nelle
città generalmente si paga lo stesso prezzo per qualsiasi percorso,
senza badare alla distanza. Però è meglio informarsi sul posto del
sistema in vigore. Viaggiare in autobus è un modo simpatico e
qualche volta anche divertente per conoscere una città, a contatto
con la gente e senza il problema di trovare un parcheggio una
volta arrivati a destinazione. E costa relativamente poco. Di solito
è più economico acquistare un blocchetto di dieci biglietti che un
biglietto solo. Chi sale senza biglietto paga una multa.

Vocabulary

occorre	it is necessary to, you need to	**acquistare**	to purchase, buy
di solito	usually	**prima di salire**	before getting on
dal giornalaio	at the newsagent's	**dal tabaccaio**	at the tobacconist's
un cartello	a sign, a notice	**in qualsiasi posto**	in any place
la vendita	the sale	**salendo**	as you get on
macchinetta	little machine	**si paga lo stesso prezzo**	you pay the same price
senza badare a	regardless of	**sul posto**	on the spot, in the place
è meglio informarsi	it's better to find out (inform oneself)	**un modo**	a way
qualche volta	sometimes	**un parcheggio**	a parking place, a car park
una multa	a fine		

Language points

salire/scendere *'to get on/off'*

'To get on' (e.g. a bus) is **salire** and 'to get off' is **scendere**. These verbs are also used to refer to getting into and out of other vehicles. The literal meanings are 'to go up' and 'to go down', respectively. **scendere** is a regular verb, **-ere** type. **salire** is irregular.

Scusi, per il duomo, dove devo scendere?
Excuse me, for the cathedral, where should I get off?

Using chi

chi, like **che**, has more than one use. It can mean 'who?' when asking questions:

Chi vuole venire con me?   **Chi è?**
Who wants to come with me?   Who is it?

It can also be used, as in this passage, to mean 'the person who, those who, anyone who':

chi sale senza biglietto
anyone who gets on without a ticket

This is much used in proverbs. In English we would say 'he who':

Chi va piano, va sano e va lontano.
(lit. 'He who goes slowly, goes safely and a long way.')
In other words: 'More haste, less speed.'

It can also mean 'some . . . others':

Per andare a Roma c'è chi preferisce l'aereo, chi la propria macchina, chi il treno.
For going to Rome, some prefer to travel by air, others to use their own car and others the train.

Impersonal (unspecified) si

There were a number of examples of this in the last passage. **si** has more than one meaning and a very common and useful one is 'one' as in 'one does such and such', i.e. in generalizations. In English we often say 'you' or 'they' instead, or use the passive: e.g. 'How do you/they do it?', 'How is it done?' This is often called impersonal **si** in grammar books, but it does refer to a person, albeit an undefined, unspecified person.

Come si fa a prendere l'autobus?
How does one go about taking the bus?

Note: You can also say:

Come si fa *per* . . . andare alla stazione?

Can you pick out the other cases of **si** in the text?

Here are some common and useful phrases with **si**:

Come si dice in italiano *useful*?
What is the Italian for *useful*?
(lit. 'How does one say . . .')

Come si $\left\{ \begin{array}{l} \textbf{scrive} \\ \textbf{pronuncia} \end{array} \right\}$ **questa parola?**

How is this word $\left\{ \begin{array}{l} \text{written?} \\ \text{pronounced?} \end{array} \right.$

Qui si parla inglese.	**Si può parcheggiare qui?**
English is spoken here.	Can one/you park here?

Si mangia bene e si paga poco.
The food is good and it's not expensive. (e.g. of a restaurant)
(lit. 'One eats well and one pays little.')

Using qualsiasi *'any'*

qualsiasi means 'any' in the sense of 'it doesn't matter which',
'whichever'.

qualsiasi percorso	any journey
qualsiasi paese	any country
qualsiasi cosa	anything (in positive sentences)

Reading 2 ろ6

L'aeroporto

1 Why is travelling by air so easy for English-speaking travellers?
**2 In what case are announcements made in English as well as
  Italian?**

Viaggiare in aereo, per una persona di madre-lingua inglese, è
facile. Perché? Perché l'aeroporto è un posto dove si usa molto la
lingua inglese. Questo è vero anche per l'aereo. E il personale
capisce sempre l'inglese. In genere tutto viene annunciato in inglese
e in italiano, soprattutto per i voli diretti verso un paese in cui la
lingua principale è l'inglese. Il vocabolario poi non è difficile. Il
viaggiatore prende un *volo*; c'è anche un verbo, *volare*. Il volo *parte*
da un aeroporto e *arriva* in un altro. Per la *partenza* il viaggiatore
deve prima fare il 'check-in', poi deve passare per l'esame elet-
tronico del bagaglio e il *controllo dei passaporti*. Poi va a una
precisa *porta* o *uscita*, da dove sale sull'aereo. Esattamente come
in tutti gli aeroporti del mondo.

Vocabulary

perché?	why?	**un volo**	a flight
perché	because	**mondo**	world
soprattutto	especially, above all		

5 Vorrei comprare/ Quanto costa?

I'd like to buy/How much does it cost?

In this unit you will learn about:

- Shopping for various items, asking how much something costs
- Comparing one thing with another
- 'False friends'
- Asking if you may do something, saying you want to or have to do something
- Saying what you would like, and what you could or ought to do
- **si può**? Asking whether something is possible
- The plurals of nouns, adjectives and definite articles
- **questo e quello** 'this and that'
- The plural subject and strong pronouns ('we, they')
- The plurals of regular verbs and some irregular ones

Dialogue 1

Vorrei una guida

Joe has just arrived in Florence and he wants to start exploring, but first he needs a guidebook and a good map. He goes into a likely-looking bookshop.

1 **What type of guidebook does Joe choose?**
2 **Is he offered a choice of maps?**

COMMESSA: Buongiorno, signore. Desidera?
JOE: Vorrei una guida della città.

COMMESSA: In italiano o in inglese?

JOE: Preferisco l'inglese, se è possibile.

COMMESSA: Ecco. C'è questa, illustrata. E' molto bella. E c'è anche questa, tascabile. E' più pratica, forse.

JOE: Posso vedere? Infatti, ha ragione. La guida piccola è più pratica. Quanto costa?

COMMESSA: 12 euro, signore.

JOE: Va bene. Prendo questa.

COMMESSA: Altro, signore?

JOE: Sì. Vorrei anche una pianta della città.

COMMESSA: Per il momento abbiamo solo questa. Guardi pure. Secondo me, è la migliore.

JOE: E' molto chiara. La prendo. Quant'è?

COMMESSA: 17 euro in tutto. La pianta costa 5 euro.

JOE: Ecco 20 euro.

COMMESSA: 18, 19, 20, ecco … Grazie, signore. ArrivederLa. Buongiorno.

JOE: Buongiorno.

Santa Maria Novella, Florence; courtesy of Suzanne Cousin.
This church, near the San Lorenzo market, also gives the main rail station its name.

Vocabulary notes

vorrei 'I'd like'. Polite way of asking for something in a shop – see below.

tascabile lit. 'pocketable'. **una tasca** means 'a pocket'.

posso vedere? 'may I see?' (see below)

ha ragione 'you're right'

abbiamo 'we have'

guardi pure 'please have a look/please do have a look'

altro? 'anything else?'

la prendo 'I'll take it', lit. 'I take it' (present tense)

quant'è? (**quanto è**) 'how much does it come to in total?', 'how much is it?' – usually referring to all the items bought

Language points

The comparative

You have met **più o meno** 'more or less'. To compare two people or things, you use **più**:

questa guida è più pratica	this guidebook is more practical
piccola	smaller
interessante	more interesting

In Italian few words actually change in the comparative form; most are simply preceded by **più**. Exceptions are:

migliore	better	**maggiore**	bigger
peggiore	worse	**minore**	smaller

But you can also say: **più buono**, **più cattivo**, **più grande** and **più piccolo**. Purists prefer the first forms, but the second are frequently heard.

To say things from the other point of view, you use **meno** 'less':

Questo libro è meno importante.
This book is not so important (less important).

Vorrei una guida meno grande.
I'd like a smaller guidebook.

To compare one thing with another, in phrases such as 'smaller than, more interesting than', use **di**:

> **Questo libro è più interessante di quello.**
> **Firenze è più piccola di Roma.**
> **Firenze è meno grande di Roma.**

Il più grande, la più grande means 'the biggest':

> **Di tutte le città italiane, Roma è la più grande.**
> **Questo ristorante è caro, ma secondo me è il migliore della città.**
> **Questa cartolina è la più bella di tutte.**

Note:

| la più bella } | di | the most beautiful } | in |
| il migliore } | | the best } | |

However, **più** can also mean 'plus' and **meno** can mean 'minus':

> **Due più due fa quattro** $2 + 2 = 4$
> **Quattro meno due fa due** $4 - 2 = 2$

Exercise 1

Vero o falso? Say if the following statements are true or false.

1 L'Italia è più grande del Canada.
2 Un albergo è più caro di un campeggio.
3 L'Everest è più alto dell'Etna.
4 L'elefante è più feroce del leone.
5 Napoli è più tranquilla di Venezia.

'False friends'

infatti is frequently used by Italians when agreeing with something someone has said. It means 'indeed' rather than 'in fact', which is **in effetti**, **in realtà**. You have seen that Italian is highly 'guessable'. Many Italian words resemble English words. Language professionals refer to such words as *cognates*. Cognates make the learner's task easier. However, there are some cases where the similarity is misleading. These words are sometimes called 'false friends'. One false friend you have already met is **simpatico**, which does not mean quite the same as 'sympathetic' in English. If a person is **simpatico**, you find him congenial, likeable but he does not necessarily feel sympathy for you.

In the cases of both of these words, it is not disastrous if you get the word wrong. Indeed it is often more a laughing matter and everyone will probably enjoy it. For instance Italians use **suggestivo** to mean 'beautiful' and it has no hint of the meaning given to 'suggestive' in English, hence Italian tourist brochures may refer to 'suggestive views'. But it makes all the difference to your Italian if you pay attention to the points where the two languages differ and try to get things right.

Common false friends

accidenti!	good heavens!	**un incidente**	an accident
attualmente	at present	**veramente**	actually
bravo	good, clever (at something)	**coraggioso**	brave
		congresso	conference
conferenza	lecture	**lettura**	reading
educato	polite	**colto, istruito**	educated
fattoria	farm	**fabbrica**	factory
ginnasio	high school	**palestra**	gymnasium
largo	wide	**grande**	large
libreria	bookshop	**biblioteca**	library
morbido	soft	**malsano, morboso**	morbid
occorrere	be necessary	**succedere**	happen, occur
sensibile	sensitive	**sensato**	sensible

Exercise 2

What does the following short paragraph mean? Watch out for the false friends!

Alberto è un ragazzo molto educato. Attualmente frequenta il ginnasio. E' uno studente molto bravo. Gli piace la lettura e va spesso nelle librerie a guardare e comprare libri.

Asking if you may do something, saying you want to or have to do something

The word **posso ...?** means 'can I, may I ...?'. You first met it in Unit 4. **posso**, like **devo**, is part of an irregular verb and one that is just as useful. Indeed there is a trio: **dovere** 'to have to', **potere** 'to be able to' and **volere** 'to want', which, combined with an infinitive, enable you to say a lot of useful things. You have already met the present of **dovere** (singular). Here are the other two and **dovere** too to help you:

potere	*volere*	*dovere*
posso	**voglio**	**devo**
puoi	**vuoi**	**devi**
può	**vuole**	**deve**

You can now make combinations. Here are a few:

posso		**parlare**
		finire
voglio		**partire**
		andare
devo		**lavorare**
		giocare
e così via		(and so on)

You can now ask other people if they are able, willing or have to do something.

Formal

Può portare questo per me?
Can you carry this for me?

Vuole andare a Firenze domani?
Do you want to go to Florence tomorrow?

Deve veramente partire? Mi dispiace.
Do you really have to leave? I'm sorry.

Informal

Puoi finire questo per me?
Can you finish this for me?

Vuoi giocare a tennis?
Do you want to play tennis?

Devi andare a Roma?
Do you have to go to Rome?

Saying what you'd like, and what you could or ought to do

When you are requesting something, in a shop for instance, it is more courteous to say **vorrei** 'I'd like' than **voglio** 'I want'. **vorrei** is the first person singular 'I' form of a different part of the verb called the *conditional*. We shall look at the conditional in detail in Unit 15. Also useful are two other first person singular conditionals:

potrei	I could
dovrei	I ought to

Dovrei andare a Roma domani, potrei partire con il treno delle 7.00, ma vorrei aspettare la telefonata di Giorgio prima di decidere.
I ought to go to Rome tomorrow, I could leave on the 7 a.m. train but I should like to wait for Giorgio's phone call before deciding.

si può? *Asking whether something is possible*

You saw in Unit 3 that you can use this to ask if something is possible. And of course you can use it to say it is impossible:

Si può prenotare un posto al cinema per questo film?
No, signore, mi dispiace, non si può.
Can one book a seat in the cinema for this film?
I'm sorry, Sir, it is not possible.

Exercise 3

Pair the sentences in the first group below with logical follow-ups from those in the second group.

1 Vado a Parigi, ma non parlo francese.
2 Non mi piace la pizza.
3 Potrei prenotare due posti per il film stasera?
4 Andiamo in questa libreria.
5 Sono stanco.

a Mi dispiace, signore, ma non si può.
b Dovrei studiare la lingua.

c Vorrei andare a dormire.
d Potrei prendere gli spaghetti alla bolognese?
e Vorrei comprare una guida della città.

Exercise 4

How would you say the following in Italian?

1 I want to go to Rome.
2 I'm sorry, I can't go to Rome.
3 May I see the book?
4 Can you play tennis tomorrow?
   Sorry, I can't. I have to go to Milan.
5 I don't want to leave tomorrow.
6 Is it possible to leave for Rome tonight?
   I'm sorry, it's not possible.
7 I'd like a beer.
8 Is it possible to pay by credit card?
   (**pagare con la carta di credito**)
9 Can you (people generally) see Etna from here?

Using secondo me

This means 'according to me' but is a very useful way of expressing the idea 'in my opinion, I think that . . .'. It can be adapted:

secondo	**me**
	te
	lui
	lei
	Paolo

Dialogue 2

Cinque cartoline per favore

Joe intends to send postcards to friends back home. He goes into a Tabaccheria, which has some attractive displays of cards.

1 How many postcards does Joe buy?
2 Which country does he plan to send them to?

TABACCAIO:	Dica.
JOE:	Posso vedere le cartoline?
TABACCAIO:	Certo, faccia pure.
JOE:	Quanto costano?
TABACCAIO:	Queste qui, normali, costano 40 centesimi l'una. Le grandi costano 55 l'una.
JOE:	Allora, prendo cinque di quelle normali e cinque grandi. Sono molto belle, le grandi, ma un po' care.
TABACCAIO:	Sì, sono bellissime, ma se deve scrivere a molte persone . . . Allora, sono 4 euro e 75 in tutto. Vuole anche i francobolli?
JOE:	Sì, mi dia dieci francobolli per gli Stati Uniti.
TABACCAIO:	Via aerea?
JOE:	Sì, grazie.
TABACCAIO:	Metto i francobolli qui nella busta con le cartoline. Le do anche dieci etichette 'via aerea'. Desidera altro?
JOE:	No, grazie. Quant'è?

Cultural point

In Italy tobacco and cigarettes come under a state monopoly and are therefore sold though licensed outlets. This explains why tobacconists also sell stamps (and, at one time, salt, which was also under a state monopoly). The post office also sells stamps, of course, along with other functions. A letter or postcard going outside Europe will need to be sent via aerea 'by air'. For mail within Italy and Europe a relatively new service: prioritaria, for which you pay extra, seems to get letters to their destinations quickly, in a way that used to be unknown in Italy.

Language points

Plurals of nouns

Singular ending		Plural ending
-o	(m.)	**-i**
-a	(f.)	**-e**
-e	(m. and f.)	**-i**

Examples

un francobollo	dieci francobolli
un palazzo	due palazzi
una cartolina	cinque cartoline
una fontana	tre fontane
uno studente	cento studenti
una torre	due torri

Exception

Monosyllabic nouns and nouns ending in a consonant or a stressed vowel do not change in the plural:

due bar

tre computer

dieci caffè

Plurals of adjectives

Adjectives form their plurals in the same way:

Singular	Plural
americano	americani
bello	belli
americana	americane
bella	belle
inglese	inglesi
interessante	interessanti

So we have:

un signore americano
due signori americani

un libro interessante
due libri interessanti

Exercise 5

The bar is very busy and the barman is working fast. But either he is flustered or he is not hearing properly. He repeats the orders to the customers, but in each case he gets it wrong. Be the customers and correct him as indicated.

Example: **Un vino rosso, vero?** No, two _____.
You say: **No, due vini rossi.**

1 Un caffè, vero? 'No, three _____.'
2 Un'aranciata, vero? 'No, four _____.'
3 Una birra, vero? 'No, five _____.'
4 Un'acqua minerale, vero? 'No, six _____.'
5 Una spremuta di arancia, vero? 'No, seven _____.'
6 Un cappuccino, vero? 'No, eight _____.'

(to customer number seven, as the barman turns away)

Oh, questo barista è decisamente strano.

Plurals of definite articles

	Singular	Plural
Feminine	la	le
	l'	le
Masculine	il	i
	l'	gli
	lo	gli

Examples

la strada	le strade
l'acqua	le acque
il francobollo	i francobolli
l'americano	gli americani
lo studente	gli studenti

Note: (1) **lo stato** –means 'the state' and hence we have **gli Stati Uniti d'America**. (2) **le**, the feminine plural article, is not short-ened when the next word starts with a vowel.

Exercise 6

Here are some nouns, sometimes with adjectives describing them.
What would be the correct word for 'the' to use with each one?

> *Example*: _____ **pianta tascabile**
> *Answer*: *la* **pianta tascabile**

1 _____ albergo caro   6 _____ studente americano
2 _____ città tranquilla   7 _____ uffici pubblici
3 _____ ragazzi educati   8 _____ monumento importante
4 _____ cartoline grandi   9 _____ scontrini
5 _____ francobolli italiani   10 _____ città italiane

Using questo/quello

These may be used as an adjective, with a noun, or as a pronoun,
standing for a noun.

> **Prendo questo.** (pr.)
> I'll have this one (referring to a masculine noun).

> **Mi piace quella fontana.** (adj.)
> I like that fountain.

> – **Vuoi comprare questa cartolina?** (adj.)
> – **No, preferisco quella.** (pr.)
> – Do you want to buy this postcard?
> – No, I prefer that one.

> **Questo** (pr.) **è più grande; quello** (pr.) **è più interessante.**
> This one is bigger; that one is more interesting.

quello, when used in front of a noun, has forms like those of the
definite article:

il palazzo	**quel palazzo**	**i palazzi**	**quei palazzi**
l'albergo	**quell'albergo**	**gli alberghi**	**quegli alberghi**
lo stato	**quello stato**	**gli stati**	**quegli stati**
la fontana	**quella fontana**	**le fontane**	**quelle fontane**
l'acqua	**quell'acqua**	**le acque**	**quelle acque**

The changes are to do with sound and the smooth flow of speech
from the tongue; the forms are those that flow for Italian. Say them
to yourself.

Exercise 7

Look back at Exercise 6. Instead of 'the' in each case, what would you put for 'that/those'?

Plural subject pronouns

> **noi**   we
> **voi**   you (more than one person)
> **loro** they

Don't forget that more often than not Italians omit the subject pronoun. However, these pronouns, unlike the singular ones (see Unit 1), can also be used after a preposition ('with, in, from'); and with **secondo**:

Noi siamo con loro.	We are with them.
Parte con voi?	Is he leaving with you?
Vuole venire con noi.	He wants to come with us.
secondo loro	in their opinion

In other words, they are also the *strong pronouns.*

Plurals of regular verbs

-are	*-ere*	*-ire*	
-iamo	-iamo	-iamo	
-ate	-ete	-ite	
-ano	-ono	-ono/iscono	

parlare	*vedere*	*partire*	*finire*
parliamo	vediamo	partiamo	finiamo
parlate	vedete	partite	finite
parlano	vedono	partono	finiscono

Look closely: the differences are small. For all verbs, the **noi** form is **-iamo**. For **voi**, the distinguishing or characteristic vowel of the infinitive appears: **-ate, -ete, -ite**. For the **loro** form, the **-are** verbs have **-ano**, the others **-ono**. Also for the **loro** form, the stress moves

from the penultimate syllable to the antepenultimate. The stressed
vowel is indicated above by the underlining. Note also, that verbs
like **finire** have the extra **-isc-** only in the third person in the plural.

Exercise 8

How would you complete the following sentences in Italian? We
give you the verb to use. Don't forget to leave out the pronoun
('we, you' etc.).

1 (We prefer) Roma a New York. (**preferire** – it works like **finire**)
2 (We arrive) a casa alle sei e mezzo. (**arrivare**)
3 (They are buying) una guida di Roma. (**comprare**)
4. Gianni e Carlo, (do you understand) l'inglese? (**capire**)
5 Anna e Giorgio (are leaving) alle otto. (**partire**)
6 Gli studenti (are having) un caffè. (**prendere**)

Using quanto costa?

Now you probably understand why the question is sometimes
quanto costa? and sometimes **quanto costano?**. **costare** is an **-are**
verb, so:

    Quanto costa?   How much does it cost?
    Quanto costano?   How much do they cost?

quant'è? or **quanto fa?** are usually used to enquire about the total
cost: 'how much does it come to?'.

Plurals of irregular verbs

essere	*avere*	*potere*	*dovere*	*volere*
siamo	abbiamo	possiamo	dobbiamo	vogliamo
siete	avete	potete	dovete	volete
sono	hanno	possono	devono	vogliono

As you study these you will realize that, for the most part, the
irregularities are sound changes in the 'root' of the verb, not in
the endings.

Exercise 9

Here are two short paragraphs. Most of the verbs have been left in the infinitive. Can you write down the correct form in each case?

(a) Mio marito ed io (1 andare) in discoteca questa sera. Generalmente la sera (2 guardare) la TV, (3 leggere) o (4 invitare) amici. Ma questa sera (5 volere) cambiare.

(b) Gli Italiani (1 lavorare) molto. Generalmente (2 cominciare) a lavorare alle 7.30, alle 8.00 o alle 8.30. A mezzogiorno molti (3 tornare) a casa per mangiare, altri (4 mangiare) in città. (5 Finire) di lavorare alle 6.00 o alle 7.00 di sera. Se (6 volere) andare al cinema o a teatro (7 dovere) mangiare rapidamente. Il teatro comincia alle 9.00.

molti	many people
altri	others, other people
se	if

Reading

Il mercato in Italia

1 Why is it easy to visit a market in Italy?
2 Why are the restaurants and bars full on market day?

Per lo straniero in Italia, un divertimento e un piacere è la visita al mercato locale. Ogni paese ha un mercato almeno una volta alla settimana e questo è vero anche nelle grandi città dove ci sono mercati di quartiere. Il turista ammira la frutta e la verdura: tutto è sempre fresco e disposto con arte per attirare il cliente. Spesso ci sono contadini che vengono dalla campagna con i loro prodotti: uova, frutta e verdura, noci, funghi, dipende dalla stagione. Generalmente c'è anche un venditore di formaggi, una bancarella di pesce e spesso un macellaio che vende la carne. In più ci sono vestiti, articoli da cucina, scarpe e sandali, borse, biancheria da casa, un po' di tutto, insomma. Il mercato è anche un luogo di incontro per la gente del paese e della campagna circostante. I bar, i ristoranti e le strade sono pieni di persone che chiacchierano con animazione.

Vocabulary

lo straniero	the foreigner	**piacere**	pleasure
un divertimento	entertainment	**almeno**	at least
la verdura	vegetables	**attirare**	to attract
contadini	peasants, farmers, country people	**uova**	eggs
		noci	walnuts
stagione	season	**formaggi**	cheeses
pesce	fish	**macellaio**	butcher
vestiti	clothes	**cucina**	kitchen, cooking
scarpe	shoes		
borse	bags, handbags	**biancheria**	household
chiacchierare	to chat, chatter	**da casa**	linen

Exercise 10

Going over and revising what you have learned is a good way of fixing it more securely in your mind. If you haven't been doing this, try reviewing Unit 1 and perhaps further units. You should find that things that seemed difficult or strange at first have become clearer.

6 Appuntamenti

Engagements

In this unit you will learn about:

- Making appointments
- Hours, days, weeks, months, seasons, years and the date
- Using the telephone and mobile phones
- Prepositions: **a** and other prepositions + definite article; prepositions generally
- Reflexive and reciprocal verbs ('to enjoy oneself', 'to speak to each other')
- More irregular verbs
- Telling people to do something – the imperative

Dialogue 1

Vorrei parlare con il signor Rossi

Angela Smith calls signor Rossi to arrange a meeting next week to discuss their new project.

1 **When would Mrs Smith like to have a meeting with Mr Rossi?**
2 **After agreeing to the meeting, what suggestion does Mr Rossi make to Mrs Smith?**

SMITH:	Pronto, ditta Rossi?
SEGRETARIA:	Sì, buongiorno. Desidera?
SMITH:	Vorrei parlare con il signor Rossi.
SEGRETARIA:	Chi parla?
SMITH:	Sono Angela Smith.
SEGRETARIA:	Ah, buongiorno signora Smith. Un attimo, per favore. Le passo subito il signor Rossi.

ROSSI:	Pronto. Buongiorno, signora, come va?
SMITH:	Bene grazie, e Lei? Senta, vengo in Italia la settimana prossima. Possiamo vederci per parlare del nuovo progetto?
ROSSI:	Buona idea. Quando Le va bene?
SMITH:	Martedì devo andare a Torino. Suggerisco mercoledì alle nove. Va bene?
ROSSI:	Sì, anche per me va bene. Mercoledì, 17 giugno.
SMITH:	Giusto.
ROSSI:	E mercoledì sera, se Lei è libera, venga a cena con me e mia moglie.
SMITH:	Grazie, è molto gentile. Accetto con piacere. Arrivederci alla settimana prossima.

| **ditta** | company, firm |
| **cena** | supper, evening meal |

Language points

Hours, days, weeks, months, years

You should be able to work out what these mean:

un secondo	**60 secondi**	=	**un minuto**
un minuto	**60 minuti**	=	**un'ora**
un'ora	**24 ore**	=	**un giorno**
un giorno	**7 giorni**	=	**una settimana**

una settimana	**4 settimane**	=	**un mese**
un mese	**12 mesi**	=	**un anno**
un anno			

Do you remember how to say 'wait a moment' (Unit 1)?

un attimo

or often

attenda/aspetti un attimo

Vocabulary

Here are some more words related to days, months and years.

oggi	today
ieri	yesterday
l'altro ieri	the day before yesterday
domani	tomorrow
dopodomani	the day after tomorrow
la settimana prossima	next week
la settimana scorsa	last week
mattino, mattina	morning (both masculine and feminine forms exist – use either)
pomeriggio	afternoon
ogni giorno	daily (adv.)
quotidiano	daily (adj.); also 'daily newspaper' (as noun)
ogni settimana	weekly
ogni mese	monthly
il giorno dopo	the day after
il giorno prima	the day before
l'indomani	the next day (the day after the one being talked about, usually in the past)
quindici giorni, due settimane	a fortnight

Do you remember the words for 'evening' and 'night'?

Exercise 1

Using the words given above, how do you think you might say the following? Don't forget, **mese** and **anno** are masculine.

1 next month
2 last month

3 next year
4 last year
5 annually

Can you guess how you might say:

6 tomorrow morning
7 yesterday afternoon

Note: 'This morning', 'this evening' and 'tonight' are usually **stamattina**, **stasera** and **stanotte** respectively, i.e. **questa** is abbreviated to **sta**. 'This afternoon' is **questo pomeriggio** or **oggi pomeriggio**.

i giorni della settimana

The days of the week:

lunedì	**venerdì**
martedì	**sabato**
mercoledì	**domenica**
giovedì	

Note: All have irregular stress and are written without capital letters. All are masculine, except **la domenica**.

arrivo lunedì	I arrive/am arriving on Monday
arrivo il lunedì	I arrive on Mondays (regularly)
a sabato	see you on Saturday
a domani	see you tomorrow
a stasera	see you this evening
alla settimana prossima	see you next week

i mesi dell'anno

The months of the year:

gennaio	**maggio**	**settembre**
febbraio	**giugno**	**ottobre**
marzo	**luglio**	**novembre**
aprile	**agosto**	**dicembre**

Again, no capital letters are used and all are masculine.

When giving the date you say:

il primo dicembre	**il due dicembre**
l'otto dicembre	**il trentun dicembre**

i.e. you use the ordinal for 'the first' only. Note also that **trentun** works like **un**, as do other numbers ending in **uno**.

There is more than one way of asking what the date is:

Qual è la data (di) oggi?
What's the date today?

Oggi è il venti aprile.
Today is the twentieth of April.

di is optional. Or, when you know the month but are not sure of the day:

Quanti ne abbiamo oggi?	**Oggi ne abbiamo 20.**
What's the date today?	It's the 20th.

Che giorno è oggi?
What day is it today?

'On' with a date is omitted:

Arrivo il diciassette giugno.
I'm arriving on the seventeenth of June.

That is the usual word order; the number is *not* put after the month. And when abbreviating, the order is the European one:

03.11.04 = **il tre novembre 2004**

To say simply 'in July' you can use either **a** or **in**:

Mark, il mio amico inglese, viene in Italia a luglio.
Mark, my English friend, is coming to Italy in July.

Exercise 2

Say these dates aloud in Italian and then write them down.

1	1 May	4	11 June
2	25 December	5*	25 April
3	14 July	6*	20 September

7 Work out the date of your own birthday, **compleanno**.

* These two dates are often used for street names. They mark respectively the liberation of Italy at the end of the Second World War; and the date in 1870 when the Papal States fell to the troops of the then recently unified Italian state, thus completing it.

le quattro stagioni

Here are the four seasons:

l'inverno   la primavera   l'estate (f.)   **l'autunno**

You say: **in inverno, in primavera, in estate, in autunno**. With **inverno** and **estate**, **di** can also be used.

al telefono *Using the telephone*

Vocabulary

telefonare *a* una persona	to telephone someone
chiamare una persona	to call someone
carta/scheda telefonica	telephone card
una cabina telefonica	telephone box
pronto	hello (**pronto** also means 'ready')
chi parla?	who is calling/speaking?
con chi parlo?	who am I talking to? who's speaking?
sono Giorgio	(this is) Giorgio speaking
c'è Carla?	is Carla there/available?
sì, c'è/no, non c'è	yes, she's here/no, she's not here
teleselezione	direct dialling
prefisso	area (or country) code (see note below)
centralino	switchboard
interno	extension
attenda (resti) in linea	hold the line
le passo . . .	I'm putting you through to . . .
mi sente?	can you hear me?
è caduta la linea	I (we)'ve been/were cut off
scusi, ho sbagliato numero	I'm sorry, I've dialled the wrong number
numero verde	freephone number (starts with 167)
segreteria telefonica	telephone answering machine
un abbonato	subscriber
un elenco telefonico	telephone directory

Note: Italian area codes must be included even when you dial from *within* that area. When dialling from outside Italy, do *not* omit the 0 of the area code. So in Milan, calling a Milan number, you dial the area code 02 and then the number. Calling from outside Italy, you dial 00 39 (code for Italy) 02 and then the number.

Italians vary in how they say telephone numbers. It is usual to say:

nove tre sei sette uno cinque sei   9367156

but some people group the numbers:

novantatrè, sessantassette, quindici, sei

We advise the first system.

The dialling tone in Italy is a short tone followed by a longer tone. When the number is ringing you hear a long tone, repeated. If the number is engaged you get a repeated short tone.

Exercise 3

Look at the information below from an Italian telephone directory and say which number you would call if:

1 You saw a building on fire.
2 You saw someone collapse in the street.
3 You saw a bridge collapse.
4 Your house had been broken into.
5 You were a child with a problem you couldn't handle and no one to turn to about it.

NUMERI DI EMERGENZA	
Soccorso pubblico di emergenza	113
Carabinieri – pronto intervento	112
Vigili del fuoco – pronto intervento	115
Soccorso stradale	803.116
Emergenza sanitaria	118
Pronto soccorso autoambulanze	118
Telefono azzurro – Linea gratuita per i bambini	1.96.96

Using mobile phones, il telefonino/il cellulare

un sms	a text message
(un esse emme esse)	(from the English: Short Message Service); also called **un messaggino (telefonico)**

The **telefonino** quickly became widely popular in Italy. It has been argued that it is another means by which the usually tight-knit Italian family keeps a check on its members!

Text messaging, however, does not seem to have developed the same lively special language as it has in English. Perhaps Italian lends itself less to creative abbreviation. The most usual thing is to eliminate the vowels in words, thus **non sono libero** becomes **nn sn libero**. For example:

che	often becomes	**ke**			
chi	often becomes	**ki**	so	**ki 6** =	**chi sei**?
per	becomes	**x**	so	**xke** =	**perché**
comunque	becomes	**cmq**			

This is particularly popular among teenagers (who also abbreviate **messaggino** to **mess** or **mex**), but rather frowned on by the generation immediately preceding them – e.g. those in their twenties. Older generations are often completely unaware of the practice. It is the teenagers too who use messages such as:

TVB = **ti voglio bene**
I love you

TVTB = **ti voglio tanto bene**
I love you so much

TAT = **ti amo tanto**
I love you

These are perhaps similar to SWALK in English and of course precede the mobile phone. However, Italian is a language of long words and suppressing some of the vowels when you text can save time!

Dialogue 2 🎧

Andiamo al cinema

Alberto telephones Marisa to ask her to go to the cinema with him.

1 Which days can Alberto not manage?
2 Where do they decide to meet?

ALBERTO: Pronto. Casa Rossini? C'è Marisa?
MARISA: Sì, sono io. Chi parla?

ALBERTO:	Ciao, Marisa. Sono Alberto. Senti, danno quel nuovo film al Lux la settimana prossima. Sai, il film che ha avuto il Leone d'oro al Festival di Venezia. Che dici? Andiamo a vederlo?
MARISA:	Sì, volentieri. Quando?
ALBERTO:	Lunedì non posso perché ho una riunione. Va bene martedì?
MARISA:	Mi dispiace, faccio sempre aerobica il martedì.
ALBERTO:	E io il mercoledì gioco sempre a tennis con Raffaele. Giovedì ti va bene?
MARISA:	Giovedì, vediamo un attimo. Il 10, vero?
ALBERTO:	Sì, il 10 ottobre.
MARISA:	(*consulting her diary*) Sì, sono libera. Per me va benissimo giovedì. Dove ci troviamo?
ALBERTO:	Andiamo a mangiare la pizza prima? Ti vengo a prendere alle 7.00.
MARISA:	Perfetto. A giovedì allora. Ciao.
ALBERTO:	Ciao, a giovedì.

Language points

Prepositions

Prepositions with the definite article

You have now met a number of examples and it is time to give you the whole picture. The spelling reflects the way **a** combines with the definite article in speech:

a + il	→	**al**	**al supermercato**
a + l' (m.)	→	**all'**	**all'aeroporto**
a + lo	→	**allo**	**allo stadio**
a + la	→	**alla**	**alla stazione**
a + l' (f.)	→	**all'**	**all'entrata**
a + i	→	**ai**	**ai negozi**
a + gli	→	**agli**	**agli scavi**
a + le	→	**alle**	**alle casse**

gli scavi   excavations (archaeological)   **la cassa**   till, cash desk

Look back to **quel** in Unit 5. It works the same way.

The same thing happens with four other common, short prepositions: **da, su, in** and **di**. The following examples are taken from earlier units:

un panorama *sulla* **valle**   *sulla* **destra,** *sulla* **sinistra**
salire *sull'***autobus**   **informarsi** *sul* **posto**
dal **tabaccaio**   *dal* **giornalaio**

In and **di** change when they combine with the article:

in + il   →   **nel**
di + il   →   **del**

metto i francobolli *nella* **busta**
i mesi *dell'***anno**
i giorni *della* **settimana**
prima *della* **partenza**
una guida *della* **città**

These forms are called *articulated prepositions*. The full table can be found in the Grammar section at the end of the book.

Warning: These very common prepositions (**a**, **di**, **da**, **in**, **su**) should be handled with care. They are arguably the trickiest thing to learn to use correctly in Italian. Nonetheless, you should not be too inhibited by this warning, as a mistake in a preposition does not usually obscure your meaning.

For example, Italian uses **a** to mean 'to' or 'in' when talking about towns and cities and **in** when talking about countries, regions etc. Direction or place (*going to* or *being in*) is indicated in the verb.

Abito	**a Roma**	I live	in Rome
	in Italia		in Italy
Devo andare	**a Roma**	I have to go	to Rome
	in Italia		to Italy

Note: You use the article as well as **in** with countries that are plural:

Devo andare	**negli Stati Uniti**
	nei Paesi Bassi (Netherlands)
	nelle Antille (West Indies)

It makes sense to learn usages as you go along. For instance **a** can mean 'to', 'in', 'at', or even 'on' in some cases:

Andiamo al cinema	Let's go to the cinema
Siamo al cinema	We are at the cinema
Abita a Roma	He lives in Rome
Marco è al telefono	Marco's on the phone

Another tricky preposition is **da**: **da** can mean 'at the house/ establishment of'. For example, **dal tabaccaio** means 'at the tobacconist's' (cf. French 'chez').

Fra and **tra** are interchangeable and mean 'among, between, through', and with an expression of time, 'in . . .'s time'.

fra Milano e Genova	between Milan and Genoa
fra un'ora	in an hour's time

Other common prepositions

Other common prepositions are listed below. There are fewer idiomatic uses with these.

con	with	**senza (di)**	without
per	for, through, by	**attraverso**	across, through
contro (di)	against	**dietro (di)**	behind
davanti a	in front of	**accanto a**	beside, next to
di fronte a	opposite	**in fondo a**	at the bottom of
sopra (di)	above	**sotto (di)**	under
in mezzo a	in the middle of	**dopo (di)**	after
prima di	before	**entro***	by (+ point in
oltre	beyond		time)

* **Finiamo entro giovedì** 'We'll finish by Thursday'

Where (**di**) is indicated above, **di** is used before a pronoun, for example:

senza di lui	without him
contro di me	against me

Exercise 4

The following information comes from the brochure of a gymnasium. Complete it by putting articulated prepositions in the blanks. We indicate which preposition you should use (e.g. **su**) but leave you to work out how it combines with the definite article. *Note*: **salute** is feminine. You should be able to work out the gender of the other nouns.

SERVIZI OFFERTI

Biblioteca (su) _____ salute e (su) _____ sport

Ampio parcheggio

La possibilità (in) _____ bella stagione di allenarsi

(a) _____ aperto tra il verde

Orario:

(da) _____ lunedì (a) _____ venerdì (da) _____
ore 9.00 (a) _____ ore 21.15

il sabato (da) _____ ore 10.00 (a) _____ ore 12.30

---

salute	health
ampio parcheggio	large car park
allenarsi	to train, to work out

And this is from an advertising brochure for a self-service restaurant:

Per il pranzo (in) _____ corso (di) _____ intervallo di

lavoro, per la cena che segue (a) _____ shopping, per

ritrovarsi con gli amici prima (di) _____ spettacolo in

una sala (di) _____ centro, per una sosta ristoratrice

fra una scoperta e l'altra (in) _____ la città in cui si fa

turismo . . . la soluzione è Brek.

---

pranzo	lunch
cena	supper
spettacolo	show
sala	hall (theatre, cinema etc.)
sosta	pause, stop
scoperta	discovery

Note: **shopping** is considered as beginning with **s** + consonant.

Reflexive/reciprocal verbs

Mi chiamo Harry.
Come si chiama?

We explained in Unit 2 that **chiamare** means 'to call' and **mi chiamo** means 'I call myself', i.e. 'my name is'. The infinitive is **chiamarsi**. A verb that works this way is called a *reflexive verb*, i.e. one that 'turns back on itself'. The present tense of **chiamarsi** is:

mi chiamo	**ci chiamiamo**
ti chiami	**vi chiamate**
si chiama	**si chiamano**

mi, **ti** etc. are called *reflexive pronouns*. In the infinitive form the reflexive pronoun follows the verb and is written joined to it. Sometimes there is a direct equivalence between an Italian verb and an English verb:

divertirsi	*to enjoy oneself*
mi diverto	I enjoy/am enjoying myself
ti diverti	you enjoy/are enjoying yourself
si diverte	he/she enjoys/is enjoying himself/herself
ci divertiamo	we are enjoying ourselves
vi divertite	you are enjoying yourselves
si divertono	they are enjoying themselves

But often this is not the case. Common reflexive verbs are:

alzarsi	to get up
coricarsi	to lie down
addormentarsi	to fall asleep
svegliarsi	to wake up
riposarsi	to rest
lavarsi	to wash (oneself)
pettinarsi	to comb/do one's hair
vestirsi	to dress, get dressed
accorgersi	to notice
sposarsi	to get married
rendersi conto	to realize

accomodarsi 'to make oneself comfortable', is used particularly in the formal invitation **s'accomodi** 'take a seat, sit down'.

In the plural some verbs are used with the reflexive pronoun to indicate the action is *reciprocal*:

Dove ci troviamo?
lit. 'Where shall we find each other?',
i.e. 'Where shall we meet?'

Non si parlano.
They don't talk/are not speaking to each other.

Si vedono ogni sabato.
They see each other each Saturday.

Grammatically sophisticated readers may be assured: the reflexive pronouns **mi**, **ti** etc. can mean both 'myself' and 'to myself', 'yourself' and 'to yourself', i.e. they can be *direct* and *indirect* objects of the verb.

Note: Common ways of saying 'goodbye' between friends are **ci vediamo** or **ci sentiamo**, meaning 'see you soon' and 'we'll telephone each other' respectively.

Exercise 5

The printer has got the following sentences muddled up. They describe what I do every morning. Put them into a more logical order.

1 Mi pettino. (5)
2 Non mi alzo subito. (2)
3 Mi vesto. (6)
4 Vado in bagno. (3)
5 Mi sveglio alle sette. (1)
6 Mi lavo. (4)

Exercise 6

Lucio has done a series of drawings of his morning routine. What does he do? Here are the verbs you need: **pettinarsi**, **fare la doccia**, **vestirsi**, **svegliarsi**, **fare colazione**, **alzarsi**, **prepararsi**.

(a)

(b)

(c)

(d)

(e)

(f)

(g)

More irregular verbs

andare	venire	fare	sapere	dire	dare
vado	vengo	faccio	so	dico	do
vai	vieni	fai	sai	dici	dai
va	viene	fa	sa	dice	dà
andiamo	veniamo	facciamo	sappiamo	diciamo	diamo
andate	venite	fate	sapete	dite	date
vanno	vengono	fanno	sanno	dicono	danno

You need to find your own way of learning these verbs. You will need them a lot – but you will also hear them a lot, which will help you.

- **Dove vai?**
- **Vado a fare la spesa. Perché non vieni con me?**
- **Buona idea, così faccio la spesa anch'io.**

- Where are you going?
- I'm going shopping. Why don't you come with me?
- Good idea, that way I'll do my shopping too.

- **Anna dice che non sa dove abita Luisa. Come facciamo a trovare la sua casa?**
- Anna says she doesn't know where Luisa lives? How shall we find her house?

Exercise 7

Here are two lists. The first contains questions and the second answers but again they have become muddled. Can you sort them out?

1 Vuoi venire con me?

2 Da dove vengono?

3 Che cosa dicono del progetto?
4 Che cosa fai?
5 Andate al mercato?
6 Dove vanno Giorgio e Maria?
7 Lucia sa che Giorgio arriva oggi?
8 Chi viene con noi?

a Sì, vogliamo un po' di frutta e di verdura.
b Sì. Viene a trovarlo stasera.
c Al cinema.
d Non posso oggi.
e Scrivo una lettera.
f Vengo io.
g Non sanno che esiste.
h Da Roma.

Telling people to do something – the imperative

You have met a number of examples of this. For instance:

Giri a destra.	**Prenda la terza sulla sinistra.**
Turn right.	Take the third on the left.
Scusi.	**Senta.**
Excuse me.	Listen.

All these are examples of the *imperative*, the form of the verb used to give orders or instructions. They were all used in the formal form, addressed to people when using **lei**. How can we make sense of this?

Formal form

-are verbs		All other verbs	
scusare	scus*i*	prendere	prend*a*
girare	gir*i*	sentire	sent*a*
parlare	parl*i*	dire	dic*a*
accomodarsi	s'accomod*i*	venire	veng*a*

The rule is that for verbs other than **-are** ones, the ending is **-a**, even if you are not quite sure what to attach it to. In fact, it is usually the first person singular of the verb, without **-o** (**veng(o)**, **dic(o)**).

But what about friends? Alberto said to Marisa: **senti**. But you have not met other forms yet, as you have mostly met formal conversations. The rule is:

Informal form

-are verbs: *-a*	All other verbs: *-i*
scus*a*	sent*i*
gir*a*	
parl*a*	

You may have observed that it is exactly the opposite of the formal form and wonder how to get it right. We suggest that you choose two imperatives you hear frequently in Italy and make them your models. For example, **scusare** and **sentire**. Your friends will say to you: **Oh scusa, Joe/Mary/Mike/Ann** (substitute your own name). In the street people you don't know will say: **Scusi, signore/ signora/signorina**, as appropriate. Similarly friends will attract your attention by saying: **Senti, Joe** etc., and people you do not know well will say: **Senta, signore** etc. These two make excellent models. Other verbs you commonly hear are:

-are verbs			
tu		*Lei*	
guarda	Joe	**guardi**	signore
aspetta		**aspetti**	

Other verbs			
tu	*Lei*	*tu*	*Lei*
prendi	**prenda**	**fa'**	**faccia**
abbi pazienza	**abbia pazienza**[1]	**va'**	**vada**
vieni	**venga**	**da'**	**dia**
di'	**dica**		

1 lit. 'have patience', i.e. 'be patient'.

In fact, for regular **-ere** and **-ire** verbs, the **tu** form of the present is also the imperative form. This is also true for some irregular verbs (e.g. **vieni**). In the case of **dire**, **fare**, **andare** and **dare**, the full form is usually abbreviated, as (') shows.

Andiamo! 'Let's go!'

To include yourself in a suggestion, you use the **noi** *form* of the verb, but without **noi**. This is also an imperative.

Telefoniamo a Gianni!	Let's call/phone Gianni!
Mangiamo alle otto!	Let's eat at 8 o'clock!
Facciamo gli spaghetti!	Let's make spaghetti!

To tell several people to do something, you use the **voi** form of the verb, again without **voi**.

Andate presto!	Go quickly!

Telling someone not to do something

You simply use **non** and the verb:

Non dica questo.
Non giri a sinistra, vada dritto.

However, when you are using **tu**, you use **non** + infinitive:

Non dire questo.
Non girare, va' dritto.

Exercise 8

You and your friend Mario are on your way, by car, to Giorgio's house. You know the way and Mario, who is driving, doesn't, so you have to give him directions. The verbs have been left out. Choose the correct ones from the list that follows to make sense of your instructions. You may use two of them twice. As Mario is a friend, you use **tu** when talking to him.

> **rallenta   prendi   girare   va'   gira   sta'**
> **facciamo   cerca   andare**

1 _____ la seconda sulla destra.
2 Qui, _____ a destra.
3 E poi _____ sempre dritto un po'.
4 Non _____ troppo veloce.
5 Ora al semaforo _____ a sinistra.
6 _____ sempre sulla sinistra perché devi girare di nuovo.
7 No, non _____ qui.
8 Ecco _____ un po'.
9 _____ questa via.
10 _____ un parcheggio in questa piazza.
11 _____ l'ultimo pezzo a piedi perché non si può parcheggiare.

Exercise 9

There's an air traffic controllers' strike – again. You are an airline employee and a passenger wants information about his flight.

You: (1)   (Yes,) signore. (Say 'tell me', using dire, indicating you are ready to listen.)

Passenger: Quando parte il mio volo?

YOU: (2) (Give me) il biglietto per favore. Mi dispiace, signore, il volo per Amsterdam ha due ore di ritardo.

PASSENGER: Ma non è possibile! Devo essere a Amsterdam a mezzogiorno.

YOU: (3) (Be patient), signore. (4) (Forgive me). Non posso fare niente. (5) (Make yourself comfortable) al bar o nel ristorante. (6) (Wait) con calma . . .

Exercise 10

Compose a text message (SMS) to someone in your office saying your flight to Amsterdam is two hours late and asking them to phone your hotel to warn them.

Reading

La domenica in Italia

1 **Why is it difficult for families to be together on Saturdays?**
2 **Can you list five activities that an Italian family might be engaged in during a winter Sunday?**
3 **Where do many people enjoy going on summer Sundays?**

La domenica è un giorno molto importante per gli Italiani. Il sabato molti adulti non lavorano ma i bambini sono a scuola la mattina. La domenica è dunque il giorno in cui tutti i membri della famiglia sono a casa. Spesso il venerdì o il sabato, si sente l'augurio 'Buona domenica!'. La domenica è il giorno in cui si invitano i familiari a pranzo a mezzogiorno. Il pomeriggio si va a fare una passeggiata in campagna o nei parchi o semplicemente si passeggia lungo la via principale della città, che è spesso zona pedonale. Certe persone, invece, d'inverno preferiscono passare il pomeriggio al cinema. Durante la stagione calcistica, i tifosi vanno allo stadio a vedere la partita. Se però devono accompagnare la famiglia a spasso, seguono la partita alla radio. E' divertente vedere questi signori camminare con la radiolina all'orecchio per seguire, anche da lontano, la loro squadra. In inverno dalle città del nord c'è l'esodo verso la montagna per sciare; invece d'estate sono il mare e la campagna che attirano i gitanti. La sera, sulle strade che vanno in città, qualsiasi città, si formano code di automobilisti che tornano

per prepararsi a una nuova settimana di lavoro. Il lunedì arriva
sempre troppo presto.

Vocabulary

dunque	so, therefore	**augurio**	wish, greeting
spesso	often	**(auguri!**	best wishes!)
i familiari	relatives	**il calcio**	soccer
pedonale	traffic-free, reserved for pedestrians	**calcistico**	to do with soccer
pedoni	pedestrians	**un tifoso**	a fan
spasso	walk or outing for pleasure	**camminare**	to walk
esodo	exodus	**orecchio**	ear
una gita	a trip, an excursion	**un gitante**	tripper
casa	house, home	**una coda**	a queue

7 Giriamo

Let's get out and about

In this unit you will learn about:

- Booking into hotels
- Saying it doesn't matter, **non importa**
- The plural of nouns and adjectives ending in **-co** and **-go**, **-ca** and **-ga**
- The verb **uscire** 'to go out'
- Saying you are going to do something: **andare a fare** ...
- Shopping for food and for clothes – and for computers
- Saying you need something, asking if someone needs something else, and saying you have enough
- Weights and measures
- Plurals of nouns ending in **-cia** and **-gia**
- Talking about colours

Dialogue 1

All'albergo (1)

Frances is touring Italy with her husband and another couple. They haven't booked accommodation because it's low season. Frances has been delegated to go into the Albergo della Fontana in a little Tuscan town to see whether they have rooms for tonight.

1 How many rooms does Frances want?
2 What are the important points about the rooms for her and her party?
3 Before deciding to take the rooms what does she ask to do?

DIRETTORE: Buona sera, signora, desidera?
FRANCES: Avete una camera?
DIRETTORE: Sì, signora. Una camera singola o doppia?

FRANCES:	In realtà, vorrei due camere, due camere doppie. Una per me e mio marito, una per i nostri amici.
DIRETTORE:	Preferite un letto matrimoniale o due letti?
FRANCES:	Veramente non importa.
DIRETTORE:	Con bagno o senza?
FRANCES:	Oh, con bagno, per favore. E preferiamo camere tranquille.
DIRETTORE:	Certo, signora. Per una notte?
FRANCES:	No, per due notti.
DIRETTORE:	Abbiamo due camere tranquille. Danno sul cortile dietro l'albergo. Ma qui in ogni modo c'è poco traffico.
FRANCES:	Potrei vedere le camere?
DIRETTORE:	Senz'altro. Prendo le chiavi. Venga pure.

Vocabulary

i nostri amici	our friends
veramente	really (**vero** means 'true'; lit. 'truly')
danno sul cortile	they overlook the courtyard (implied 'at the back of the hotel')
in ogni modo	in any case **c'è poco traffico** there's not much
senz'altro	of course traffic

More vocabulary for hotels

una camera singola/doppia	a single/double room
una camera a un letto	a single room (room with one bed)
a due letti	a double (room with two beds)
matrimoniale	a room with a double bed (Italian double beds are generous)
con bagno	with bath
doccia	shower
aria condizionata	air-conditioning

Cultural point

Quite often Italian hotels do not have a dining room, so some hotels have a room charge without breakfast. They can usually provide a continental breakfast, however some guests may prefer to go to a nearby bar. The bar is the place to go for really good coffee (see Unit 1). If your hotel does not have a restaurant, that

leaves you free to try a variety places to eat during your stay.
And you may well find you eat better than you would have done
in a hotel.

Language points

non importa *'it doesn't matter'*

non importa means 'it doesn't matter, it's not important'. **importa**
is a verb (**importare**), and the subject (which is not stated) is 'it'.
A verb used in this way is called an *impersonal* verb, that is, the
subject is not a person. Look out for others.

The plural of nouns and adjectives ending in -co *and* -go, -ca *and* -ga

Most nouns and adjectives ending in **-go** keep the hard **g** sound in
the plural and therefore insert an **h** to indicate this:

> **un albergo**   **due alberghi**

Nouns ending in **-co** are less predictable. Generally speaking those
in which the *penultimate* syllable bears the main stress keep the
hard **c** and therefore insert an **h**:

> **un arco etrusco**   **due archi etruschi**
> **un vino bianco**   **due vini bianchi**

Exception:

> **un amico**   **due amici**

When the stress is on the *antepenultimate* syllable, however, there
is usually a sound change:

> **un medico simpatico**   **due medici simpatici**

Note: Feminine nouns and adjectives in the feminine ending in
-ca and **-ga** all keep the hard sound and insert the **h**, including:

> **un'amica**   **due amiche**

These points fall into place the more Italian you hear. Lists of
exceptions are confusing for the beginner, so we are not giving
them here. However, **amico** is such a common word, you should
learn it. And remember: if in doubt, consult a dictionary. At this

stage don't worry too much, as mistakes do not usually impair communication. As your Italian becomes more sophisticated you can gradually aim to get these details correct.

Exercise 1

In the hotel conversation singulars and plurals were used:

una camera   due camere   un letto   due letti

Here are some more words, sometimes with adjectives, to put into the plural (remind yourself of the forms first, Unit 5). In numbers 1 to 8, change to two of everything.

Example: **un letto**
Answer: **due letti**

1   un giorno
2   una settimana
3   un mese interessante
4   un nuovo progetto

5   una banca
6   un giornale
7   un cappuccino
8   una birra

In the next group you have definite articles ('the'). Make the whole word group plural.

Example: **il francobollo francese**
Answer: **i francobolli francesi**

9   il nuovo film
10   lo spettacolo
11   il giornale interessante
12   il supermercato francese

13   la nuova galleria
14   la strada che va in città
15   l'adulto responsabile
16   il vino rosso

Dialogue 2

All'albergo (2)

Having satisfied herself the rooms are pleasant, Frances continues the conversation.

1 What is and what is not included in the price?
2 Where is the garage?

FRANCES: Qual è il prezzo di una camera per una notte?
DIRETTORE: 105 euro, signora.

FRANCES: E' inclusa la colazione?
DIRETTORE: No, signora. Sono inclusi le tasse e il servizio, ma la
             colazione non è compresa nel prezzo.
FRANCES: Va bene. Vado a chiamare mio marito e i nostri
             amici. Oh, c'è un garage?
DIRETTORE: Sì, signora. Quando esce, giri a sinistra. Poi deve
             passare sotto l'arco, a sinistra. Il garage è dietro
             l'albergo, in fondo al cortile. Posso avere un docu-
             mento, per cortesia?
FRANCES: Ecco il mio passaporto.

Vocabulary

compreso, incluso	included (very similar in meaning, from **comprendere**, **includere**)
quando esce	when you go out
in fondo a	at the bottom of, at the end of
per cortesia	please (this is another way of saying 'please', as is **per piacere**)
un documento	an identification document (usually a passport or an identity card)

Language points

Using uscire *'to go out'*

esco	usciamo
esci	uscite
esce	escono

Using andare

Vado a chiamare mio marito

When you say you are going to do something, you need to use **a** after **andare**, before the second verb.

Vado a mangiare.
I am going to eat.

Andate a vedere il nuovo film?
Are you going to see the new film?

Va a lavorare.
He/she is going to work.

Exercise 2

Joe McDonald needs to book into a hotel for the night. Here is his conversation with the receptionist. Unfortunately the printer has got the order all wrong and forgotten to indicate whether Joe or the receptionist is talking. Can you sort it out so that it makes sense?

1 Per quante notti?

2 Singola o doppia?

3 60 euro.

4 Abbiamo una singola con doccia. Va bene?

5 E' compresa la colazione?

6 Ecco la chiave. E' il numero 32.

7 Va bene.

8 Buona sera. Avete una camera?

9 No, non è compresa.

10 Una notte.

11 Grazie.

12 Posso avere un documento?

13 Singola.

14 Qual è il prezzo?

15 Certo, ecco la mia carta d'identità.

Dialogue 3

Vorrei un po' di frutta

Mrs Rossi is shopping for fruit and vegetables.

1 **The fruit seller says the small oranges have certain qualities. What are they?**

2 **Which other fruit does she want?**

3 **How much will her apples cost her?**

FRUTTIVENDOLO:	Buongiorno, signora. Desidera?
SIG.RA ROSSI:	Buongiorno. Vorrei un po' di frutta. Quanto costano le arance?
FRUTTIVENDOLO:	1 euro e 49 centesimi al chilo le grandi, 1,19 le piccole. Sono molto dolci, quelle piccole, ottime per la spremuta.
SIG.RA ROSSI:	Allora, un chilo. E ho bisogno anche di banane.
FRUTTIVENDOLO:	Quante?
SIG.RA ROSSI:	Cinque o sei. Ecco, così va bene. E due pompelmi.
FRUTTIVENDOLO:	Benissimo, signora. Altro?
SIG.RA ROSSI:	Ci sono delle mele buone?
FRUTTIVENDOLO:	Queste a 1,96 al chilo, del Trentino, sono molto buone.
SIG.RA ROSSI:	Mezzo chilo, per favore.
FRUTTIVENDOLO:	Ecco. E poi?
SIG.RA ROSSI:	Basta così per oggi. Quant'è?
FRUTTIVENDOLO:	3 euro e 75 centesimi, signora.
SIG.RA ROSSI:	Ecco (*giving him a 10 euro note*).
FRUTTIVENDOLO:	Quattro, cinque e cinque, dieci. Grazie, signora, arrivederLa, buongiorno.

Vocabulary

ho bisogno di	I need (see below)
del Trentino	from the Trentino (in northern Italy)
basta così	that'll be all (lit. 'it's enough like that')

Shop in the Mercato di Mezzo, Bologna.
Courtesy EPT Emilia Romagna.

Language points

Using avere bisogno di

Ho bisogno di ...

avere bisogno di (lit. 'to have need of') corresponds to the English 'to need':

Ho bisogno di francobolli.
I need some (postage) stamps.

Ho bisogno di sapere la risposta.
I need to know the answer.

Hai bisogno di me?
Do you need me?

Using altro?

When asking a customer if she (he) needs anything else a shop-keeper may say **altro?** which means 'anything else?' in this context. **altro** is the word for 'other':

un altro caffè	another coffee
l'altro giorno	the other day

Take note of the way you say 'two, three' etc. and 'more/other':

altri due caffè	two more coffees
altre tre persone	three other people

Other ways of encouraging the customer to buy more are:

E poi?	And then? Next?
Dopo?	After (that)?
E' tutto?	Is that all?

And ways of saying 'no' are:

No, grazie	No, thank you
Basta, grazie	That's all, thanks
No, basta così	No (lit. 'it's sufficient like that')
No, va bene così	No (lit. 'it's all right like that')

così means 'in this way, in that way, thus'.

Using basta

bastare is a verb but normally used only in the third person singular and plural. It can have a specific subject:

Bastano queste banane?
Are these enough bananas?

Bastano dieci euro?
Are 10 euros enough?

Or it can be used impersonally followed by an infinitive or a noun:

Basta chiedere.
It's sufficient to ask.
(i.e. 'All you need do is ask'.)

– E' lontano. Si può arrivare in una giornata?
– It's a long way. Can one get there in one day?

– Basta partire presto.
– So long as one starts early.
(lit. 'All you need do is start early'.)

Basta telefonare.
All you need to do is telephone.

Or, from a leaflet about cancer prevention:

Basta una telefonata per prenotare una visita preventiva gratuita per te e per i tuoi cari ...
All it needs is a telephone call to book a free check-up for you and your loved ones ...

Weights and measures

The metric system is used in Italy, as elsewhere in Europe. For weight, the basic measures are the gram (**grammo**) and the kilogram (**chilogrammo**), 1,000 grams. Lightweight items such as ham, sweets/candies, are sold by the **etto**. **Un etto** = 100 grams, which is just under 4 oz. So you have:

un etto   = 100 grammi
mezzo chilo = 5 etti = 500 grammi
un chilo   = 1.000 grammi

The liquid measure is the litre:

un litro
mezzo litro
un quarto (di litro)

la frutta *'fruit'*

The word **frutta** is similar to the English collective noun 'fruit', i.e.
you do not usually use it in the plural. In season, the following are
commonly found (the singular is given for clarity):

l'albicocca	apricot	**l'arancia**	orange
la ciliegia	cherry	**la fragola**	strawberry
il limone	lemon	**la mela**	apple
il melone	melon	**la pera**	pear
la pesca	peach	**il pompelmo**	grapefruit
la prugna	plum	**la susina**	plum (also)

l'uva   grapes (**uva** is a singular noun meaning 'grapes'):

L'uva è molto buona.
The grapes are very good.

Un chilo di uva bianca, per piacere.
A kilo of white grapes, please.

Plurals of nouns ending in -cia, -gia

A stressed **-i** remains in the plural:

la farmacia
le farmacie
un'allergia
molte allergie

If the **-i-** is there only to show that the **-c-** or **-g-** is soft, then:

(a) **-cia**, **-gia**, preceded by a vowel becomes **-cie**, **-gie**:

  una ciliegia   **un chilo di ciliegie**

(b) **-cia**, **-gia**, preceded by a consonant becomes **-ce**, **-ge**:

  un'arancia   **un chilo di arance**

Difficult? Yes, but we needed to tell you before the next exercise. When you are speaking Italian, in the case of (a) and (b) it makes no difference to the sound, so don't worry. But, in the next exercise, try to get it right, while it is fresh in your mind. You can always look it up when you have to write.

Exercise 3

You are at a fruit stall in a market. Ask how much the fruits listed above cost. There is one 'trick question' – watch out for it.

Dialogue 4

Ho bisogno di formaggio

Mrs Rossi is in a grocer's shop.

1 How much 'pecorino' does Mrs Rossi buy?
2 What else does she buy besides cheese?

COMMESSO:	Buongiorno, signora, desidera?
SIG.RA ROSSI:	Ho bisogno di formaggio oggi. C'è del pecorino?
COMMESSO:	Dolce o piccante?
SIG.RA ROSSI:	Piccante. Tre etti.
COMMESSO:	Ecco. Altro?
SIG.RA ROSSI:	Sì. Del prosciutto crudo.
COMMESSO:	Prosciutto di Parma o nostrano?
SIG.RA ROSSI:	Quanto costano?
COMMESSO:	Il nostrano 32 euro e 90 centesimi al chilo, quello di Parma 35,60. E' molto buono quello nostrano.
SIG.RA ROSSI:	Allora lo prendo. Basta un etto.
COMMESSO:	*Slices some and then weighs it* 120 grammi. Va bene così?
SIG.RA ROSSI:	Sì, va bene. Quant'è?
COMMESSO:	4 euro e 30 centesimi il pecorino. E poi, 3,30 il prosciutto. 7,60 in tutto. Grazie, arrivederLa. Buongiorno.

Cultural point

Italy boasts a wide variety of cheeses. The Po Plain produces **grana padano** and **parmigiano reggiano**, which are very similar to each other. They are both made from cow's milk and are fairly hard, depending on how long they have been matured; more importantly, maturing affects the flavour. Another popular cheese is **pecorino**, which is made with ewes' milk. According to how long it has been matured it is **dolce** 'mild' or **piccante** 'strong flavoured'. All these cheeses are used for grating as well as being delicious eaten as cheese. Grated cheese is much used in Italian cooking, on pasta, risotto, soups etc. Another very special Italian speciality is **prosciutto crudo,** cured ham. It is usually known in English as 'Parma ham' although ham is cured in a similar way in other parts of Italy; **prosciutto** can also be **cotto** 'cooked'.

Exercise 4

Say out loud and then write down in words the prices in Dialogue 4.

Language points

The partitive, 'some . . .'

To express the idea 'some' ('not all') of something, you use the articulated preposition **del**, i.e. **di** + the definite article:

del formaggio	some cheese
delle mele	some apples
del prosciutto	some ham

Prices

When giving the price 'per kilo, per litre' etc. Italian uses: **al chilo, al litro**:

30 euro al chilo

Exercise 5

Sig.ra Rossi has made a shopping list. How would she tell the shop assistant she wants *some* of the following?

>*Example*: **banane**
>*Answer*: **Vorrei delle banane**

1 limoni
2 francobolli
3 caffè
4 formaggio
5 uva

6 acqua minerale
7 arance
8 pesche
9 pane

Quantity

When you specify a quantity, however, you just use **di**:

un chilo di mele
un litro di vino
un po' di formaggio
un etto di prosciutto

Dialogue 5

Ci sono altri colori?

*Joe, in Florence, wants to buy presents to take home. He, like many other tourists, goes to the very large street market near the church of San Lorenzo. He is looking at sweaters ('a sweater' is **una maglia**), with his young sister in mind. There is one he likes displayed on a stall.*

1 Who does the salesgirl assume he is buying for?
2 What colour sweater catches his eye?
3 Why does he take an 'L'?

JOE: (*trying to attract the salesperson's attention*) Senta! Posso vedere quella maglia?
VENDITRICE: Sì, signore. E' molto bella, questa maglia. Fatta a mano.

JOE:	Quanto costa?
VENDITRICE:	Solo 30 euro. E' per Sua moglie?
JOE:	No, per mia sorella. Ha 16 anni. Ci sono altri colori?
VENDITRICE:	(*pointing to a pile of sweaters*) Sì signore. Guardi. C'è verde, rosa, blu, beige …
JOE:	Mi piace quella verde.
VENDITRICE:	Sua sorella, com'è? Di che misura ha bisogno?
JOE:	Le piace portare le maglie grandi.
VENDITRICE:	Allora deve prendere una "L".
JOE:	Va bene. Prendo quella verde.

Vocabulary notes

fatto/a a mano   'handmade' (made by hand)
misura   'size' (used for clothes, shoes etc.)

Language point

Colours, i colori

The singular of **i colori** is **il colore**.

azzurro	blue (darker than **celeste**)
bianco	white
giallo	yellow
grigio	grey
nero	black
rosso	red
celeste	blue (sky blue, paler than **azzurro**)
arancione	orange
marrone	brown
verde	green
blu	dark or navy blue
rosa	pink
viola	violet

The colours have been grouped above according to the way the adjectives work. The ones in the first group have four forms: **rosso, rossa, rossi, rosse**:

buoni vini rossi   good red wines

Those in the second group have two forms: **verde**, **verdi**:

una mela verde   one (a) green apple
due mele verdi   two green apples

Those in the last group have one form only:

una maglia blu   a dark blue sweater
due maglie blu   two dark blue sweaters

Note: **chiaro** 'light' (when used of a colour), also 'clear'; **scuro** 'dark'.

verde chiaro   light green   **verde scuro**   dark green

Exercise 6

It takes a while to absorb verb forms. Here is some more practice. The verb is given in the infinitive. Write the correct form for the various subjects suggested. Where it might be more usual to leave the subject pronoun out, it is put in brackets.

> *Example*: *lavorare*
> **Carlo. Carlo lavora. Anna e Paola.**
> **Anna e Paola lavorano.**

1 *comprare*
  Anna, che cosa (a) _____ (tu)?
  Io (b) _____ un libro.
  Gianna, tu e Piero, che cosa (c) _____?
  (Noi) (d) _____ una maglia per Piero.

2 *leggere*
  Io (a) _____ poco. Non ho tempo.
  Paolo invece (b) _____ molto.
  Si dice che gli Italiani (c) _____ poco. Non so se è vero.

3 *preferire*
  Io (a) _____ la maglia rossa.
  Giorgio invece (b) _____ quella celeste.

4 *parlare*
  Questi studenti (a) _____ russo, francese e italiano.
  Io invece (b) _____ solo italiano.
  Mario (c) _____ inglese e francese?
  E tu? (d) _____ un'altra lingua?

5 *vivere*

Giorgio e Anna (a) _____ in città.

Noi (b) _____ in campagna.

Reading

Il mio primo computer

Il pc ideale per un bambino? Processore di ultima generazione e memoria potente. Inutile, invece, il modello più recente.

1 **This is part of an article in a women's magazine. It is about buying a computer. For what sort of use?**
2 **In the last sentence, what is buying a computer for the purpose described compared to?**

Con l'inizio della scuola è bene che il bambino impari a usare il pc vero e proprio, magari con mouse e tastiera semplificati. "Per un bimbo tra i 7 e gli 11 anni è sufficiente un pc di media potenza, fisso (i portatili costano di più e sono più delicati), con stampante a getto di inchiostro, cd rom, scheda audio e casse, modem per poter navigare in internet," spiega l'esperto. "Verificate che la macchina sia dotata di processore di ultima generazione e abbia una memoria Ram almeno di 128 Megabyte, meglio se è più alta, altrimenti si rischia di non poter utilizzare cd rom e giochi elettronici."

Trappole

"Non cadete nell'errore di rincorrere il modello più recente. La differenza reale tra il più potente dei pc è nell'ordine della frazione di secondo. Attenzione piuttosto alla garanzia e alla serietà del rivenditore . . . Spiegate chiaramente al venditore l'uso che intendete farne . . . E ricordate che per andare a fare la spesa non c'è bisogno della Ferrari, basta una Cinquecento."

(*Anna*, Family Life section, 18 febbraio 2003)

Vocabulary notes

inutile 'useless'. Opposite of **utile** 'useful'.
bambino, bimbo 'child'. There is a feminine form, ending in **-a**.
   When used in a general way, as here, the masculine includes the feminine.

vero e proprio 'proper' (lit. 'real and proper'). An earlier part of the article, not included here, talked about toy computers for pre-school children.

dotato/a di 'equipped, provided with'

si rischia 'one risks' (**rischiare** 'to risk')

non cadete nell'errore 'don't fall into the error of . . .' (**cadere** 'to fall')

nell'ordine della frazione di secondo 'in the order of a fraction of a second'

l'uso che intendete farne 'the use you intend to make of it'

ricordate 'remember' (**ricordare** 'to remember')

Computer vocabulary notes

You will recognize as English much of Italian computer vocabulary. Here are some words you may not have been able to guess:

tastiera 'keyboard'

media potenza 'medium power'

fisso 'fixed'. In this case 'desktop'.

portatile 'portable'. An adjective used as the noun for laptop (computer).

stampante (f.) 'printer' (**stampare** 'to print')

getto di inchiostro 'ink-jet' (**laser** 'laser')

scheda audio 'audio card' (cf. **scheda telefonica**)

casse 'loudspeakers'

navigare in internet 'to surf the internet'

ultima generazione 'last generation'. We would probably say 'latest generation'.

memoria 'memory'

giochi elettronici 'computer games' (**un gioco**)

Shopping vocabulary notes

verificare 'to check'

attenzione 'be careful'

garanzia 'guarantee'

serietà 'trustworthiness' (in this context). A **rivenditore serio** is one who can be trusted.

rivenditore 'retailer' (in this context). Really a reseller, i.e. seller of second-hand goods.

venditore 'salesman'

fare la spesa 'to do the shopping'. Usually implies the regular household shopping.

Unusual verb forms

There are three examples in this passage of the present subjunctive. They need not worry you and possibly you did not notice them. They are **impari** (first line), **sia** and **abbia**. You will probably agree that the meaning is guessable. We will deal with them later in the book.

8 Un po' di geografia

A little geography

In this unit you will learn about:

- The basics of the geography of Italy
- Vocabulary for landscape and places, distances and area
- Forming the past participle e.g. cultivated, walked
- The passive
- Adverbs
- Expressing your likes – **mi piacciono, mi piacerebbe**
- Personal pronouns, indirect object form ('to me, to him')
- Using **c'è/ci sono**, 'there is'/'there are'
- The 'north/south divide'

Reading 1

Un po' di geografia

On the following page is a map of Italy. Use it, and the text on p. 123, to answer the questions below.

Are the following statements true or false?

1 The summit of Mont Blanc is in Italy.
2 The highest mountains in Europe are to be found in the Apennines.
3 Three-quarters of Italy's land area is flat.
4 Water for crops is not a problem for agriculture on the Po Plain.
5 Milan and Turin have recently developed manufacturing industry.
6 The Alps are volcanic mountains.

Italy: physical

7 **Etna is an extinct volcano.**
8 **Sicily is the southernmost island of Italy.**
9 **Tourism is very important to the Italian economy.**

L'Italia è una penisola a forma di stivale. Montagne e colline occupano una superficie pari a oltre tre quarti del territorio italiano. L'Italia è povera di pianure.

by far

neighbouring

Al nord un arco di montagne, le Alpi, la separa dai paesi confinanti. Nell'arco alpino si trovano le montagne più alte d'Europa: il Monte Bianco, m. 4,810, il Monte Rosa, m. 4,634, e il Cervino, m. 4,478, chiamato 'Matterhorn' in inglese. Di questi tre, solo il Monte Rosa ha la cima interamente in territorio italiano.

Ai piedi delle montagne si estende da ovest ad est la Pianura Padana, cioè del fiume Po. Il Po, il più grande fiume italiano, è lungo 652 km. La pianura, di gran lunga la più grande d'Italia, (46,000 km²) è irrigata dalle abbondanti acque che scendono dalle montagne. Perciò è da secoli intensamente coltivata. Sulla ricchezza di questa agricoltura fiorente è basato lo sviluppo dell'industria che è oggi l'attività economica dominante della pianura. Città come Milano e Torino hanno una lunga storia industriale; più recente è lo sviluppo eccezionale in città medie di industrie varie che vanno dall'abbigliamento e gli alimenti, ai prodotti 'high-tec'.

La pianura è chiusa a sud da un'altra catena di montagne: gli Appennini, che si allungano per 1,190 km. fino a Reggio Calabria e anche in Sicilia. Gli Appennini sono montagne vulcaniche. Tutti conoscono il nome di due vulcani italiani: il Vesuvio, attualmente inattivo, e l'Etna, ancora in attività.

La Sicilia e la Sardegna sono due grandi isole italiane. Ci sono poi numerose isole piccole, tra cui Lampedusa, a sud-ovest dell' isola di Malta, che è più vicina alle coste della Tunisia che a quelle siciliane. Il mare e le isole, con le montagne e la campagna, costituiscono mete turistiche piacevolissime. Va ricordato che il turismo è un settore importantissimo dell'economia italiana.

allungarsi
- to stretch

Vocabulary

stivale (*m.*)	boot	**fiorente**	flourishing
pari a	equal to	**sviluppo**	development
povero/a	poor	**alimenti**	foods
cioè (**ciò è**)	that is, i.e.	**chiuso/a**	closed
di gran lunga	by far, by a long chalk	**catena**	chain
		meta	destination
è da secoli coltivata	it has been cultivated for centuries	**piacevole**	pleasant

Vocabulary for landscape and places

paese	(1) country (e.g France, New Zealand); (2) village
confine	border, boundary
frontiera	frontier
luogo	place
posto	(1) place; (2) seat; (3) job
città	city, town (not necessarily very large)
centro	centre (often **centro storico**, the old, central part of a city)
periferia	outskirts, suburbs
villaggio	village (as well as **paese**)
frazione	outlying village of a **comune**
bosco	wood
cima	summit
collina	hill
costa	coast
fiume	river
isola	island
pianura	plain
spiaggia	beach
superficie	surface

Cultural point

Italy is divided into twenty administrative regions (see map on p. x). The regions have responsibility for matters such as regional planning, economic development etc., though very much under central control. Each region (**regione** (f.)) is divided into provinces (**provincia**). Provinces have more limited functions. The basic level of local administration is the municipality (**comune** (m.)). **comuni** vary immensely in size and include cities such as Rome and Milan. They are now subdivided into **circoscrizioni** (wards) in a move to involve people at local level. At each level of administration there is an elected council, which delegates executive powers to a **giunta**, composed of **assessori**. The **comune** and **giunta** are chaired by a mayor (**sindaco**). Mayors are now directly elected by the citizens.

Language points

The points of the compass

The words for the points of the compass each have corresponding adjectives:

nord – settentrionale	**sud – meridionale**
est – orientale	**ovest – occidentale**

The compass points can be combined as in English: **sud-ovest**, **nord-est**. Given the shape of Italy, it is more frequent to talk of the north and south than east and west; the north of the country and south are in fact very different. It is common to refer to the south as **il mezzogiorno** (which also means 'south').

Measuring distances and area

chilometro (km)
metro (m)   **un chilometro = mille metri**
decimetro (dm)   **un metro = cento centimetri**
centimetro (cm)   **un centimetro = dieci millimetri**
millimetro (mm)
un chilometro quadrato (1 km^2) = one square kilometre
un ettaro = 100 m^2 = 2.471 acres

Past participles

These correspond to the English form ending in '-ed' (e.g. 'cultivated', 'irrigated', 'walked', 'talked' etc.). The passage contained a number:

Questa pianura è *irrigata* . . .
E' intensivamente *coltivata*.
Sulla ricchezza . . . è *basato* lo sviluppo . . .
   (= lo sviluppo è basato)

The past participle is formed according to the type of verb:

-are verbs:	drop **-are**, add **-ato**:	**parlare**	**parlato**
-ere verbs:	drop **-ere**, add **-uto**:	**cadere**	**caduto**
-ire verbs:	drop **-ire**, add **-ito**:	**finire**	**finito**

In English there are irregular forms (e.g. 'thought', 'seen', 'gone'), and so there are in Italian, particularly in the second group. There is a list of common ones in the 'Grammar summary' at the end of the book.

Some past participles are often used as adjectives: **una porta aperta/chiusa** 'an open/shut door'. Past participles are much used in newspaper headlines:

Città inondata, ospedale evacuato
City flooded, hospital evacuated

Sulla riforma, governo battuto due volte.
Government beaten twice on the reform.

Cultural point

You may like to try reading some Italian newspapers, especially the section called **cronaca**, which contains news items of a non-political sort (crime, road accidents etc.), as a way of getting language practice. Start with the headlines. Newspapers tend to be relatively local in Italy. The best known are probably *Il Corriere della Sera*, the Milan daily, and *La Stampa*, the Turin daily; both date back to the nineteenth century. Much more recent is *La Repubblica*, a national paper founded in the late twentieth century. *Il Sole 24 Ore* is business orientated; whereas the *Gazzetta dello Sport* is what it says it is, a sports daily.

The passive

The passive is formed with **essere** and a past participle, just as in English it is formed with 'to be' and the past participle:

La pianura è *coltivata*.
The plain is cultivated.

Lo sviluppo è *basato* sulla ricchezza dell'agricoltura.
Development is based on the wealth of the agriculture.

Il servizio è *incluso*.
Service is included.

Note: The past participle agrees with the subject, behaving like an adjective.

To say who or what things were done by, i.e. to express the agent, use **da**:

L'albergo è gestito dal proprietario.
The hotel is managed by the owner.

La pianura è circondata da montagne.
The plain is surrounded by mountains.

A common use is after **deve essere**, **può essere**:

Il lavoro deve essere finito domani.
The work must be finished tomorrow

Exercise 1

You are a busy executive and are getting your secretary organized. How will you tell him/her:

1 The fax must be sent this morning.
   (spedire un fax)
2 The meeting can be organized for Monday.
   (organizzare una riunione)
3 The hotel can be booked by telephone.
   (prenotare un albergo)
4 The booking can be confirmed by fax.
   (confermare una prenotazione)
5 The tickets must be collected at midday.
   (ritirare i biglietti)
6 Rome can be informed by fax.
   (informare Roma via fax)
7 The taxi can be called in (**fra**) 10 minutes.
   (chiamare un taxi)

You need not worry too much about the passive as it works the same way as the passive in English. It tends to belong to formal language. We shall meet it and the past participle again. However, don't forget *impersonal si*. We met it in Unit 4 and it often conveys ideas which in English would be in the passive:

Qui si parla italiano.
Italian is spoken here.

Come si scrive questa parola?
How is this word written/spelt?

Cultural point

Several times in the year a public holiday falls close to a weekend and Italians, and others working in Italy, like to make a long weekend of it, taking a holiday on the days between the weekend and the public holiday. This is called: **fare il ponte**, making a bridge.

Dialogue 1

Fare il ponte nel Bel Paese

Here, George, an American working temporarily in Milan, asks a colleague for advice about how he and Jane, his wife, might spend the long weekend.

1 **Why does George ask Andrea for advice?**
2 **What does George want to avoid?**
3 **What conflict is there between George's and Jane's interests?**
4 **In which town is there a Roman arena?**
5 **What is the name of the really restful place Andrea suggests?**

GEORGE: Senti, Andrea, mi puoi dare un consiglio? Vorrei suggerimenti per il fine settimana del 25 aprile. Jane ed io abbiamo pensato di fare il ponte e partire per quattro o cinque giorni. Tu che conosci bene l'Italia, che cosa mi suggerisci? Vogliamo a tutti i costi andare via e cambiare aria.

ANDREA: Cosa preferite, città o campagna? Un lago forse? O il mare? C'è anche la montagna.

GEORGE: A Jane piace visitare le città. S'interessa molto di architettura, di cose antiche. Io vorrei riposarmi, non vorrei passare troppo tempo in macchina. E mi piacciono di più i posti tranquilli, i paesi piccoli, i panorami belli.

ANDREA: Perché non andate nel Veneto?

GEORGE: Conosciamo già Venezia e ci piacerebbe evitare posti troppo affollati.

ANDREA: Appunto. Nel Veneto puoi trovare città per Jane e posti più tranquilli per te. Ad esempio, Verona è una città vivacissima, ricca di monumenti.

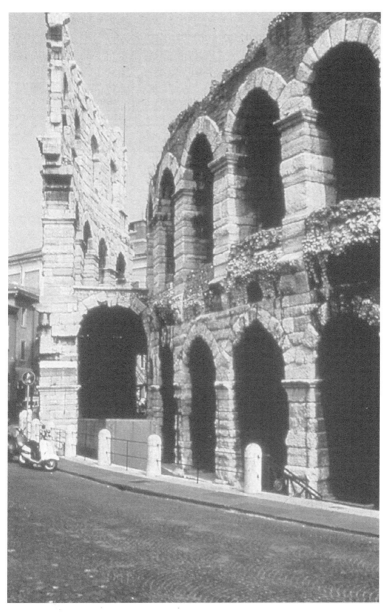

Verona, the Roman Arena. Courtesy Archivio Provincia di Verona.

GEORGE: Davvero? Che cosa c'è da vedere a Verona?
ANDREA: C'è l'Arena, un anfiteatro romano, c'è la chiesa di S.
          Zeno, romanica, bellissima; ci sono anche altri monu-
          menti e tanti angoli pittoreschi. Poi potreste continuare
          verso Vicenza e vedere qualche opera del Palladio.*
          Per te c'è Marostica, una cittadina medievale; c'è
          Asolo, un posto veramente riposante, in una bellissima
          posizione in collina. E poi ...
GEORGE: Vedo che non mancano le possibilità; grazie.

* Palladio was a Renaissance architect.

Language points

Using -issimo/-issima

bellissimo/bellissima

Often, instead of using the word **molto** to convey the idea 'very',
Italians use **-issimo/-issima**. Just remove the final vowel of the
adjective and add **-issimo/-issima**.

Exercise 2

Jane and George are telling someone about their weekend. George
echoes everything Jane says.

> *Example*: J: **Verona è una città molto interessante.**
> G: **Interessantissima.**

J: Il Veneto è molto bello.
G: (1) _____

J: Marostica è una cittadina molto simpatica.
G: (2) _____

J: Asolo è un posto molto tranquillo.
G: (3) _____

J: Le ville del Palladio sono molto eleganti.
G: (4) _____

J: E' stato un weekend molto piacevole.
G: (5) _____

Adverbs

To form an adverb, add **-mente** to the feminine of the adjective:

lento/a	**lentamente**

Adjectives ending in **-e**:

semplice	**semplicemente**

Adjectives ending in **-ale** and **-are** lose the **-e**:

finale	**finalmente**
attuale	**attualmente**
regolare	**regolarmente**

Common adverbs *not* formed from adjectives are:

bene	well	**male**	badly
presto	quickly	**sempre**	always
spesso	often	**subito**	at once

-issimo can be added to four of these adverbs:

bene	**sto benissimo**	**spesso**	**viene spessissimo**
male	**canta malissimo**	**presto**	**partiamo prestissimo**

Note: **molto** can be an adverb and an adjective. As an adverb it is invariable.

I libri sono molto interessanti. (adv.)
The books are very interesting.

Ho molti libri sulla geografia italiana. (adj.)
I have lots of books on Italian geography.

Exercise 3

Complete these statements inserting an adverb formed from the adjective given:

1 La porta si chiude _____ (automatico).
2 Anna è contenta e canta _____ mentre lavora (allegro).
3 Non hanno molto tempo e così mangiano _____ (veloce).
4 Il treno viaggia _____ (lento).
5 Il dottor Rossi fa molto _____ (buono) il suo lavoro.
6 Anna mi telefona _____ (regolare).

Expressing your likes

mi piacciono

You will remember **mi piace** (see Unit 2) means 'it is pleasing to me'. Therefore when it is a *plural* thing you like, for example, quiet places (as George does), then you have to say 'quiet places are pleasing to me', **mi piacciono i posti tranquilli**.

Exercise 4

How would you say you like:

1 Roma   2 le montagne
3 visitare monumenti storici   4 le isole piccolissime
5 questi spaghetti (**spaghetti** are plural, as you can see from the form and the adjective, **questi**)

But what about talking about *other* people's likes? You need to be able to say 'it is/they are pleasing to you, to him' etc. Here's how:

mi	
ti	
gli	
le	**piace/piacciono**
ci	
vi	
gli	

These pronouns are called *indirect object pronouns*: 'pronouns' because they stand instead of nouns, 'indirect object' because they contain the idea 'to me', not simply 'me'. To express this particular idea in English, we have a direct object: 'I like *it*'. But remember that in Italian what you are saying is 'it is pleasing *to me*'.

Exercise 5

How would you ask: (a) a friend (i.e. using **tu**); (b) an acquaintance (i.e. using **Lei**); (c) two people (using **voi**):

1 Do you like Italian wines?
2 Do you like Venice?
3 Do you like studying Italian?

mi piacerebbe

This means 'it would be pleasing to me': in other words 'I should like'. It is the same tense of the verb you met in **vorrei** 'I should like'. They are very similar in meaning, but you will usually use **vorrei** when choosing/asking for things (e.g. when making purchases, ordering drinks, food etc.). **mi piacerebbe** has a plural form for use when what you would like is plural: **mi piacerebbero**.

You can talk about what *other* people would like in the same way as with **piace**:

mi
ti
gli
le   **piacerebbe/piacerebbero**
ci
vi
gli

mi piacerebbe is frequently followed by verbs:

Mi piacerebbe visitare le isole Tremiti.
Ci piacerebbe vedere il Vesuvio.

Exercise 6

(a) Here are some things you might like to do when you are in Italy. Translate these sentences:

1 Mi piacerebbe vedere il Campidoglio.
2 Mi piacerebbe andare in gondola a Venezia.
3 Mi piacerebbe gettare una moneta nella fontana di Trevi.
4 Mi piacerebbe assistere ad una gara di Formula 1 a Imola.
5 Mi piacerebbe sciare sulle pendici dell'Etna.
6 Mi piacerebbe visitare Pompei ed Ercolano.
7 Mi piacerebbe vedere lo Stromboli, il vulcano nelle isole Eolie.

(b) Now add some suggestions of your own.

Using qualche *'some'*

Qualche opera del Palladio

This means 'some works by Palladio'. **qualche** means *some* but it is always followed by a singular noun:

qualche volta	sometimes
qualche libro	some books
qualche cosa	something (often abbreviated to: **qualcosa**)

One use of da

Che cosa c'è da vedere a Verona?

Note this use of the preposition **da** (see Unit 6). Similarly:

Cosa c'è da fare?
What is there to do?

C'è qualcosa da mangiare?
Is there something to eat?

Cosa prende da bere?
What will you have to drink?

Using c'è, ci sono

These mean 'there is, there are': **c'è** is the same as **ci è**.

A Verona c'è un teatro romano.
A Venezia ci sono tanti canali.

Exercise 7

Here is a list of some of the interesting places and artefacts to be seen in the little Tuscan town of Cortona. Answer the question: **A Cortona, che cosa c'è da vedere?**, deciding whether you should say **c'è** or **ci sono**. Translate your answers.

1 Il lampadario etrusco nel Museo dell'Accademia Etrusca.
2 La via Crucis a mosaico di Gino Severini.[1]
3 Le strade pittoresche del quartiere alto della città.
4 Il panorama sulla Val di Chiana.
5 Le opere del pittore Luca Signorelli.[2]
6 La fortezza Medicea.
7 I dipinti del Beato Angelico[3] nel Museo Diocesano.

1 **Gino Severini**, 1883–1966, was also born in Cortona although he lived and worked mostly in Paris.
2 **Luca Signorelli**, 1445–1523, was born in Cortona.
3 **Il Beato Angelico**, a Dominican monk and painter, *c.* 1400–1455, is usually known in English as 'Fra Angelico'.

Reading 2

Nord–Sud

1 **What is the essence of the problem of the south?**
2 **What six differences between north and south are quoted as lying behind the economic differences?**
3 **Why might tourists be attracted to the south?**

Il "problema del mezzogiorno" è da anni un' importante questione della politica italiana. In che cosa consiste il problema? Nel fatto che il sud è in genere più povero del nord.

Perché? Ci sono tanti motivi: una storia diversa, costumi diversi, un clima diverso, terreno diverso, una più lunga e più diffusa industrializzazione nel nord ... perfino il fatto che il sud è più lontano dal centro economico dell'Europa. Non solo questo, ma la forma allungata e montagnosa dell'Italia rende difficile i collegamenti nord-sud. In più, il crimine organizzato è senza dubbio un forte freno allo sviluppo economico del Mezzogiorno. Il problema è molto complesso e sembra difficile da risolvere.

Per il turista però le differenze sono altre. Il sud è ricco di resti dell'antica civiltà greca, ad esempio. Ci sono città e villaggi affascinanti, paesaggi e coste bellissime e tra la gente un calore umano che forse si perde in una società più prospera.

9 Buon appetito

Enjoy your meal

In this unit you will learn about:

- Italian food
- Ordering a meal
- Object pronouns, direct and indirect, e.g. 'me, her, them', 'to me, to her, to them'
- **Come mai?** 'How's that?', 'How come?'
- Making your point clear – those little words
- **viene fatto, va fatto** – 'it's done, it should be done' – another form of the passive
- **ci vuole, ci vogliono** 'you need, one needs'

Dialogue 1 ⌒

Al ristorante

Mr and Mrs Rossi have taken Angela to one of their favourite restaurants. They are just finishing their antipasto.

1 **Why does signora Rossi say ham and melon is good in the summer?**
2 **How does the waiter describe the fish?**
3 **In spite of its name, 'manzo alla California' is a speciality of an Italian region according to the waiter. Which one?**

ANGELA:	E' molto saporito questo prosciutto. Mi piace moltissimo prosciutto e melone.
SIG.RA ROSSI:	Sì, d'estate è buono, è leggero.
CAMERIERE:	*(taking plates away)* E come primo, cosa prendete, signori?

SIG. ROSSI:	(*consulting the menu*) Cosa prende per primo, signora? Ci sono i tortellini, il risotto, gli gnocchi, le tagliatelle al pomodoro e basilico, al pesto ...
ANGELA:	(*looking at her copy*) Per me il passato di verdura.
SIG.RA ROSSI:	Buona scelta. Lo prendo anch'io. E tu, Massimo?
SIG. ROSSI:	Per me, il risotto.
CAMERIERE:	E come secondo? Abbiamo dell'ottimo pesce stasera. Oppure c'è un arrosto di vitello speciale ...
ANGELA:	Che cosa è il 'manzo alla California'?
CAMERIERE:	E' una specialità lombarda, signora. E' uno stufato di manzo cotto molto lentamente con aceto di vino e panna. (*They make their selection.*)

Vocabulary

prosciutto e melone	Parma ham and melon (considered a dish, hence the singular verb)
passato di verdura	sieved or liquidized vegetable soup
uno stufato di manzo	a beef stew

It is assumed readers have eaten pasta and know dishes such as **tortellini**, **gnocchi**; they are virtually untranslatable but any book on Italian food will explain them.

Cultural point

i pasti del giorno 'the meals of the day' for Italians are **prima colazione** breakfast, which some have at home: coffee or hot chocolate, or perhaps tea, plus biscuits, bread and jam – quite simple. The main meal of the day is **pranzo**, sometimes eaten in the evening. In that case the midday meal is often called **colazione**. Supper is **cena**. There are regional variations and of course living in a big city implies different rhythms, dictated by travelling times, from those enjoyed by people in less congested areas. Children usually have a snack between lunch and supper, called **la merenda**. **uno spuntino** is a snack taken by adults between meals or can be instead of a meal, for instance a quick snack lunch.

An Italian main meal (lunch or dinner) normally consists of **il primo** (pasta, rice or soup), followed by **il secondo** (a meat or fish course, which is accompanied by a **contorno** (vegetable)). A celebration meal or a meal out in a restaurant starts with **antipasto**, then **il primo**, then sometimes fish, and then the meat course. Bread, **il pane**, is an essential accompaniment. A family meal often finishes with cheese and/or fruit. A **dolce** (dessert) is served on special occasions. Weight- and health-conscious Italians are tending to cut down on the number of courses in a meal nowadays. Feel free to skip a course from time to time in a restaurant. When your hostess has gone to the trouble of cooking it, it is rather more delicate a matter – and often too delicious to resist.

More vocabulary notes for meals and food

verdure	'vegetables'
ristorante	'restaurant' (usually fairly big)
trattoria	'restaurant' (small, usually family-run)
pizzeria	specializes in **pizza** but often offers other dishes, particularly **pasta**
tavola calda	serves 'fast food', Italian-style, to take away, or to eat in the shop
self-service	just what it says: the food is usually good

There is a wide variety of fish available. Names are sometimes local – you'll have to to be bold and take a chance.

Alla carta

Secondi piatti

carne	meat	**pollo**	chicken
vitello	veal	**tacchino**	turkey
manzo	beef	**maiale**	pork
agnello	lamb	**bistecca**	steak
pesce	fish	**trota**	trout
salmone	salmon	**calamaro**	squid

Contorni

carote	carrots	**cipolle**	onions
fagioli	beans (dried)	**fagiolini**	French beans
funghi	mushrooms	**melanzane**	aubergine, eggplant
porcini	porcini, ceps*	**piselli**	peas
peperoncini	chillis	**peperoni**	peppers
patate	potatoes	**pomodori**	tomatoes
spinaci (pl.)	spinach	**zucchini**	baby marrows
insalata mista	mixed salad	**insalata verde**	green salad

Vocabulary

odori	herbs	**tartufo**	truffle
aglio	garlic	**sale**	salt
basilico	basil	**pepe**	pepper
maggiorana	marjoram	**aceto**	vinegar
prezzemolo	parsley	**olio d'oliva**	olive oil
rosmarino	rosemary		
salvia	sage	**al forno**	roast, in the oven
timo	thyme	**bollito**	stewed
		alla griglia	grilled
panna	cream	**stufato**	a stew
polenta[†]		**arrosto**	a roast
riso	rice		

* *Bolelus edulis.*
† Polenta is made with maize flour and was once the staple diet of northern Italy. It is a thick, solid paste which is cooked and then sliced. Nowadays it is served with meat or fish dishes.

cucinare	to prepare food, cook – a person does this to food
cuocere	to be subjected to heat etc., to cook – food does this

alla fiorentina, alla veneziana, alla milanese etc. mean prepared Florentine-, Venetian- or Milanese-style. Menus can be difficult to understand, partly because cooking varies from region to region and partly because imaginative cooks invent dishes. Don't be afraid to ask for explanations.

Direct object pronouns ('him, her, it, them')

Signora Rossi, hearing Angela order the vegetable soup, says:

Buona idea. *La* prendo anch'io.
A good idea. I'll have *it* too.

See also Unit 5: Joe, choosing a map, said:

La prendo.
I'll have it.

Here are some more examples:

Dov'è il giornale? Non *lo* vedo.
Where is the newspaper? I can't see *it*.

Giorgio non vuole venire stasera. *Lo* capisco.
Giorgio doesn't want to come this evening. I understand *him*.

Cerco i miei occhiali. Non *li* trovo.
I'm looking for my glasses. I can't find *them*.

Mi piacciono molto le lasagne al forno. *Le* prendo.
I love lasagne. I'll have *them*.

I miei nonni abitano qui vicino. *Li* vediamo quasi ogni giorno.
My grandparents live near here. We see *them* nearly every day.

Do you see the way the pronoun works? It depends whether the noun being replaced is masculine or feminine, singular or plural.

	Singular		*Plural*	
Masculine	**lo**	him, it	**li**	them
Feminine	**la**	her, it	**le**	them

Notice also that the pronoun is placed *before* the verb.

You have already met the *indirect object* pronouns. The difficulty for most English-speaking people is to understand the idea of *direct* and *indirect object.* Here are a couple of examples in English. Are the words in italic direct or indirect objects?

He sees *me.*   He speaks *to me.*
They know *her.*   They talk *to her.*

In the first column you have a direct object, in the second, an indirect. The direct object is directly affected by the action of the verb; the indirect object has a preposition before the pronoun. A more complicated case in English would be:

They gave it to me.

What is *it* and what is *to me*, grammatically? They are direct and indirect objects respectively. *It* was given. I benefited indirectly – it was given *to me.*

Exercise 1

You are having a meal in a restaurant. Your host asks you whether you like various dishes. Say you do and that you will have it.

Example: HOST: **C'è prosciutto e melone come antipasto. Le piace?**
            YOU: **Sì, mi piace. Lo prendo.**

HOST: Come primo ci sono lasagne al forno. Le piacciono?
YOU: (1) _____

HOST: Come secondo c'è bistecca alla fiorentina. Le piace?
YOU: (2) _____

HOST: E come contorno, ci sono spinaci. Le piacciono?
YOU: (3) _____

Exercise 2

Things are being very irritating. You can't see them, you can't find them, you can't understand them – and you are getting into quite a state. You need help (**aiuto**). Here is what you say, in English. But your Italian friend won't understand if you say it that way, so say it in Italian.

> Where's Mary's letter? I can't find it. And the magazine?
> I can't see it. Where are the stamps for the postcards?
> I can't find them. Can you see the pen? I can't find it.
> And this bill (**conto**), I don't understand it. Help!

More about object pronouns

The indirect object pronouns are:

mi	to me	**ci**	to us
ti	to you	**vi**	to you
gli	to him	**gli**	to them
le	to her, to you		

mi, **ti**, **ci**, **vi**, are also *direct object pronouns*:

mi	me	**ci**	us
ti	you	**vi**	you

So the problem of difference arises only in the third person:

lo	him	**gli**	to him
la	her	**le**	to her
La	you	**Le**	to you
li	them (m.)	**gli**	to them (m. and f.)
le	them (f.)		

Note: Confusion between **gli** singular and plural doesn't arise because you only use a pronoun when you have used a noun immediately previously. Some grammar books will mention a plural indirect object pronoun, **loro**, but it is rarely used in speech.

What did you notice about the position of the object pronoun, whether direct or indirect? It usually goes just before the verb:

Carla	**mi/ti/lo/la/ci/vi/li/le**	**conosce molto bene**
Carla	**mi/ti/gli/le/ci/vi/gli**	**scrive ogni settimana**

Note: When **loro** is used, it must follow the verb: **Carla scrive loro**.

Exercise 3

Here are some sentences very similar to ones you have met. In each case, translate the pronoun (which has been left in English).

1 Mio figlio abita a Toronto. _____ scrive ogni domenica. (to me)
   Quando arriva la lettera _____ leggo sempre tre o quattro volte. (it)
2 Il signor Marini _____ conosce bene. (us) _____ dà qualche volta delle riviste italiane. (to us)
3 (Al telefono) _____ passo subito il signor Anselmi. (to you, formal)
4 Per la riunione _____ va bene giovedì? (to you, informal)
5 Anna è una mia carissima amica. _____vedo quasi ogni settimana. (her)
6 L'autobus _____ porta in centro. _____ lascia proprio davanti al municipio. (you)

For question 6, try to do each sort: informal singular, formal singular, and the plural – i.e. the object pronouns corresponding to **tu**, **Lei** and **voi**.

Exercise 4

How would you say the following to an Italian friend?

1 Signor Galli knows me well. I see him every week. He telephones me often.
2 Do you know Mr and Mrs Fabrizi? Do you like them? I see them every Sunday. I speak to them on the telephone almost every day.
3 I am writing you a letter. I am sending you the photos (**le foto**) of Gianni.

Dialogue 2 🎧

La cucina italiana

Angela enjoys cooking. She asks signora Rossi about Italian food.

1 **Why, according to Mrs Rossi, is it difficult to talk about Italian cooking?**
2 **Why do they use rice a lot in the Po Plain?**

3 **What does Mrs Rossi say Sicily produces well?**
4 **Why is olive oil not used in the cooking of Lombardy?**
5 **What is used in its place?**

SIG.RA R:	Veramente parlare di 'cucina italiana' è difficile. Ancora oggi la cucina è diversa da una regione all'altra.
ANGELA:	Ah, sì? Come mai?
SIG.RA R:	Dev'essere la geografia, penso; cioè il clima e il terreno. Ad esempio, qui nella Pianura Padana, c'è molta acqua e ci sono risaie. Così si mangiano piatti a base di riso, come il risotto alla milanese. Invece, la Sicilia è molto più arida, ma anche più calda. Produce verdure buonissime, frutta, agrumi. Allora si usano questi in cucina.
ANGELA:	Certo, capisco. Ci dev'essere una differenza di clima notevole tra la Sicilia e la Lombardia.
SIG.RA R:	Sì. Qui abbiamo anche bestiame e naturalmente carne molto buona e latte, panna, formaggi e così via. Ma non abbiamo olive, così nella nostra cucina il burro viene usato più spesso. In quella siciliana si usa quasi esclusivamente l'olio di oliva. Anche in tutta l'Italia centrale si usa l'olio di oliva.
CAMERIERE:	(*bringing the pasta course, **il primo***) I passati di verdura? Per chi sono?
SIG.RA R:	Per la signora e per me. (*Attention turns to the **primo**.*)

Vocabulary

piatti a base di riso	dishes based on rice
così via	and so on

Language points

Come mai? *'How's that?', 'How come?'*

Come mai? means 'How's that?', 'Why?', 'How come?'. The expression implies surprise as well as asking 'why'. A simple 'why' is **perché?**

Making your point clear

When we talk or write, we use various words to clarify and structure what we are saying or writing. They catch the ear of the foreign
learner since they seem to crop up frequently and he/she wonders
what they mean. Such words:

(a) clarify – **cioè** 'that is, i.e.': **Dev'essere la geografia, penso: cioè
il clima e il terreno**;

(b) exemplify – **ad esempio** 'for example' (the **d** is added to **a**
because of the vowel that follows, but this is optional, a question of style; the same can be done with **e** 'and');

(c) contrast – **invece** 'on the other hand, instead';

(d) indicate the consequences – **dunque** 'therefore, so'; **così** 'so,
thus': **così si mangiano piatti a base di riso**; **così** also means 'in
this way' (for example, **Così fan tutte** 'All women behave this
way'; here **fan** is an abbreviation for **fanno**).

Other words of this sort include **comunque** 'anyway, however',
often used to introduce a final remark that is seen as concluding
the argument:

**So che non ti piace e che è difficile; comunque il direttore lo
vuole così. Non c'è scelta.**
I know you don't like it and that it's difficult. However the
director wants it that way. There's no choice.

Look out for others. They often have very minimal meaning.

Saying how things are done

viene fatto così

When saying how things are generally done, it is common to use
venire plus the past participle rather than **essere**. (See Unit 8 – the
passive – but don't forget impersonal/indefinite **si** – Unit 4.)

Il burro viene usato spesso nella cucina settentrionale.
Butter is often used in northern cookery.

va fatto

When saying what should be done it is usual to use **andare** + past participle:

L'ambiente naturale va conservato.
The natural environment should be preserved.

Il vino bianco va bevuto fresco.
White wine should be drunk chilled.

In discussions, you will hear:

Va ricordato che . . .   It should be remembered that . . .
Va detto che . . .   It should be said that . . .

Dialogue 3 🎧

Una ricetta

In the restaurant Angela pursues the topic of Italian food.

1 What kind of recipe does Angela ask for?
2 What are the ingredients for the dish Mrs Rossi describes?
3 What additions does she say would make it more authentically Sicilian?

ANGELA: Signora Rossi, si vede che Lei sa molto sulla cucina italiana. Avrebbe qualche buona ricetta da darmi? Mi piace molto la pasta.

SIG.RA R: Conosco una ricetta siciliana molto buona. In Sicilia la pasta viene spesso servita mescolata con verdure. Il piatto si chiama "pasta con i broccoli" o in dialetto siciliano: "pasta chi vruoccoli". Io lo preparo così: ci vogliono olio, aglio, broccoli, maccheroni e parmigiano. Butto i broccoli in acqua bollente salata. Una volta cotti, li tolgo dall'acqua e li metto in una zuppiera con olio di oliva, aglio e parmigiano. Metto la pasta nell'acqua dei broccoli. Quando la pasta è cotta, la scolo e la metto sui broccoli, mescolando velocemente. Mmm, buoni, buoni . . .

ANGELA: Grazie. Provo la ricetta appena torno a casa.

SIG.RA R: Per fare un piatto autenticamente siciliano ci vuole anche un po' di peperoncino. Si possono aggiungere anche acciughe o sardine e perfino uva passa e pinoli. Ma così come lo faccio, piace alla mia famiglia.

Vocabulary

si vede che	it's clear that (lit. 'one can see that')
avrebbe qualche buona ricetta da darmi?	would you have some good recipes to give me?
mescolata (mescolare)	mixed (to mix)
parmigiano	Parmesan cheese (it goes without saying here that it is grated)
butto	I throw
acqua bollente salata	boiling salted water
una volta cotti	once they are cooked
li tolgo (togliere) dall'acqua	I take them out of the water
li metto in una zuppiera	I put them in a soup tureen
mescolando	tossing, mixing
si possono aggiungere acciughe e sardine	anchovies and sardines can be added (plural verb)

Language point

Using ci vuole, ci vogliono *'you need, one needs'*

ci vuole un po' di peperoncino
ci vogliono olio, aglio, broccoli ecc.

The expression means 'you need, one needs', but it is impersonal. If what is needed is singular, you use **ci vuole**, if it is plural, **ci vogliono**.

Per arrabbiarsi ci vogliono 65 muscoli, per sorridere solo 19.
Fa' economia, sorridi!
To get angry you need 65 muscles, to smile only 19.
Economize, smile!
(Handwritten notice commonly seen in offices etc.)

si può, si possono work in a similar way – see the conversation above.

10 Buone vacanze

Have a good holiday

In this unit you will learn about:

- Talking about holidays
- Saying where you've been
- The family
- Possessive adjectives ('my, his, our')
- Saying how old someone is
- Talking about the weather
- Saying something's about to happen
- Exclamations

Dialogue 1 🎧

Vacanze in Sicilia

Enrico bumps into his friend Aldo whom he hasn't seen for a few weeks.

1 Why is Aldo feeling so well?
2 Why is Enrico surprised to learn what he has been doing?
3 What does Aldo recommend to Enrico and why?
4 What are Enrico's holiday plans?
5 Aldo's children seem to intend to spend their holidays very constructively. What are their plans?

ENRICO:	Ciao, Aldo, come va? E' un po' che non ti vedo.
ALDO:	Infatti, sono appena tornato dalle vacanze. E perciò sto benissimo.
ENRICO:	Come mai le vacanze così presto? Siamo solo al 15 maggio. Tu di solito vai all'estero in agosto.

ALDO:	Ma quest'anno non siamo andati all'estero, siamo rimasti in Italia. Siamo andati in Sicilia. Per questo siamo partiti così presto, per evitare il gran caldo.
ENRICO:	Capisco. Il tempo è stato bello?
ALDO:	Sì, bellissimo. Non troppo caldo, ma un cielo sempre sereno.
ENRICO:	E la Sicilia? Non la conosco.
ALDO:	Guarda, è una meraviglia. C'è tanto da vedere, dai templi greci ad Agrigento al duomo di Cefalù. E poi dei paesaggi incantevoli e un mare spettacolare. E si mangia bene, i vini sono ottimi. Dovresti andarci anche tu con Anna.
ENRICO:	Forse l'anno prossimo. Anche noi quest'anno rimaniamo in Italia. Andiamo nel Gargano a luglio. E i ragazzi, sono venuti con voi? O sono rimasti qui per la scuola?
ALDO:	Per la prima volta non sono venuti con noi. Anche per questo siamo potuti partire presto. Infatti i figli sono grandi ormai e quest'estate vanno via per conto loro. Marco ha 16 anni e va a fare un corso di inglese in Irlanda. Maria invece va in Francia a fare un corso di vela.

The Greek temple at Segesta.

Vocabulary

è un po' che non ti vedo	I haven't seen you for a while
sono appena tornato	I've just come back
all'estero	abroad
dovresti andarci anche tu	you ought to go there too
per conto loro	on their own (account)

Language points

Talking about where you've been, il passato prossimo

To talk about what you did in the past, or have done recently, you use a tense called the **passato prossimo** 'the near past', usually called the *present perfect* in English. For verbs that refer to coming, going, arriving, departing, staying, the **passato prossimo** is formed with the present tense of **essere** and the past participle:

> *Sono* appena *tornato* dalle vacanze.
> I have just come back from holiday.

> Non *siamo andati* all'estero.
> We didn't go abroad.

> *Siamo rimasti* in Italia.
> We stayed in Italy.

> *Siamo partiti* così presto.
> We went away so early.

> Il tempo *è stato* bello.
> The weather was lovely.

> Non sono venuti con noi.
> They didn't come with us.

Note: This is not the same as the passive. Only *transitive* verbs, verbs that can have a direct object, can be used in the passive. (**Scrivo una lettera. La lettera è scritta da me.**) The verbs we are looking at here cannot have a direct object: they are *intransitive*. In Italian it is impossible to say **vado la città**; you have to say **vado alla città** or **in città**. You need a preposition: the object is not a direct but an indirect object. The past participle does however agree with the subject in the same way as in the passive:

$$\left.\begin{array}{l}\textbf{Enrico è andato}\\ \textbf{Maria è andata}\\ \textbf{I bambini sono andati}\\ \textbf{Le signore sono andate}\end{array}\right\} \quad \textbf{in Sicilia}$$

Commonly used verbs that make their past in this way are: **andare, venire, arrivare, partire, entrare, uscire, salire, scendere, nascere, morire, rimanere, restare, essere,** all verbs to do with *movement* or *a state* or *change of state*. The following have irregular past participles:

venire	**venuto**	**nascere**	**nato**
rimanere	**rimasto**	**morire**	**morto**

Warning: The **passato prossimo** can be translated into English by more than one English tense, according to circumstances (see the examples above: 'I have just come back ...', 'we went away ...'). The tense systems of Italian and English are different and it is unhelpful to hope to think from one language to the other on a 'one-to-one' basis. It's not like putting sentences into a code. For example, in the present tense **mangio** can mean 'I eat' or 'I am eating'. It is more helpful to try to understand the way the system of tenses works in Italian. Remember: the **passato prossimo** is used for a completed action or event in the past. Here are some more examples:

Ieri mattina sono andato a trovare Carla. Il pomeriggio sono rimasto a casa e Giorgio è venuto a parlare del nuovo progetto. La sera io, lui e le nostre mogli siamo andati a vedere il nuovo film.
Yesterday morning I went to see Carla. In the afternoon I stayed at home and Giorgio came to talk about the new project. In the evening I, he and our wives went to see the new film.

– **Non siete venuti alla festa sabato?**
– **No, siamo andati a Parigi e siamo tornati solo ieri sera.**
– You didn't come to the party on Saturday.
– No, we went to Paris and we only got back yesterday evening.

– **Dov'è Giorgio?**
– **E' sceso in cantina a prendere il vino. Arriva subito – eccolo.**
– Where's Giorgio?
– He's gone down to the cellar to get the wine. He'll be here straight away – here he is.

in cantina

Exercise 1

You've been away for a couple of days and, on your return, you bump into a friend at the airport. Complete the conversation below. To help you where the subject might be unclear the pronoun has been indicated between square brackets. It would not normally be used, omit it.

AMICO: Ciao, come stai? Da dove arrivi?

TU: [Io] (1 essere) a Zurigo per affari. E tu?

AMICO: [Io] (2 andare) in Svezia per lavoro.

TU: (3 andare)[tu] da solo?

AMICO: No, (4 andare) [io] con due colleghi. (5 partire) [noi] insieme ma loro (6 rimanere) a Stoccolma per altri due giorni.

Exercise 2

Here is a report of a visit by a team from another company that took place last week. They came to discuss a joint venture the two companies are hoping to undertake together. Choose the correct forms for the verbs. They must be in the **passato prossimo**.

La delegazione (1) (*arrivare*) il 20 giugno. L'amministratore delegato (2) (*andare*) all'aeroporto a dare il benvenuto ai membri della delegazione. Poi questi (3) (*andare*) in albergo. Il primo incontro formale (4) (*essere*) molto cordiale ma quando (5) (*arrivare*) alla questione del finanziamento (6) (*venire*) fuori varie difficoltà.

Vocabulary

La mia famiglia

il nonno	grandfather	**la nonna**	grandmother
il padre	father	**la madre**	mother
il fratello	brother	**la sorella**	sister
il figlio	son	**la figlia**	daughter
lo zio	uncle	**la zia**	aunt
il cugino	cousin (m.)	**la cugina**	cousin (f.)
il nipote	nephew, grandson	**la nipote**	niece, granddaughter
il marito	husband	**la moglie**	wife

il cognato	brother-in-law	la cognata	sister-in-law
il suocero	father-in-law	la suocera	mother-in-law
il genero	son-in-law	la nuora	daughter-in-law

Plurals

i nonni	grandparents
i genitori	parents
i parenti	relations (not just mother and father, see above)
i fratelli	brothers, or brothers and sisters
le sorelle	sisters
i figli	sons, or sons and daughters
le figlie	daughters
gli zii	uncles or uncles and aunts
le zie	aunts

Cultural point

Nipote can be both nephew/niece and grandson/granddaughter. Many people use the form **nipotino, nipotina** for 'grandson, grand-daughter'. For 'boyfriend, girlfriend' it is usual to use the words **ragazzo**, **ragazza** (which also mean 'boy, girl'). When there is a formal intention to marry, then **fidanzato**, **fidanzata** 'fiancé(e)', is used. And note that when talking in the plural, the masculine can include the feminine too, e.g. **fratelli** can be 'brothers and sisters' or just 'brothers' (see also: **gli zii, i figli**). On the other hand **sorelle** can only be 'sisters' (see p. 154).

Exercise 3

Here is a family tree. Complete the sentences below with the correct word.

Note: **Andrea** = Andrew; **Nicola** = Nicholas – i.e. they are boys' names.

Example: **Emilio è il figlio di Alberto.**

1 Nicola è _____ di Carla.   6 Antonietta è _____ di Arturo.
2 Andrea è _____ di Rosa.   7 Rosa è _____ di Alberto.
3 Anna è _____ di Paolo.   8 Paolo è _____ di Arturo.
4 Margherita è _____ di Aldo. 9 Anna è _____ di Margherita.
5 Aldo è _____ di Pietro.   10 Aldo è _____ di Silvia.

Exercise 4

Carlo has drawn his family tree (**albero genealogico**).

Draw your family tree and label it for an Italian friend.

Possessive adjectives

When Carlo refers to his relations he writes:

   mio fratello   **mio nonno**   **mia sorella**   **mio padre**

This usage is in fact an *exception*, used when you are talking about family members in the singular. Here are some examples of how you usually express possession:

   La mia famiglia è grande.
   My family is large.

   Le mie sorelle sono sposate.
   My sisters are married.

   I tuoi nonni, dove abitano?
   Where do your grandparents live?

   Il nostro amico, Carlo, è appena tornato da Lisbona.
   Our friend, Carlo, has just come back from Lisbon.

Il suo nuovo direttore è un uomo molto difficile.
His new manager is a very difficult man.

Dov'è il mio libro?
Where is my book?

Mi piace la vostra nuova casa.
I like your new house.

Conoscete i nostri amici?
Do you know our friends?

You will note that the *definite article* is used, as well as the possessive. The words used to express possession are adjectives and have to agree with the noun they qualify. The forms are:

my	il mio	la mia	i miei	le mie	(io)
your	il tuo	la tua	i tuoi	le tue	(tu)
his/her	il suo	la sua	i suoi	le sue	(lui/lei)
your (formal)	il Suo	la Sua	i Suoi	le Sue	(Lei)
our	il nostro	la nostra	i nostri	le nostre	(noi)
your	il vostro	la vostra	i vostri	le vostre	(voi)
their	il loro	la loro	i loro	le loro	(loro)

Notes

(a) You cannot distinguish in Italian between 'his' and 'her'. **e' la sua macchina** means 'it's his/her car', according to the context.

(b) **il tuo** etc. is used when talking to someone to whom you say **tu**, a friend, a relation, a colleague, a child: **Usi la tua macchina ogni giorno?**

   il Suo etc. is for when you are talking to someone whom you address as **Lei**, i.e. someone with whom your relationship is formal: **Signor Martini, Lei usa la Sua macchina ogni giorno?**

   il vostro etc. is used when talking to more than one person: **Voi usate la vostra macchina ogni giorno?**

(c) **il loro** etc.: **loro** is invariable. Also, **il loro** is an exception to the rule about omitting the definite article when talking about a relative: **Il loro padre.**

(d) When referring to their family, Italians often call them simply: **i miei.**

(e) The possessives can also be used as *pronouns:*

   Non trovo l'ombrello. I can't find my umbrella.
   Non preoccuparti. Prendi il mio. Don't worry. Take mine.

A saying

Natale con i tuoi, Pasqua con chi vuoi.
Christmas with your family, Easter with whoever you like.

Exercise 5

Gianni is showing you some
photos. Ask him if the people
are members of his family and
if the buildings etc. belong to
him.

Example: **E' la tua casa?**

Now imagine that you had
only recently met the person
showing you the photos, perhaps in a hotel
while on holiday. You would use **Lei**. How would you
change your questions?

Saying how old someone is

Talking about his son, Aldo says: **Marco ha sedici anni**. To express age, you use **avere** + the number + years. In answer to the question **Quanti anni hai?** Marco might say:

Ho sedici anni. *or* **Ne ho sedici.**

ne means 'of them', here referring to years. You need either **anni** after the number or **ne** before the verb.

Exercise 6

Work out how you would say

1 your own age
2 that of your children if you have any
3 that of your brothers and sisters
4 and of your grandparents etc.

You will get sentences like:

Ho trentaquattro anni.
Mio figlio, Bill, ha tre anni e mia figlia, Clare, ne ha due.
Mia sorella ha quarant'anni e mio fratello ne ha trentotto.
Mio nonno ha novantadue anni.

Dialogue 2 🎧

Il tempo

Aldo is telephoning a business colleague who is in Venice. It's January and it is just before lunch.

1 Is Aldo's colleague having good weather in Venice?
2 Why are the ski buffs likely to be happier in the near future?

ALDO: Che tempo fa a Venezia?
COLLEGA: Oggi c'è un bel sole e ora, a mezzogiorno, fa quasi
           caldo. Ieri e lunedì però il tempo è stato brutto: nebbia
           umida, e che freddo! E da te?
ALDO: Qui fa bello. La notte però la temperatura scende sotto
           zero. In montagna non nevica e gli sciatori si lamen-
           tano perché non c'è neve. Ma secondo le previsioni, il
           tempo sta per cambiare.

Talking about the weather

The standard question about the weather is **Che tempo fa?** You
can answer in the following ways:

Fa bel tempo   or **Il tempo è bello**   The weather is fine
Fa brutto tempo   **brutto**   bad/nasty
                                     freddo   cold
                                     caldo   hot

or

Fa bello   It's fine/lovely
brutto   nasty/bad
freddo   cold
caldo   hot

In other words: either (1) start your sentence with **Fa** and add an adjective or the set phrases **bel tempo**, **brutto tempo**; or (2) start with **il tempo è** and add adjectives. Other possible answers are:

C'è	**il sole**	It's sunny/the sun is shining
	la nebbia	foggy
	vento	windy

| **Piove** | It's raining | **la pioggia** | rain |
| **Nevica** | It's snowing | **la neve** | snow |

More weather vocabulary

le previsioni del tempo	the weather forecast or, often: **il meteo**
cielo sereno	clear sky
nuvoloso	cloudy
mare mosso	rough sea
calmo	calm
un temporale	a storm
il maltempo	bad weather
la grandine	hail (hailstones)

Every so often you will read the headline in the newspaper:

Mezza Italia in tilt per il maltempo
Half Italy in chaos because of the bad weather

and know that heavy snow or rain, high winds or thick fog has upset road, rail or air traffic.

Sta per cambiare

Using stare + per *'about to'*

Il tempo sta per cambiare
'The weather is about to change'

Use the present of **stare** + **per** + the infinitive to say 'to be about to, to be on the point of', e.g:

Stiamo per partire
We are about to leave/on the point of leaving

Il treno sta per arrivare
The train is about to arrive/on the point of arriving

The present tense of **stare** is:

sto	**stiamo**
stai	**state**
sta	**stanno**

Exclamations

Che can be used with adjectives or nouns to make exclamations.

Che freddo!	What cold!
Che pioggia!	What rain!
Che scemo!	What a silly boy/man

Exercise 7

The language of weather forecasts tends to be technical but similar to English. There is usually, however, a drawing to help. We have reproduced one below which refers to the weather on Christmas Eve. Many people's image of Italy is of sunshine and warmth. Study the drawing and then answer the questions.

By courtesy of *La Stampa*.

1 What is the weather going to be like on the coast north of Rome?
2. What are the seas around all of the peninsula going to be like?
3 What is likely to fall on the Alps and the Apennines?
4 What is going to fall in Sardinia? It will also fall in the heel of Italy south of Bari and in the Po Plain.
5 In the instep of Italy (Basilicata) something particularly nasty seems to be in store. What is it?

Reading 🎧

un clima — masculine.
dappertutto. everywhere

Il clima italiano

1 If you are flying to Milan in November, what might be a problem?
2 Why do those who can leave the northern cities in the summer head for the sea or the mountains?
3 In what way is the climate of the Adriatic Coast different from that of the Tyrrhenian coast?
4 If you like really hot weather, where in Italy should you choose for your holiday?
(It may be helpful when reading this passage to refer to the map of Italy, p. 122)

Come per la cucina italiana, così anche per il clima non si può parlare di "clima italiano". Varia da regione a regione. Le montagne del nord hanno un clima alpino: inverni freddi, estati calde di giorno ma con notti relativamente fresche. La pianura padana invece ha un clima continentale: inverni freddi, estati molto calde. Un grosso problema in questa zona è l'umidità: d'inverno c'è spesso nebbia e d'estate il tasso d'umidità è alto. In tutta l'Italia le zone costiere godono di un clima mite, grazie all'influenza del mare. Ma c'è una differenza tra la costa adriatica e quella tirrenica: infatti quest'ultima ha un clima generalmente più mite. D'inverno la costa adriatica è battuta qualche volta da venti freddi da nord-est, cioè dall'Europa centrale. Sull'Appennino influisce l'altitudine: d'inverno fa più freddo che sulla costa alla stessa latitudine. E poi, più si va verso sud, più il clima diventa caldo. Naturalmente, dappertutto ci sono momenti in cui il tempo è eccezionale, essendo particolarmente freddo o insolitamente caldo.
unusually

Vocabulary

godere di un clima mite	to enjoy a mild climate
quest'ultima	the latter
battuto	hit by, beaten by
alla stessa latitudine	at the same latitude

11 Che cosa ha visto?

What did you see?

In this unit you will learn about:

- **Polizia e carabinieri** – the Italian police
- Saying what you did/have done
- Saying **niente**, **nulla** 'nothing'; and **qualcosa** 'something'
- The gerund, **essendo, vendendo**
- Saying how long something has been going on for:
  da + present tense
- Diminutives (**casetta** 'little house') and other suffixes
- Letters and emails to friends

Dialogue 1

Un giallo

The apartment next door to Mrs Mancini's has been burgled. She is being interviewed by the carabinieri.

1 **Who left home first, Mrs Mancini or her family?**
2 **Where did she go the first time she went out?**
3 **Why did she come back again before going to work?**
4 **What did she notice as she left the house the second time?**
5 **What did not seem strange to her at the time but does now?**
6 **Why did she find it strange that her neighbours' door was open?**

CARABINIERE: Signora, ci racconti che cosa ha fatto questa mattina.

SIG.RA M: Ecco. Mi sono alzata verso le sei e mezzo, come al solito. Ho preparato la colazione per mio marito

	e i miei figli. Loro sono usciti verso le sette e mezzo e io poco dopo.
CARABINIERE	Non ha notato niente di strano in quel momento?
SIG.RA M:	No, niente.
CARABINIERE:	E poi?
SIG.RA M:	E poi sono andata al mercato. Ho fatto la spesa. Siccome ho comprato carne, frutta e verdura, ho portato tutto a casa e ho messo la carne e la verdura nel frigo. E poi sono andata al lavoro verso le nove meno un quarto.
CARABINIERE:	E tutto Le è sembrato normale?
SIG.RA M:	Sì. Ma adesso mi ricordo che ho notato una grande macchina bianca, una Volvo, parcheggiata davanti a casa nostra. Dentro ho visto due uomini.
CARABINIERE:	Mi può descrivere questi uomini?
SIG.RA M:	Ma questo è il fatto strano: quando sono uscita di casa hanno girato la testa dall'altra parte. Cosi non ho visto la loro faccia. Sul momento non l'ho trovato strano, ma ora . . .
CARABINIERE;	E poi?
SIG.RA M:	E poi sono andata a lavorare e quando sono tornata a casa all'una ho trovato aperta la porta dell'appartamento dei miei vicini. Sono in vacanza all'estero, così ho subito pensato a un furto e ho chiamato i carabinieri.
CARABINIERE:	Ha fatto molto bene, signora. Allora, torniamo a quella macchina bianca . . .

Vocabulary

ci racconti	tell us
non ha notato niente di strano?	you didn't notice anything strange?
siccome	since (in the sense of 'because')
frigo (short for **frigorifero**)	fridge
mi ricordo	I remember
hanno girato la testa	they turned their heads
dall'altra parte	the other way
i miei vicini	my neighbours

A carabiniere examining works of art which have been recovered by the force. Courtesy Comando Generale dell'Arma dei Carabinieri.

Cultural point

The **Arma dei Carabinieri** is a military corps, under the Ministry of Defence. It originated as the Royal Guard of the Kingdom of Piedmont and Sardinia in the days before Italy was unified. Italy also has a police force: **la Polizia di Stato**, set up after the Unification of Italy, under the Ministry of the Interior. Their websites give an idea of the two: www.carabinieri.it and www.poliziadistato. it. There are also other corps such as the **Guardia di Finanza**, under the Ministry of Finance, who deal with tax evasion and smuggling. Each **comune** also has **vigili urbani**.

Language points

More about the passato prossimo, *saying what you did*

The **passato prossimo** of most verbs is formed with the present tense of **avere** + the past participle:

– Che cosa *ha fatto* questa mattina?
– *Ho preparato* la colazione ...

Make a list of other examples of the **passato prossimo** in the Dialogue above. You should have found:

avere	*essere*
ha notato	*mi sono alzata*
ho fatto la spesa	loro *sono usciti*
ho comprato	*sono andata* al mercato
ho portato	*sono andata* al lavoro
ho messo	tutto Le *è sembrato* normale?
ho notato	*sono uscita*
ho visto	*sono andata* a lavorare
hanno girato	*sono tornata*
non *ho visto*	
non l'*ho trovato* strano	
ho trovato	
ho subito *pensato*	
ho chiamato	
ha fatto bene	

You will perhaps have noticed:

1 that when the **passato prossimo** is formed with **avere** the past participle does *not* agree with the subject;
2 **messo** is a new past participle to you; it comes from **mettere** 'to put'.

The passato prossimo **of reflexive verbs**

The second verb in the conversation, **mi sono alzata**, is not one of the verbs of movement or state which you learned were conjugated with **essere**. It is a reflexive or pronominal verb (see Unit 6). Reflexive verbs also form their **passato prossimo** with **essere**.

The passato prossimo **of impersonal verbs**

Verbs used impersonally also usually make their **passato prossimo** with **essere: Tutto Le è *sembrato* normale?** 'Did everything seem normal to you?' (**sembra** means 'it seems').

Mi è *piaciuto* molto il film.
I liked the film a lot.

Che cosa è *successo*?
What's happened?/What happened?

(**succedere** means 'to happen'; **succede** means 'it happens, it is happening'.)

With verbs relating to weather phenomena such as **nevicare, piovere**, both **avere** and **essere** are used. **essere** is considered the better usage.

E' nevicato **in montagna ieri. Qui è *piovuto*.**
Ha nevicato **in montagna ieri. Qui *ha piovuto*.**
It snowed in the mountains yesterday. Here it rained.

Exercise 1

You and your husband/wife/friend(s) had a busy weekend. Tell someone about it. Here is what you did:

Sabato	*mattina*
	fare la spesa
	comprare un vestito nuovo per me
	pomeriggio
	andare a una mostra interessante
	sera
	essere a cena da vecchi amici
Domenica	fare una gita con amici che hanno una barca a vela
	andare in mare con questi amici
	pranzare sulla barca
	fare il bagno
	prendere il sole
	cenare in un ristorante sul porto

Exercise 2

You are an Italian private detective (**investigatore privato**) and you have been asked to follow a certain lady. Report on what she did yesterday. We give you the verbs in the infinitive.

1 uscire di casa alle nove e mezzo
2 salire su un taxi
3 andare alla Banca Nazionale del Lavoro in Piazza Garibaldi
4 uscire dalla banca dopo un quarto d'ora
5 andare a piedi al bar Roma
6 sedersi all'interno del bar
7 ordinare un cappuccino
8 essere raggiunta da un uomo alto, bello, elegante
9 uscire dal bar con quest'uomo
10 salire su una Mercedes con lui
11 andare in un ristorante sul lago
12 verso le tre lasciare il ristorante, sempre in compagnia dell'uomo

YOUR CLIENT: E poi?
YOU: E poi, niente. Li ho perduti. Ho avuto un incidente con la mia macchina.
YOUR CLIENT: Pazienza. In ogni modo, quell'uomo alto e elegante, che guida una Mercedes, è probabilmente suo fratello.

Using niente/nulla *and* qualcosa

niente means 'nothing/not . . . anything'. The **carabiniere** asks Mrs Mancini:

Non **ha notato** *niente* **di strano?**
You didn't notice anything strange?

To use **niente** with a verb, you must have **non** before the verb:

Non **ho visto** *niente.*
I saw nothing/I didn't see anything.

Non **capisco** *niente.*
I understand nothing/I don't understand anything.

nulla also means 'nothing' and is used in the same way as **niente**:

Non **abbiamo visto** *nulla.*
We didn't see anything/we saw nothing.

Note: 'Something' is normally **qualcosa**, or the longer form **qualche cosa**:

E' successo qualcosa.
Something has happened.

Hai visto qualcosa?
Did you see something/anything?

'Something'/'nothing' + adjective is **qualcosa/niente/nulla di ...**:

E' successo *qualcosa di* **strano.**
Something strange has happened.

Qualcosa di **bello.**
Something lovely.

Non **ha detto** *nulla di* **interessante.**
He didn't say anything interesting.

Non **so** *nulla di* **buono di lui.**
I don't know anything good about him.

'Something'/'nothing' + verb is **qualcosa da/niente da/nulla da ...**:

Vuoi *qualcosa da* **mangiare?**
Do you want something/anything to eat?

Ho *qualcosa da* **fare.**
I have something to do.

Non **ha** *niente da* **fare.**
He/she has nothing to do. He/she hasn't anything to do.

Non **c'è** *nulla da* **mangiare.**
There's nothing to eat.

(See also p. 134 for a similar use of **da**.)

Exercise 3

Things went badly today. Your husband wants to know about a number of things you intended to do but you had no success, so answers to these questions are negative. Use **non ... niente**.

1 Hai comprato la camicetta che volevi?
2 Hai letto l'articolo di Sergio Romano sul giornale di ieri?

3 Hai finito di scrivere la lettera alla nonna?
4 Hai almeno mangiato bene a mezzogiorno? C'era quel buon prosciutto da finire.
5 Ma insomma, che cosa hai fatto oggi?
   Sono stata poco bene e così _____ .

Reading 🎧

La lettera di un'amica

When you write letters to your friends you will often want to talk about what you have been doing. Here is a letter from a friend.

1 **Marina says a lot has happened since she last wrote. What three events does she write about?**
2 **Why was 23 May a special day for Marina?**
3 **What keeps Marina busy in spite of the fact that she has retired?**
4 **What did Marina and her husband find difficult when she retired? What has helped them resolve the problem?**

Cara Sara,

Ti ringrazio per la tua lettera. Mi scuso per questo lungo silenzio. Sappi almeno che sei spesso stata presente nei miei pensieri.

Nel frattempo sono successe molte cose. Piero, essendo ormai ben inserito nel suo lavoro di avvocato, si è sposato con la sua ragazza. Si conoscono da quasi dieci anni. Hanno una casa piccola ma fra un mese trasloceranno nella casa che abbiamo comprato vendendo la nostra casetta di Desenzano.

La seconda grande notizia è stata la nascita di Andrea, figlio di Paola. E' nato il giorno del mio compleanno, il 23 maggio. E' un bambino simpaticissimo con occhi grigio-blu e un carattere allegro. Ora ha nove mesi e tutti gli vogliamo molto bene.

Terzo avvenimento: sono andata in pensione il primo di settembre. Ma ho molto da fare e non mi annoio. Lavoro sempre come consulente e scrittrice. Poi mi occupo spesso di Andrea mentre Paola lavora. Infine i miei genitori che sono vecchi e deboli hanno bisogno di aiuto. Così sono sempre occupata.

Anche mio marito è in pensione: all'inizio è stato difficile ma ormai ci siamo abituati. La nostra casa è grande e ognuno ha il suo studio, il proprio spazio.

Non mi resta che scusarmi ancora per il ritardo nello scrivere. Con molto affetto, buon lavoro e fatti sentire,

Un abbraccio,

Marina

Vocabulary

ti ringrazio	I thank you
mi scuso	I apologize (I excuse myself)
sappi	I want you to know that (the **tu** imperative/command form from **sapere**; the formal form (**Lei**) is **sappia**)
nei miei pensieri	in my thoughts
nel frattempo	in the meanwhile
ben inserito nel suo lavoro	nicely settled in his work
traslocheranno	they will move
tutti gli vogliamo molto bene	we all love him very much
sono andata in pensione	I retired
non mi annoio	I'm not bored (**annoiarsi** 'to be bored')
mi occupo di Andrea	I take care of Andrea
ci siamo abituati	we have got used to it, we are used to it
fatti sentire	keep in touch/write soon (lit. 'make yourself heard')

Language points

The gerund, essendo, vendendo

Marina writes:

Piero, *essendo* ormai ben inserito nel suo lavoro di avvocato, si è sposato.
Piero, now being well settled (since he is now settled) in his work as a lawyer, got married.

La casa che abbiamo comprato *vendendo* la nostra casetta di Desenzano
The house we bought by selling our little house in Desenzano

This form is called the *gerund*. In all cases, take the infinitive as the base and remove the ending: for **-are** verbs then add **-ando** and for all the others **-endo**.

-are	*-ere*	*-ire*		
parlare	decidere	capire	essere	avere
parlando	decidendo	capendo	essendo	avendo

The only verbs that are irregular are **dire**, **fare**, **bere** and a few others (**produrre** and similar verbs with infinitives ending in **-rre**). All have infinitives that have become shortened (from **dicere**, **facere**, **bevere**, **producere**). The gerund is based on the old infinitive:

> **dicendo   facendo   bevendo   producendo**

Knowing about this older form of the infinitive also helps explain other forms of these verbs. **dare** and **stare** behave regularly: **dando, stando**.

The gerund is used:

1 to explain *how* or *why*, as in the examples in the letter:

> **Facendo il lavoro così, lo rendi più difficile.**
> (By) doing the work this way, you make it more difficult.

2 to convey one action happening at the same time as another ('while, on, as'):

> **Andando a Roma, mi sono fermato una notte a Firenze.**
> (While) going to Rome, I stopped for a night in Florence.

> **Uscendo di casa, Giorgio ha visto l'amico Aldo.**
> As he left (on leaving) home, Giorgio saw his friend Aldo.

Do not assume the gerund will always translate the English form ending in '-ing'. The gerund is a verbal form. When the form ending in '-ing' is a noun, in Italian it is more likely to be expressed by an infinitive. For instance, Marina says:

> **... il ritardo nello scrivere**
> ... the delay in writing

Compare:

> **Mi piace leggere.**
> I like reading.

This is a difficult point. As always, try to imitate what you hear and read. And don't worry too much about mistakes.

Sbagliando si impara.
One learns by making mistakes.

Exercise 4

Below are some pairs of sentences. Combine them using the gerund. This will make the style more interesting.

Example: **Faccio passeggiate in campagna. Mi piace guardare i fiori e gli alberi.**

Facendo passeggiate in campagna, mi piace guardare i fiori e gli alberi.

(a) These sentences are about Sergio's morning routine.

1 Sergio va al lavoro ogni mattina. Compra il giornale.
2 E' di Firenze. Compra *la Nazione**.
3 Prende un espresso al bar. Legge il giornale.

* *La Nazione* is the Florentine daily newspaper.

(b) These sentences are about your friends.

1 I miei amici hanno una casa in campagna. Passano spesso il fine settimana lì.
2 Il loro giardino è grande. Hanno sempre del lavoro da fare.
3 Hanno un orto (vegetable garden, kitchen garden). Hanno sempre frutta e verdura fresca a tavola.

Another use of da, *saying how long something has been going on for*

Si conoscono da dieci anni

When you talk about what you have been doing you use the **passato prossimo**. An exception to this is when you want to convey the idea that something has been happening *for* a certain amount of time and is still happening. Marina said Piero and his girlfriend 'have known each other *for* ten years'. Here are some more examples:

Studio l'italiano da due mesi.
I have been studying Italian for two months.

Gianni lavora da due anni in quella ditta.
Gianni has been working for that firm for two years.

Non lo vedo da tre anni.
I haven't seen him for three years.

You say what is going on, using the present tense, and then use
da plus the amount of time. This is another use of the preposition
da. You can also use **da** followed by a point in time, meaning 'since'
in English:

E' qui da venerdì.
He's been here since Friday.

Abitiamo a Roma da giugno dell'anno scorso.
We have been living in Rome since June last year.

Exercise 5

Here are some things Pietro does and the date when he started
doing them. Imagine it is now December 2006. Write down how
long he has been doing these things. Then also write down how
you would say this in English.

Example: **Fuma la pipa.**   **2000**
            Pietro fuma la pipa da sei anni.

1	Suona il pianoforte.	1982
2	Lavora come ingegnere.	2002
3	Conosce Antonio.	1992
4	Studia il francese.	2005, settembre
5	Esce con Alessia.	2003
6	Abita a Milano.	1995

You could also have said: **Pietro fuma la pipa dal 2000** etc.

Diminutives and other suffixes

Marina talks about a little house (**una casetta**) in Desenzano (on
Lake Garda) which they have sold to help Piero buy a house.
Rather than saying **una piccola casa** she alters the word **casa** by
adding a suffix (an extra syllable at the end of a word), **-etta**. You
will remember how this device is used with adjectives to convey
the idea 'very': **bello**, **bellissimo**. There are a number of such
suffixes.

Warning: it takes time for the non-native speaker to get them right. However, it is useful to be able to recognize them. Here are some common ones.

- **-etto**, **-ino** can be added to nouns and adjectives to convey an idea of smallness:

fratellino	little brother
orchestrina	small orchestra (such as plays for a bar in Piazza San Marco in Venice – see Unit 1)
piazzetta	little square (indeed the square which lies at right angles to Piazza San Marco and which leads to the waterfront is called la Piazzetta)

- **-ino** is also commonly added to certain adjectives and adverbs, modifying their meaning:

caro	dear	**piano**	softly, slowly
carino	pretty, cute, sweet	**pianino**	very softly, slowly

- **-one** indicates bigness; it can be added to nouns, adjectives and the adverb **bene**. When it is added to feminine words they change gender and become masculine:

una donna	woman	**un libro**	a book
un donnone	a big woman	**un librone**	a big book

– Come sta?	**– Benone.**
– How are you?	– Fine.

- **-accio** indicates the speaker considers the person or object nasty or worthless:

parola	word	**tempo**	weather
parolaccia	swear word	**tempaccio**	dreadful weather
parolacce (pl.)	bad language		

- **-astro** added to words for colour is equivalent to the English '-ish':

bianco	white
biancastro	whitish

Note: **fratellastro**, **sorellastra**, **figliastro/a** are used to mean 'step-brother, stepsister, stepson, stepdaughter' respectively.

Listen for these suffixes. There are others, but it is best to use only those you have heard. Sometimes the words formed come to stand in their own right, for example **telefonino** is the usual everyday word for a 'cellular telephone', **spago** is 'string', **spaghetti** are long pieces of pasta in the shape of strings.

Letters and emails

Letter-writing is being eclipsed by emails and telephone calls. However, much of what follows applies equally to emails and to letters. When writing to a friend, use **caro**, **cara** and the friend's name. If you start your emails 'Hi, Guido!' you will probably use **Ciao, Guido!** in Italian. The salutation at the end depends on the intimacy of the relationship. Possible endings are:

affettuosamente	yours affectionately
saluti affettuosi	affectionate greetings
cari saluti	warm (lit. 'dear') greetings
un abbraccio	much love (lit. 'a hug, an embrace')

When writing to someone you know fairly well but with whom you have a fairly formal relationship, using **Lei**, you may start **Caro signor Rossi**, and end **Cordialmente** or **Cordiali saluti**. It is considered a courtesy to use a capital letter for **Lei** and related words, e.g:

> *La* **ringrazio della** *Sua* **gentile ospitalità.**

When writing to someone you do not know or with whom your relationship is very formal, you write:

> **Egregio Signore** (to a man)   **Gentile Signora** (to a woman)

When the surname is not used, a capital letter for the title is customary. You can still end with **cordiali saluti**, or use **distinti saluti** which is more formal.

Emails tend to be less formal but that will depend on the circumstances. The word for email is **una email** or, more commonly, **una mail**. The Italian name for the system is **posta elettronica**.

Exercise 6

Write a letter or an email to an imaginary Italian friend telling him/her what you did last weekend. You should try to use some of the expressions in this unit but of course you are free to try to say whatever you like.

12 Ecco la mia casa

This is my home

In this unit you will learn about:

- How to talk about houses and flats
- **maggiore**, **minore** 'elder, younger'; **morire**, **nascere** 'to die, to be born'; **nel** 'in'
- Ways of giving reasons: **perché**, **a causa di**, **grazie a**
- The various uses of **ci**
- The pronoun **ne** 'of it, of them, some'
- Trends in housing in Italy

Reading 1

La cugina italiana

1 Who is Gabriella?
2 Why does Angela go to see her?
3 Does Angela visit Gabriella often?
4 What sort of district is the one Gabriella lives in?

La sorella maggiore della mamma di Angela Smith ha sposato un italiano. Questa sorella è morta qualche anno fa, ma la mamma di Angela ha mantenuto i contatti con i suoi figli, i cugini di Angela. Una in particolare scrive regolarmente. Si chiama Gabriella. La mamma di Angela le ha chiesto di andare a trovare questa cugina. E' la prima volta che Angela va da Gabriella. Gabriella le fa vedere la sua casa, che si trova al quarto piano di un palazzo costruito nel 1967. E' in una zona residenziale nella periferia di Torino, nata negli anni del boom, del 'miracolo italiano', per gente che veniva a lavorare nella grande industria automobilistica. Oggi nella zona ci sono molti palazzi simili ma le strade sono larghe, ci sono alberi e spazio. E' un quartiere tranquillo.

Gabriella

Vocabulary

sorella maggiore	elder sister
qualche anno fa	some years ago
questa sorella è morta	this sister died
le fa vedere	shows her

Language points

maggiore, minore

As well as meaning 'bigger', **maggiore** is also used to mean 'elder', referring to brothers and sisters. **minore** means 'younger'.

Using morire, nascere

morire (past participle: **morto**) 'to die' is irregular, as is **nascere** (past participle **nato**) 'to be born'. Both verbs form the **passato prossimo** with **essere**:

E' morto il presidente.   **Anna è nata nel 1954.**
The president has died.   Anna was born in 1954.

nel *'in'*

Notice you say **nel 1967** 'in 1967', as in the example above, **nel 1954**. You always do this for 'in' with a year.

Exercise 1

Use the information in this family tree to complete the paragraph below.

Alberto sp. 1957 Anna
n. 1935 | n. 1937

Marco sp. 1985 Mara
n. 1960 | n. 1963

Paolo | Nicola
1962–1980 | n. 1973

Anna | Alfredo | Paolo
n. 1987 | n. 1990 | n. 1992

Alberto ha (1) _____ Anna a Napoli (2) _____ 1957. Poco dopo sono emigrati negli Stati Uniti. Hanno avuto tre figli. Il (3) _____, Marco, (4) _____ nel 1960. Da studente è tornato in Italia a trovare i cugini italiani e così ha conosciuto Mara. Si sono sposati nel (5) _____. Vivono a Chicago e ormai hanno anche loro tre (6) _____, Anna, (7) _____ nel 1987, Alfredo, nel 1990, e Paolo, nel 1992. Paolo, il secondo figlio di Alberto e di Anna (8) _____ in un incidente stradale nel 1980. Nicola, il figlio (9) _____ di Alberto e di Anna, è medico. Per il momento non è (10) _____ e così non ha figli.

Vocabulary

La casa

appartamento	flat, apartment	**palazzo**	apartment building, block of flats, palace
il pian terreno	the ground floor		
al pian terreno	on the ground floor		
		il primo piano	the first floor
il secondo piano	the second floor	**ascensore**	lift

il seminterrato	basement, semi-	scala	staircase
	basement (partly	entrata	entrance hall
	below ground)	stanza	room
soggiorno	living room,	sala da pranzo	dining room
	sitting room	cucina	kitchen
bagno	bathroom	camera	bedroom
ripostiglio	boxroom, store	(da letto)	
cantina	cellar	balcone	balcony
terrazza/o*	terrace		

* Often used of a large balcony. Both masculine and feminine forms exist.

Cultural point

Stanza is a general word for 'room', particularly in a house.

Quante stanze ci sono nella casa?
How many rooms are there in the house?

sala also means 'room' but in a home its use is limited to **sala da pranzo**: **sala** is used for spacious rooms in public buildings, e.g. **sala d'attesa** 'waiting room', **sala da ballo** 'dance hall', **sala operatoria** 'operating theatre'. (*Note also*: **saletta** 'little room', **salone** 'large, spacious room'.) **camera** also means 'room', but its use is usually limited, in the context of a home or a hotel, to 'bedroom', sometimes given the longer name of **camera da letto**. **stanza** is used in **stanza da bagno**, although often the bathroom is just **il bagno**.

Floors are counted European-style. **il pian terreno** is the ground floor at ground level. **il primo piano** is one floor up from ground level. 'On' a particular floor is **al**:

al terzo piano
on the third floor (fourth floor American-style counting)

Dialogue 1

Ecco il mio appartamento

Gabriella shows Angela her apartment.

1 **What does Gabriella particularly like about her living room?**
2 **What does Angela approve of about the kitchen?**
3 **Would Gabriella like a second bathroom?**

tramonti
— sunset.

4 Where is the garage?
5 What does Gabriella have in the basement?

GABRIELLA: Questo è il soggiorno. Mi piace perché dà verso ovest
             e riceve il sole al tramonto.
ANGELA: E' spazioso e anche molto luminoso.
GABRIELLA: Sì, a causa delle porte-finestre che danno sul balcone.
             Ed ecco la cucina.
ANGELA: E' bella e grande. Ci si può mangiare senza diffi-
             coltà.
GABRIELLA: Sì, serve anche da sala da pranzo. Poi c'è il bagno.
             E in fondo al corridoio ci sono le camere.
ANGELA: E quella porta lì è un altro bagno?
GABRIELLA: Purtroppo no. Ne abbiamo uno solo. E' un
             ripostiglio. E' molto utile.
ANGELA: Immagino. Avete anche il garage?
GABRIELLA: Sì. Ma è dietro il palazzo, nel cortile. Abbiamo anche
             la cantina nel seminterrato.
ANGELA: Hai detto che avete un balcone?
GABRIELLA: Ne abbiamo due, uno davanti e uno più piccolo
             dietro. Vieni a vedere.

Vocabulary

dà verso ovest   it looks west
serve anche da sala da pranzo it also acts/serves as a dining room

Language points

Ways of giving reasons

perché is used followed by a verb; **a causa di** by a noun:

Mangio perché ho fame.
I'm eating because I'm hungry.

Mangio a causa della fame.
I'm eating because of hunger.

On the other hand if the reason is positive, you can say **grazie a**:

Grazie al bel tempo, mangiamo fuori.
Thanks to the good weather, we are eating outside.

Various uses of ci

ci si può mangiare   one can eat in it/there

ci here replaces **nella cucina**. In the letter in the previous unit, Marina wrote:

ci **siamo abituati**   we are used to it

ci has a number of functions:

1 As a *pronoun* replacing **in** or **a** + noun (in English 'in it, to it, at it, in them, to them, at them, there'). Used in this way, **ci** may be replaced by **vi** but **vi** is not common in everyday speech. Notice that **ci** (or **vi**) goes in front of the verb:

> – **Vai spesso a Roma?**
> – *Ci* **vado una volta al mese.**
> – Do you go to Rome often?
> – I go there once a month.

> **Mi piace molto la campagna.** *Ci* **sto volentieri.**
> I like the country. I like being there
> (lit. 'I stay in it willingly').

2 *With verbs* which need an **a** before the object, such as **credere** 'to believe', **riuscire** 'to succeed, to manage', **ci** is used as follows:

> **Tu credi *a* quello che dice? Io non *ci* credo.**
> Do you believe what he says? I don't believe it.

> **Riesci *ad* aprire questa bottiglia? Io non *ci* riesco.**
> Can you open this bottle? I can't manage it.

3 As a *subject* ('there') + **essere**:

> *C'*è **un libro sul tavolo.**
> There's a book on the table.

> *Ci* **sono due macchine davanti alla porta.**
> There are two cars outside the door.

Again, **vi** can replace **ci** but again it is not common in spoken Italian.

4 As a *personal pronoun*, direct and indirect object ('us, to us'):

> **Anna *ci* ha visti al ristorante.**
> Anna saw us in the restaurant.

> **Maurizio *ci* telefona spesso. (telefonare *a* qualcuno)**
> Maurizio telephones us often.

Note: The past participle agrees with a direct object pronoun (as in **ci ha visti**).

5 As a reflexive and reciprocal pronoun:

> ***Ci* divertiamo molto.**
> We are enjoying ourselves/enjoy ourselves a lot.

> ***Ci* scriviamo una volta alla settimana.**
> We write to each other once a week.

Exercise 2

Answer these questions using **ci** instead of repeating the place.

> *Example*: **Paolo va a Roma sabato? (domenica)**
> **No, ci va domenica.**

1 Anna, da quanto tempo abita a Genova? (due anni)
2 Vai da Giorgio domani? (se ho tempo)
3 Sei stato a New York quest'anno? (due anni fa)
4 I tuoi genitori, quando traslocano nella loro nuova casa? (a maggio)

Using ne

> **Ne abbiamo uno solo** (lit. 'We have only one of them')

ne means, according to the context, 'of it, of them, some'. It is used in sentences where the speaker is saying how many or how much of something is being referred to. In English the 'of it, of them' would normally not be necessary:

– **Quante macchine hai?**	– **Ne ho una sola.**
– How many cars do you have?	– I only have one.
– **Hai dei francobolli?**	– **Sì, ne ho due o tre.**
– Have you any stamps?	– Yes, I have two or three (of them).
– **E' buono il gelato?**	– **Sì, ne vuoi un po'?**
– Is the ice cream good?	– Yes, do you want a little (of it)?

Sono belle le mele, ne prendo un chilo.
The apples are lovely, I'll have a kilo (of them).

– **Ti piacciono gli spinaci?**   – **Sì, ne mangio spesso.**
– Do you like spinach?   – Yes, I eat it often.

Exercise 3

Answer 'yes' to the following questions about your family home (imaginary) using the information given.

Example: **Avete un bagno? (2)**
            Ne abbiamo due.

1 Quante camere avete?   (4)
2 Quanti piani avete?   (3)
3 Quante stanze avete?   (7 in tutto)
4 Avete anche un garage?   (1 solo)
5 Avete un giardino?   (2 – uno davanti e uno dietro)

Now give the real answers referring to the house where you actually live.

Using ci *and* ne *together*

Ce n'è per tutti

Sometimes when you are asked whether there is something, you need to use both **ci** and **ne**:

– **Mamma, sono qui con i miei amici. C'è qualcosa da mangiare?**
– **Sì, c'è una torta.**
– **E' grande? Siamo in sette.**
– **Non preoccuparti. Ce n'è per tutti.**

– Mum, I've got my friends with me. Is there anything to eat?
– Yes, there's a cake.
– Is it big? There are seven of us.
– Don't worry. There is some/enough (of it) for everybody.

When you have **ci** followed by **ne**, **ci** changes and rhymes with **ne**. In the example, of course, the **ne** was followed by **è** and so shortened.

– **Ci sono delle macchine davanti alla casa?**
– **Si, ce ne sono tre.**
– Are there any cars outside the house?
– Yes, there are three (of them).

Exercise 4

Below is the plan of some houses being built on the edge of a small town. Land is relatively cheap and the builder is offering small houses built on three floors rather than flats. Study the plans and answer the questions.

Piano seminterrato   Piano rialzato   1° Piano
                                             Planimetrie indicative

Note: **box** is another word for **garage**. **una tavernetta** is usually furnished simply and used for parties. To have one seems to be something of a status symbol. **una lavanderia** is a place for doing the washing. **uno spogliatoio** is a place where you can take off and leave your clothes, for instance at a gymnasium or a swimming pool. **piano rialzato** is a floor a little above ground level.

Example: – **Quanti bagni ci sono?**
               – **Ce ne sono due.**

1 Quanti piani ci sono in questa casa?
2 Nel box quante macchine ci sono?

3 Quanti terrazzi ci sono?
4 Quante camere ci sono?
5 C'è una cantina?

Exercise 5

You have enjoyed a holiday in Tuscany. The agent is checking you out of the house as you leave. You ask about a different villa for your stay next year. Explain the following points to him. Keep it simple. You can use: **abbiamo bisogno di** 'we need', **vorremmo** 'we should like', or, more firmly, **vogliamo** 'we want'.

1 You want to come back next year but not to the same villa.
2 Next year you want a view over the valley.
3 Next year your friends, the Simpsons, are going to come with you, so you need four bedrooms.
4 You prefer to have two rooms downstairs (i.e. not just one big room, so use **stanza**).
5 You also want two or more bathrooms next year.
6 And, above all, you want a quiet house, away from the road. This year's house has been noisy (**rumoroso**).

Exercise 6

Write a simple description of your own house and draw a floor plan, labelling the rooms.

Reading 2 🎧

Dove vivono gli Italiani

1 What is the new trend as far as bathrooms go?
2 Which room is sometimes missing?
3 What is the latest trend as far as a place to live is concerned?
4 How did some families acquire their house in the country?
5 What did the many Italians who left the land and moved into the cities in the 1950s and 1960s do there?
6 What change in lifestyle is making it possible to reverse this trend nowadays?

Oggi la maggior parte degli Italiani vive in città e così l'alloggio è un appartamento. In genere gli appartamenti hanno stanze spaziose. Un appartamento tipico comprende un'entrata, un soggiorno, una, due o tre camere, un bagno e una cucina. Sempre di più i costruttori forniscono "doppi servizi", cioè due bagni. Il secondo bagno di solito non ha la vasca ma solo la doccia. Con una famiglia di due o tre persone è molto pratico. Non c'è sempre la sala da pranzo; piuttosto c'è il tinello, cioè una sala piccola dove si può mangiare ma con un angolo cucina. Generalmente l'appartamento ha un balcone.

Sempre di più però gli Italiani vogliono fuggire dalla grande città per vivere in periferia, in città più piccole o addirittura in campagna. Parecchie famiglie inoltre, pur vivendo in città, possiedono una casa in campagna. Spesso è la casa dei nonni, abbandonata negli anni '50, '60, periodo in cui moltissimi Italiani andavano a lavorare nelle fabbriche in città. Ora, poiché quasi ogni famiglia dispone di una macchina, è possibile tornare a vivere in campagna, o almeno andare in campagna ogni fine settimana e trovare pace e aria pulita.

Vocabulary

la maggior parte	the majority
addirittura	even
parecchie famiglie	several families
inoltre	furthermore, besides
pur vivendo	even though they live
poiché	since, as

13 La vita è cambiata

Life has changed

In this unit you will learn about:

- Saying what things were like
- Saying what you used to do
- Saying what was happening at the time of a particular event
- Saying something is going on at this very moment (**stare** + gerund): the present continuous
- How to say 'no' firmly; more negatives
- **passato remoto**: past events that no longer matter
- **neppure** 'not even, neither'
- Word power: ways of guessing meanings

Dialogue 1

Nel 1967

Having shown Angela her flat, Gabriella offers her a cup of tea. Thanks to her English mother, she knows how to make a good one. They are sitting on the balcony.

1 **From Gabriella's balcony what can be seen all around?**
2 **When she first came to live there what did she look out over?**
3 **What was there opposite the building?**
4 **What was the road like?**
5 **There was a factory there, surrounded by fields. How did the workers get to work?**
6 **Why are there fewer workers at the factory these days?**

GABRIELLA: Ecco il tè.
ANGELA: Si sta bene qui. C'è anche posto per mangiare fuori.

GABRIELLA: Sì. Anche se ci sono palazzi tutto intorno, è tranquillo. Ma sai, quando siamo venuti a vivere qui c'era tutta campagna in questa zona, tutti prati.

ANGELA: Davvero?

GABRIELLA: Proprio di fronte, c'era una cascina, con animali, mucche, pecore. La strada non era ancora asfaltata. Io, quando andavo a fare la spesa, mettevo un paio di scarpe vecchie, perché camminavo sulla terra, sul fango. Poi quando arrivavo sulla strada buona, cambiavo scarpe. Non potevo mica andare in giro con le scarpe coperte di fango. Ma non volevo mettere scarpe belle per camminare su questa strada!

ANGELA: La zona è molto cambiata, allora.

GABRIELLA: Sì, molto. A quell'epoca, la fabbrica era già qui ma era isolata in mezzo ai campi. Gli operai arrivavano con il tram o con pullman privati.

ANGELA: E oggi?

GABRIELLA: Oggi la zona sta cambiando di nuovo. Ora ci sono meno operai alla fabbrica. Usano invece robot. E la gente preferisce vivere fuori, in centri piccoli piuttosto che nella grande città. Ci sono molti appartamenti vuoti nella zona.

Vocabulary

prati	meadows
camminavo sulla terra, sul fango	I used to walk on earth, on mud
non potevo mica	I really couldn't (see below)
andare in giro	go around
la fabbrica era già qui	the factory was already here
gli operai	the workers (industrial workers)
piuttosto che	rather than

Language points

The imperfect: saying what things were like

To talk about completed actions in the past you use the **passato prossimo**. But sometimes you want to look at the past in another way. To describe the way things were in the past you use the *imperfect* tense, **l'imperfetto**. The name does not mean there is something wrong with it; it comes from Latin and means 'not finished'. When you use the imperfect, you are not interested in whether the action or event is finished. Gabriella uses it to describe what her district was like when she and her husband first came there as a young married couple:

> **Quando siamo venuti a vivere qui c'***era* **la campagna.**
> When we came to live here, it was the country.

> **Di fronte c'***era* **una cascina.** Opposite there was a farm.
> **La strada non *era* asfaltata.** The road wasn't made up.

Notice Gabriella says **quando siamo venuti** – that was an event which happened at a specific point in time and then was over and done with so she uses the **passato prossimo**.

The imperfect again: saying what you used to do

You also use the **imperfetto** for repeated or habitual actions in the past:

Quando *andavo* **a fare la spesa,** *mettevo* **un paio di scarpe vecchie, perché** *camminavo* **sulla terra, sul fango. Poi quando** *arrivavo* **sulla strada buona,** *cambiavo* **scarpe.**
When I went shopping, I used to put on a pair of old shoes because I used to be walking on dirt, on mud. Then when I got to the good (made-up) road, I used to change shoes.

The **imperfetto** is easy to form: you just take the **-re** off the end of the infinitive and add the endings as shown below:

cambiare	*mettere*	*preferire*
cambia*vo*	mette*vo*	preferi*vo*
cambia*vi*	mette*vi*	preferi*vi*
cambia*va*	mette*va*	preferi*va*
cambia*vamo*	mette*vamo*	preferi*vamo*
cambia*vate*	mette*vate*	preferi*vate*
cambi*a̱vano*	mett*e̱vano*	preferi*vano*

The stress falls on the penultimate syllable *except* in the third person plural when, as in the present, it falls on the antepenultimate syllable, the third syllable from the end of the word. Very few verbs are irregular, although **essere**, as you might expect, is; the others are verbs whose infinitives have become shortened in modern Italian from earlier longer forms (see Unit 11, the gerund).

essere	*fare*	*dire*	*bere*	*produrre*
ero	facevo	dicevo	bevevo	producevo
eri	facevi	dicevi	bevevi	producevi
era	faceva	diceva	beveva	produceva
eravamo	facevamo	dicevamo	bevevamo	producevamo
eravate	facevate	dicevate	bevevate	producevate
e̱rano	face̱vano	dice̱vano	beve̱vano	produce̱vano

Also similar to the gerund are:

> *dare*: davo, davi, dava, davamo, davate, da̱vano
> *stare*: stavo, stavi, stava, stavamo, stavate, sta̱vano

Note: When Gabriella said **cambiavo scarpe**, in English she might have said 'I used to change my shoes, I changed my shoes, I would change my shoes', all with the same meaning.

The imperfect is also used for actions that were going on when another event occurred:

> *Parlavo* con Angela quando il telefono ha suonato. Sapete chi *era*? *Era* proprio la mamma di Angela che *chiamava*.
> I was talking to Angela when the telephone rang. Do you know who it was? It was Angela's mother calling.

In English we would use 'I was talking'. As was said in relation to the **passato prossimo** it is wiser and more profitable to try to avoid thinking of English and to see the Italian tense system in its own terms. You have two past tenses, one for actions viewed as completed and the other for setting the scene, describing, and also for habitual actions or events. (English has five.)

Exercise 1

Last summer you attended an enjoyable party at the country house of some friends of yours. Here you are recalling some of it. We have helped you, except that you have to put the verbs into the correct tense. Since you are describing the day and your friends, you will need to use the tense for descriptions, the imperfect.

Il tempo (1 essere) così bello. (2 Fare) caldo ma non troppo. La campagna (3 avere) ancora il bel verde della primavera. I fiori (4 avere) un profumo delicatissimo. Tutti gli amici (5 essere) lì. Anna (6 portare), come al solito, un vestito molto elegante. Il colore, un giallo chiaro, le (7 andare) benissimo. Aldo (8 avere) una maglia fatta a mano, molto grande. (9 Sembrare) strano e preoccupato. Infatti abbiamo saputo che la sua ditta (10 avere) dei problemi. Meno male che c' (11 essere) anche Roberto che gli ha parlato e ha potuto aiutarlo. Anche per questo la festa è stata bella, un grande successo.

Vocabulary

i fiori	the flowers
le andava benissimo	it suited her very well
abbiamo saputo	we learned (note how the tense of **sapere** tells us that this happened at a precise time, hence the translation)
la sua ditta	his firm, company
meno male	thank goodness, just as well, luckily

Exercise 2

As a free exercise, describe in writing a happy scene you have been part of in the last year.

Exercise 3

When you were a child, were things very different? Mario is talking about his childhood around 1960. Complete what he says, but be careful: often he includes his brothers and sisters or all the family in what he says, so he will say 'we. . .'.

Quando ero bambino, le cose (1 essere) diverse. Mio nonno
(2 essere) pescatore. Noi (3 abitare) in Liguria. Mio padre
invece (4 lavorare) in un bar. Noi bambini (5 guardare) la
TV nel bar, non a casa. A casa non (6 avere) la TV. Mia
madre (7 fare) la casalinga. (8 Essere) cinque fratelli e la
mamma (9 avere) molto lavoro da fare. Non (10 mangiare)
spesso la carne ma naturalmente mio nonno (11 portare)
a casa molto pesce. Mia madre (12 fare) i nostri vestiti.
Non (13 essere) ricchi come la gente oggi. Ma (14 divertirsi)
molto. (15 Essere) felici.

pescatore	fisherman
fare la casalinga	she was a housewife

Exercise 4

Has life changed a lot since you were a child? Write down some of the things you used to do, and things that people did then and they no longer do today. This is another open-ended exercise.

Exercise 5

There's been an accident. Nothing serious, thank goodness, but two cars have hit each other at the traffic lights and the drivers are looking for witnesses to support their views of what happened. There's a bar on the corner so they ask the customers **Che cosa ha visto?** Complete the answers.

SIGNORE ANZIANO: Ma, non ho visto niente. (1 Leggere) il giornale.
DUE GIOVANI   Non abbiamo visto niente. (2 Parlarsi)

INNAMORATI:	e (3 guardarsi).
CAMERIERE:	Non ho visto niente. (4 Essere) al bar. (5 Aspettare) il barista che (6 fare) due cappuccini.
SIGNORA CON BAMBINO:	Scusi, non ho visto niente. (7 Aiutare) il bambino a mangiare il gelato.
AUTOMOBILISTA:	Ma possibile, tutta questa gente e non hanno visto niente!

due giovani innamorati   two young people in love

Do you feel now that you understand better the three uses of the imperfect? In Exercise 1 it was used to describe what things were like on one particular day in the past; in Exercise 3 it was used partly for that and partly to say what people habitually did in the past. In Exercise 5 it was used to say what people were doing at a point in time in the past.

The present continuous: stare *+ gerund*

La zona sta cambiando

Gabriella talks about what her district was like when she and her husband first moved there. She goes on to say that the area is changing again: **la zona sta cambiando**. When there is a need to emphasize that something is happening now, at this moment, Italian uses **stare** + gerund, the *present continuous*. This seems similar to the English present continuous: 'the area is changing'. But it is not used as much as the English version. It is used *only* when you want to *emphasize* that the action is taking place now.

– **Dov'è Carlo?**
– **E' in cucina, *sta preparando* la cena.**
– Where is Carlo?
– He's in the kitchen, he's getting supper ready.

– **Che cosa *stai facendo*?**
– ***Sto cercando* di riparare la macchina.**
– What are you doing?
– I am trying to repair the car.

Exercise 6

The telephone rings and you answer it. The caller would like to speak to almost anyone in the household except you but they are all busy. Explain what they are doing. *sta facendo la doccia*

1 Vorrei parlare con Paolo. (Tell the caller Paolo is having a shower.) Non può venire al telefono. *sta facendo una besciamella*
2 E Aldo? (Tell the caller Aldo is making a béchamel sauce, **una besciamella**.) Non può venire al telefono in questo momento.
3 E Maria? (She's reading a story (**un racconto**) to little Anna.)
4 E Margherita? (She's out. She's doing the shopping.)
5 E il nonno? (He's asleep.) *sta leggendo*

non c'è sta facendo la spesa

YOU: Senta. Dico a tutti che Lei ha chiamato e La faccio richia- *sta dormendo*
       mare appena possibile.
       (Look, I'll tell everyone you called and I'll get them to call you back as soon as possible.)

Postscript: stare *+ gerund*

The imperfect of **stare** + gerund can be used to say what *was going on* at a certain point of time in the past when there is a need to emphasize that the action was in progress.

Ho chiamato Giorgio ma stava facendo la doccia. Così ho lasciato un messaggio a sua moglie.
I called George but he was having a shower. So I left a message with his wife.

Scusa, ti ho interrotto. Cosa stavi dicendo?
I'm sorry, I've interrupted you. What were you saying?

More negatives

Non ... mica

Non potevo mica andare in giro con le scarpe coperte di fango, said Gabriella: 'I couldn't go round in shoes covered in mud'. You learned (see Unit 3) that to make a sentence negative you simply put **non** immediately before the verb. In Unit 11 you met **non ... niente/nulla**. Here Gabriella uses a commonly heard form:

non ... mica. It is used to strengthen the negative. (In English you might say 'I couldn't go round in shoes covered in mud, could I?'.) Other ways of emphasizing the negative are **non ... affatto**, **non ... per niente**, **non ... per nulla**. **Mica** belongs very much to the spoken language. The other forms are more acceptable in writing.

> *Non* è *mica* **vero**/*non* è *affatto* **vero**.
> It's not true at all.

> *Non* **lo conosco** *mica*/*non* **lo conosco** *affatto*.
> I don't know him at all.

> *Non* **lo conosco** *per niente*.
> I don't know him at all.

> *Non* è *per nulla* **vero**.
> It isn't true at all.

The remote past, passato remoto

There is another past tense called, in Italian, the **passato remoto**. It is little used in spoken Italian in the north; in the centre of Italy, it is more common and it is used a lot in the south. Strictly its use is for completed events and actions in a remote past that has no link with the present, i.e. it is similar to the **passato prossimo** but for a remote, not a recent, past. Because storytelling implies a remoteness from the events being recounted, it is usually used in novels and, of course, in history books. Some Italians use it when recounting something that has happened to them but which they now regard as finished. They become 'storytellers' temporarily. Many native speakers hardly ever use the **passato remoto** and the foreign learner can safely defer learning it until he is an advanced student. For completeness and for recognition when necessary, the forms are given in the 'Grammar summary'.

Cultural point

Gabriella talked about the changes in her neighbourhood in Turin since she moved there in 1967. From a zone where a factory had been built on a greenfield site, it developed into a built-up area, becoming part of the city; and now the factory has automated much of the work, or moved it away from northern Italy, so people are tending to move away, seeking a different lifestyle in small towns.

Italy has undergone huge and very rapid change since the Second World War ended in 1945. It needs to be remembered that before the war Italy was a backward, rural society and in 1945 was emerging from twenty years of Fascist rule as well as from being a battleground. Italians had an opportunity to build their country afresh. It was a time of hope and optimism, not only in Italy.

By 1995,* the fiftieth anniversary of the end of the war, things were very different: Italy was one of the foremost industrialized countries in the world and living standards had never been higher, but society was very different and, furthermore, the political system was in crisis. The framework set up by the post-war constitution, popularly known as the First Republic, had collapsed following revelations of widespread corruption in politics and business. In March 1994 a new government, which many had hoped would usher in a Second Republic, was elected, but just before the end of the year it had fallen. The much hoped for Second Republic seemed to have failed.

Reading

The article that follows appeared in *La Stampa* on 2 January 1995. The year marked the fiftieth anniversary of the end of the Second World War. We reproduce extracts, by kind permission of the writer, Lietta Tornabuoni, because it gives some idea of this social change, even though yet more years have passed. The changes since 1995 are of a different order and politically not a great deal has been achieved.

Read the passage carefully, more than once, listening to the recording if you have it. Many of the words are guessable and you should find you can answer the questions below after two or three readings, if not sooner. Then read the notes and finally come back to the passage again. At that stage you can look up any words you haven't managed to work out.

1 **In the opinion of the writer, what one thing did Italy have for the first time ever at the end of the Second World War?**
2 **List at least three material goods that Italians did not have at the time.**

---

* When the first edition of *Colloquial Italian* was written.

3 The writer says fewer than 7 per cent of Italians had all of
   three basic amenities. What were they?
4 What did almost two million Italians do between 1946 and
   1957? Why?
5 What do you learn about the Italian language at the end of the
   Second World War?
6 According to Lietta Tornabuoni, what values guided people at
   the end of the Second World War, and how do they compare
   with 1995 values (which are also not very different from
   today's)?
7 At the end, the writer lists a number of aspects of life that
   have improved and one that has not. What is that?

l'Italia 1945–1995

Con gli occhi aperti

Cinquant'anni fa, finita la seconda guerra mondiale, c'era in Italia,
per la prima volta, la democrazia. Non c'erano la televisione,
la lavatrice, la plastica, l'automobile come veicolo di massa, la
pubblicità come linguaggio collettivo, l'elettronica coi suoi computers. Non c'era granché da mangiare, nelle macerie belliche
mancavano gli alloggi: e neppure il sette per cento delle famiglie
aveva in casa elettricità, acqua potabile e gabinetto insieme. Non
c'era lavoro, bisognava andarselo a cercare fuori, tra il 1946 e il
1957 quasi due milioni di persone emigrarono per lavorare nelle
Americhe o in Europa: erano gli unici viaggi degli Italiani e per
chi restava i salari erano miseri. Non c'era una lingua comune,
davvero usata, quotidiana: al di là dei libri, della scuola, delle leggi
o dei documenti, l'italiano rimaneva un'astrazione, si parlavano i
dialetti. Non c'era la pratica del consumo, ma l'etica del risparmio;
non la pratica dell'edonismo, ma l'etica del sacrificio. Paese rurale,
l'Italia era pure un paese sottosviluppato.

In cinquant'anni, la nostra vita è immensamente cambiata,
migliorata. Meno fame, meno fatica, meno freddo, meno malattie,
più benessere, più libertà, più diritti, più informazione, più divertimento: sono dati indiscutibili ... Certo è che all'evoluzione del
modo di vivere non ha corrisposto l'evoluzione del sistema
politico. ...

(Lietta Tornabuoni, *La Stampa*, 2 gennaio 1995)

Vocabulary

non c'era granchè da mangiare	there wasn't much to eat
macerie belliche	rubble, ruins, left by the war
mancavano gli alloggi	there was a housing shortage
bisognava andarselo a cercare fuori	it was necessary to go off and find it for oneself outside (Italy)
le Americhe	the Americas, North and South
misero/a	paltry, poor, wretched
al di là di	beyond, outside
risparmio	saving, thrift
sottosviluppato	underdeveloped

Language points

coi (con + i)

> **Coi suoi computers**

coi is **con** + **i**. Some speakers and writers join **con** to **il** (**col**) and **i** (**coi**). It is, however, quite acceptable to say and write **con il** and **con i**.

Some more negatives: neppure, neanche, nemmeno

neppure means 'not even, neither'. **neanche** and **nemmeno** mean the same and work the same way.

> *Non* ho *neppure* 10 euro
> *neanche*
> *nemmeno*

As with **niente**, **nulla**, **mica**, **affatto**, there needs to be a **non** before the verb. (See also Unit 15.)

emigrarono

emigrarono means 'emigrated'. This is a **passato remoto**, third person plural. The writer considers the phenomenon of mass emigration as belonging to the past, as indeed it does. Italy is now experiencing *immigration* from poorer countries, particularly North Africa and Eastern Europe.

Word power

Superficially, the passage looks difficult. This is partly because to an eye brought up on the English language, words of Latin origin seem erudite. Italian however has grown from Latin, with various other influences mixed in. Words of Latin origin are part and parcel of the normal everyday vocabulary of the man or woman in the Italian street. So rule number one when faced with a passage in Italian is: expect Latinisms.

The passage also contains quite a high proportion of abstract words and this gives the reader a *feeling* it is difficult. But such words are particularly guessable. Intelligent guessing is invaluable when dealing with a foreign language. Using a dictionary takes time and you may not always have one handy. When faced with a word you have not met before you should try to guess. Here are three possible approaches:

1 Does it look like a word I know in English? **democrazia** was an easy one. Or **veicolo**. Slip in an 'h': 'vehicle'.

2 Sometimes you may not be able to make the link with an English word but you may recognize part of the word as being similar to an Italian word you know. For example, **lavatrice** contains **lava** and you may be able to link that with **lavare** 'to wash', and then guess that a **lavatrice** is some sort of person or machine that washes.

   novità may not immediately suggest 'novelty' to you, but it may make you think of **nuovo**. Or, to return to the first strategy, perhaps that would take you to 'innovation' and from there to 'something new'. In the case of **sottosviluppato**, you have met **sotto** 'under' and **sviluppo** 'development'. **migliorata**: do you remember **migliore** 'better'? And **benessere** is **bene** + **essere** 'to be well'. What would **malessere** mean?

3 Occasionally neither of these approaches works but you may be able to guess from the context. For instance you have not so far met the word **gabinetto**, used in **elettricità, acqua potabile e gabinetto insieme**. You will realize from the rest of the sentence

that the author is saying that, in 1945, most Italian homes did not have available all three of certain basic conveniences, which we take for granted today. So you might be able to guess that the third of the trio was a *flush lavatory*. This type of guessing is however to be used with caution as it can lead the guesser astray.

14 Alla salute!

Here's to your health!

In this unit you will learn about:

- The difference between **sera/serata, giorno/giornata**
- Object pronouns: with the infinitive, the imperative and **ecco**; the order when there are two of them
- The human body: **il corpo umano**
- Saying you are not well
- Saying you have given something up – another negative

Dialogue 1 ◠

Una distorsione alla caviglia

Enzo had planned to go to the cinema yesterday evening with his friends Piero and Elena. However he had a bad cold, so he stayed at home. Now he is telephoning them to hear what they thought of the film.

1 **How is Enzo's cold today?**
2 **Did Piero and Elena enjoy the film?**
3 **What must Elena avoid doing for a week?**

ENZO: Pronto. Ciao Piero, sei tu? Come stai?
PIERO: Io bene, grazie, e il tuo raffreddore?
ENZO: Un po' meglio oggi, grazie. Scusa se non sono venuto con voi ieri. Stavo proprio male. E il film? Come l'avete trovato? Vi è piaciuto?
PIERO: Ma non ci siamo andati.
ENZO: Come mai? Che cosa è successo?

PIERO: Beh, uscendo di casa Elena è caduta e si è fatta una brutta distorsione alla caviglia. Così invece di andare al cinema, abbiamo passato la serata al pronto soccorso.

ENZO: Oh, mi dispiace. Come va adesso Elena?

PIERO: E qui, accanto a me, sdraiata, con il piede su un cuscino. Non deve assolutamente mettere il piede a terra per sette giorni. Vuoi parlarle? Te la passo. Ciao.

Vocabulary

una brutta distorsione alla caviglia	a nasty ankle sprain
pronto soccorso	hospital emergency service
sdraiata	lying down

Language points

Using sera/serata, giorno/giornata

sera refers to the evening as a point in time, i.e. as opposed to the morning or the afternoon.

> **Vuoi andare dalla nonna questa *sera* o domani *pomeriggio*?**
> Do you want to go to grandmother's this evening or tomorrow afternoon?

Lavorare dalla *mattina* alla *sera*.
To work from morning to night (evening).

You use **serata** when thinking about the evening as a period of time, about how the evening is spent. Hence:

Abbiamo passato la *serata* al pronto soccorso.
We spent the evening at the hospital emergency department.

le lunghe *serate* invernali
the long winter evenings

Compare also **giorno/giornata**. **giorno** is used for the day as a point in time:

– Che *giorno* è oggi?   – E' mercoledì.
– What day is it today?   – It's Wednesday.

Ci sono sette *giorni* in una settimana.
There are seven days in a week.

You use **giornata** when you are thinking about *how* the daylight hours are spent, the conditions and events in them:

E' stata davvero una *giornata* bellissima.
It really was a lovely day (meaning 'the weather was wonderful', or 'we had a marvellous time').

People wish you **Buona giornata!** 'Have a nice day!' and **Buona serata!** 'Have a nice evening!' as opposed to **Buongiorno, Buona sera**, which are simply greetings without thought about how the day or evening might be spent. The same distinction is true but less commonly met for: **mattina/mattinata** and **anno/annata**. **Un'annata buona** is used in agricultural circles when talking about a 'good year' referring to the quality of the crop that year. When making a rather imprecise appointment you might say:

Passo da te in mattinata/in serata/in giornata.
I'll call on you during the morning/the evening/the day.

More about personal pronouns: object form

Here are three points about the position of pronouns.

(1)   You will remember you were told these pronouns are placed immediately before the verb, but Piero says:

Vuoi parlar*le*?
Do you want to talk to her?

When used with an infinitive, the object pronoun *follows* the infinitive with its final **e** removed and since the two run together in the sound, they are written joined to it:

Carlo sta suonando il pianoforte. Mi piace *sentirlo*.
Carlo's playing the piano. I like to hear him.

Dicono che il nuovo film è molto bello. Andiamo a *vederlo* stasera.
They say the new film is very good. Let's go and see it this evening.

Pronto, Carla? Ciao. Senti, è arrivato Bernardo. Perché non vieni a *trovarlo* domani da noi?
Hello, is that Carla? Hi. Bernardo's arrived. Why don't you come and see him at our house tomorrow?

Usually the infinitive will follow another verb as in the above examples, but not necessarily:

***Dargli* la mia macchina? Neanche per sogno.**
Give him my car? Never in a thousand years
(lit. 'not even in a dream').

When the first verb is one from that useful trio **volere**, **dovere**, **potere**, the pronoun may be put either before that verb or after the infinitive:

– **Hai telefonato a Giorgio?**
– **Non ancora. *Gli* devo telefonare oggi.**
  Devo telefonar*gli* oggi.
– Have you telephoned Giorgio?
– Not yet. I must ring him today.

– **Hai finito il libro che stavi leggendo?**
– **No. *Lo* vorrei finire oggi. /Vorrei finir*lo* oggi.**
– Have you finished the book you were reading?
– No. I'd like to finish it today.

– **Quando può fare questa riparazione?**
– ***La* posso fare domani. /Posso far*la* domani.**
– When can you do this repair?
– I can do it tomorrow.

It is simpler for the learner to stick to the second model, thus treating all verbs the same way, but be prepared for the other usage.

(2)   The direct object pronouns are also attached to **ecco**:

– **Ecco*mi*.**	– **Ecco*ci*.**
– Here I am.	– Here we are.
– **Dov'è Giorgio?**	– **Sta arrivando. Ecco*lo*.**
– Where's Giorgio?	– He's coming. Here he is.

Dove abbiamo lasciato la macchina? Ah, ecco*la*.
Where did we leave the car? Ah, there it is.

(3)   Imperatives: the object pronouns, including reflexive pronouns, are attached to the ends of imperatives (although there is one exception).

Scusa*mi*, Maria. Ti ho fatto male?
Forgive me, Maria. Did I hurt you?

Non preoccupar*ti*.
Don't worry.

In this case you have an imperative formed with the infinitive.

Dite*lo* coi fiori.	Say it with flowers.
Accomodate*vi*.	Take a seat.
Divertiamo*ci*.	Let's enjoy ourselves.

Di*mmi*, Gianni, cosa pensi?
Tell me, Gianni, what do you think?

Note: The doubling of the **m** in **dimmi** is a small point. The verbs in which this happens are **andare (va')**, **dare (da')**, **dire (di')**, **fare (fa')** and **stare (sta')**. The **tu** form of the imperative of these verbs is a monosyllable. The initial consonant of any object pronoun doubles when it is attached to these monosyllables. This applies to all the object pronouns *except* **gli**. However, the one most commonly heard is **mi**:

Fa*mmi* vedere la foto.
Show me the photo (make/let me see the photo).

Fa*cci* un piacere.	Do us a favour.
Da*mmi* la tua valigia.	Give me your suitcase.
Da*mmi* la mano.	Give me your hand.
Da*gli* la mia chiave.	Give him my key.

The *exception* to the rule that the object pronoun is attached to the end of the imperative is the formal, third person imperative. In this case the pronoun precedes the verb:

Mi scusi, signore. Le ho fatto male?
I am sorry, sir. Did I hurt you?

Mi dica.	Tell me. (see below)
S'accomodi.	Take a seat/ sit down.

It helps to use commonly heard forms as models for these rather tricky points. You will hear:

From your friends (**tu** form)	From people you do not know well (**Lei**)
Scusami	**Mi scusi**
Dimmi	**Mi dica**
Siediti	**Si sieda**
	S'accomodi

dimmi/mi dica are often heard. When you claim a friend's attention by saying his/her name, the response will very often be **dimmi** or **dimmi tutto**. And it is very common for a waiter, a shop assistant etc. to say **mi dica** to indicate he/she is ready to listen to you.

Exercise 1

Finish these remarks as indicated. You will need to use a pronoun.

Example: **Ho finito di leggere il giornale.**
(Do you want to see it?)
Answer: **Vuoi vederlo tu?/Lo vuoi vedere tu?**

1 Gianni è un amico molto caro.
(He comes to see us often.)
2 Sabato è il compleanno di Andrea.
(I'd like to invite him to supper.)
3 Hai già scritto al signor Lombardi?
(No, I must write to him today.)
4 Buongiorno, signora.
(Can I help you?)
5 Sei mai stato a Parigi?
(No, I hope to go there this year.)

Exercise 2

Answer the following using **ecco** and a pronoun:

1 Dove sono i bambini?
2 Ha il passaporto, signore?

3 Dove sei?
4 Mi dà le chiavi, per piacere?

Exercise 3

How would you say the following (a) to a person you do not know well, i.e. using **Lei**, and (b) to a friend?

1 Enjoy yourself!
2 Do me a favour.

3 Give me the key, please.
4 Tell him to come tomorrow.

Combining pronouns

You saw in Unit 12 that when **ci** and **ne** occur in the same sentence, **ci** comes first and changes to **ce**: *Ce ne* **sono tre**. This also happens with **mi**, **ti**, **ci** ('us, to us'), **vi** and the reflexive pronoun **si** before another object pronoun. Piero says:

> **Te la passo.**
> I'll pass her to you.

Similarly:

> **Me lo dici?**
> Are you going to tell me?
> (lit. 'Are you telling me?')

> **Ce li manda.**
> He's sending them to us.

The order is always:

> (1)   **mi**, **ti**, **si**, **ci**, **vi**, **si**

followed by:

> (2)   **lo**, **la**, **li**, **le**, **ne**.

Note: Remember: **Ce n'è per tutti**, Unit 13, where **ci** is a subject pronoun. The change to **ce** applies to **ci** whether used as subject or object, referring to a person or an object, or meaning 'there' if there is another pronoun following.

What about **gli**, **le** singular and **gli** plural? All three become:
glie and precede **lo**, **la**, **li**, **le**. The resulting sound group is written
as one word:

> *Glielo* **dico domani.** I'll tell you (it) tomorrow.
> him
> her
> them

Without a context the Italian phrase could mean any of the English
versions. How are you going to learn this? Find some model
sentences. A once popular song with the '**orchestrine**' in Venice
went:

> **Me lo dai? me lo dai? me lo dai un bel bacin?**
> Will you give me . . . a nice little kiss?

(**bacin** is a diminutive of **bacio** 'a kiss'.) The line from the song
could be transformed:

> **Me la dai? Me li dai? Me le dai? Me ne dai?**
> Will you give it/them/some of them to me?

> **Te lo do. Te la do. Te li do. Te le do. Te ne do.**
> I am giving (will give) it/them/some of them to you.

> **Glielo do. Gliela do. Glieli do. Gliele do. Gliene do. ecc.**
> I am giving it/some of it to him/her/them. etc.

Exercise 4

Complete the following using a double pronoun:

> *Example*: **– Pronto. C'è il signor Rossi?**
> (I'll put you through straight away)
> *Answer*: **– Glielo passo subito.**

1 – Hai fatto quel lavoro per me?
   (I'll do it for you tomorrow.)
2 – Scusi, signorina. Non capisco questo modulo.*
   (I'll explain it to you.)
3 – Ho comprato un nuovo frigo.
   (They are bringing it to us tomorrow.)
4 – Sai che Alberto ha un nuovo lavoro?
   (Yes, he told me about it† on Saturday)

* **modulo** 'form' (to fill in)   † use **parlare di**

The human body: il corpo humano

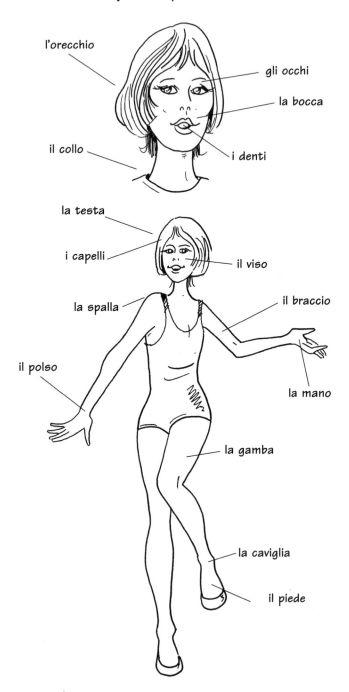

Vocabulary

Altre parole utili

la gola	throat	**il cuore**	heart
lo stomaco	stomach	**la pelle**	skin
il sangue	blood	**i polmoni**	the lungs
i reni	the kidneys	**il fegato**	the liver

It is usual not to use the possessive adjective with parts of the body unless it is necessary to make clear whose body the part belongs to (i.e. in rather unusual circumstances).

> **Elena è accanto a me con il piede su un cuscino.**
> **Si è fatta una brutta distorsione alla caviglia.**

There is no doubt whose foot is on the cushion – Elena's. And the same goes for the ankle. Similarly:

> **Mi lavo le mani.**
> I am washing/wash my hands.

Dialogue 2

Dal medico

1 **What are the patient's symptoms?**
2 **What is the doctor's diagnosis?**
3 **What treatment does he recommend?**

MEDICO: Buongiorno, signore.

PAZIENTE: Buongiorno, dottore. Ho mal di gola, e mal di testa e mi fa male anche lo stomaco, non ho appetito e mi sento stanco da morire.

MEDICO: Vediamo un po'. (*He takes the patient's temperature and examines him.*) Lei ha la febbre alta. Dovrebbe essere a letto.

PAZIENTE: Che cosa è, dottore?

MEDICO: È solo questa brutta influenza che c'è in giro quest'anno. Le do delle pastiglie e uno sciroppo ma è molto importante tornare a casa, mettersi a letto e riposarsi bene. Bisogna anche bere molto: acqua, tè leggero, eccetera. Niente alcool. E non deve tornare a lavorare se non quando non avrà più la febbre.

Vocabulary

mi sento stanco da morire	I feel dead tired
vediamo un po'	let's see, let's have a look
Lei ha la febbre alta	you have a high temperature
	(**avere** *la* **febbre**)
questa brutta influenza che c'è in giro	this nasty influenza that is going round
niente alcool	no alcohol
se non quando non avrà più la febbre	until you no longer have a temperature

Saying you are not well

stare male	to be unwell
sto meglio	I feel/am better
sto bene	I'm well
sentirsi bene/male	to feel well/ill
non mi sento bene	I don't feel well
si sente male	he feels poorly
ti senti meglio?	do you feel better?

ho mal di testa	I have a headache
stomaco	stomach-ache
schiena	back ache
denti	toothache
gola	sore throat

mi fa male la caviglia	my ankle hurts
mi fanno male gli occhi*	my eyes hurt

* 'Eyes' are of course plural, hence also the plural verb.

The word for 'pain' is **dolore** (m.). 'A prescription' is **una ricetta**. And you have already met the false friend: **essere ricoverato/a** 'to be admitted to hospital'. **ricoverare qualcuno d'urgenza** means 'to admit someone to hospital as an emergency case'.

Language point

Using non . . . più *'no longer, not any more'*

Quando *non* avrà *più* la febbre
When you no longer have a high temperature

Avrà is the future of 'have' – see Unit 16.

Una volta Paolo mi scriveva regolarmente ma da un po'
***non* mi scrive *più*.**
At one time Paolo used to write to me regularly but for a
while he hasn't written any more.

As with the other negatives, you must put **non** before the verb.
With a **passato prossimo** the **più** goes before the past particple:

Non ha più detto niente.
He didn't say anything (any) more.

Exercise 5

You are being asked by your doctor about your habits. Answer
saying you used to do all these things but you don't any more.

Example: **Mangia cioccolata?**
Answer: **Una volta, sì, ne mangiavo ma ora non ne
mangio più.**

1 Fuma? 3 Mangia carne rossa?
2 Beve molto? 4 Dorme male?

Exercise 6

Things have changed. Write a new sentence based on the one given
saying that it's not happening any more. Say what the resulting
sentence means.

Example: **Ci parlavamo spesso.**
Answer: **Non ci parliamo più.**
We don't talk to each other anymore.

1 Lo vedevo spesso. 3 Lo aiutavo.
2 Mi scriveva spesso. 4 Ci telefonavamo.

Cultural point

Italy has a National Health Service, under the Minstero della Salute (www.ministero.salute.it), which, in conception, was based on the British health service, although it was introduced well over thirty years later. It is financed by contributions paid by workers but, as in other countries, is struggling to cope with increasing demands on it.

Prescription charges (**il ticket)** have long been payable. They vary according to the patient's means and also are frequently changed by governments in the annual budget provisions. Sufferers from certain, usually long-term, illnesses, are exempt. There are also charges for various services such as blood tests, X-rays etc.

There is no parallel private service but there are many private organizations, which have agreements with the National Health Service to carry out such tests. Many people prefer to use them because they are quick and efficient, whereas the waiting time for tests in hospital is long. The patient again pays **il ticket,** the standard charge.

Italians tend also to go straight to a specialist they trust (**uno specialista di fiducia**) rather than going first to their general practitioner. They will usually do this privately, i.e. they will pay a fee. Voluntary workers also play a part in provision. For instance, the main organization collecting blood from donors, AVIS, is a voluntary organisation (www.avis.it).

15 Buona fortuna!

Good luck!

In this unit you will learn about:

- Saying what you would do if: the conditional
- How to say 'never', 'not yet', 'no one' and 'neither . . . nor'
- Offering to do something, insisting on doing something
- The imperfect subjunctive: saying if something *were* the case
- The subjunctive and other moods/modes
- The pluperfect subjunctive and the past conditional
- Ways of saying 'perhaps': **forse**, **può darsi** and **magari**
- A way of expressing doubt: **chissà**?

Dialogue 1 🎧

La lotteria

*In Italy there are various lotteries, some of which have very big prizes. One is the **lotteria gratta e vinci** – scratch and win. You buy a card and scratch the pictures on it with a coin: you see immediately whether or not you have won. Three friends, Edoardo, Filippo and Elisa, are enjoying a coffee on the terrace outside a bar . . .*

1 **Does Filippo often buy lottery tickets?**
2 **What would he do if he won?**
3 **And Elisa?**

EDOARDO: Compriamo dei biglietti della lotteria?
FILIPPO: Io non vinco mai niente alla lotteria.
ELISA: Compri spesso i biglietti?
FILIPPO: Raramente.

ELISA: Per questo non vinci mai. Come vuoi vincere se non compri biglietti? Dai, compriamo dei biglietti.

FILIPPO: Va bene.

EDOARDO: Vado io a prenderli.

ELISA: Che cosa faresti se vincessi?

FILIPPO: Mah, non lo so. Comprerei una macchina nuova. Magari vi porterei a fare il giro del mondo. E tu Elisa?

ELISA: Comprerei una casa al mare. Ci metterei un pianoforte a coda. Prenderei delle lezioni di piano e passerei le mie giornate a suonare. Inviterei anche gli amici. Quando non suonassi, starei in cucina a preparare dei buoni piatti. Sarebbe una festa continua ...

EDOARDO: Allora, ecco il tuo biglietto, Elisa. E il tuo, Filippo. Gratta e vedi se hai vinto.

FILIPPO: Sì, ho vinto!

ELISA: Oh, che bello. Facciamo il giro del mondo!

FILIPPO: Macchè giro del mondo! Ho vinto cinquanta euro!

Vocabulary notes

dai 'go on, come on'. From **dare** and used to encourage someone to do something.

vado io a prenderli 'I'll go and get them'

ho vinto 'I've won'. **vincere** has an irregular past participle: **vinto**.

macchè 'You're joking!' (rough translation). It expresses strong contradiction of what has just been said.

cinquanta euro 50 euros. At the time of writing this might buy a modest restaurant meal for the three friends.

Language points

Saying what you would do if: the conditional

You have met this quite often: **vorrei**, **dovrei**, **potrei**, **mi piacerebbe** etc. And now you have heard people talk about *what they would do if* they won money in a lottery. The base for the conditional is the infinitive without the final **-e**. Here are several verbs: pick out the ending:

dire	*fare*	*dare*	*prendere*	*partire*
dir*ei*	far*ei*	dar*ei*	prender*ei*	partir*ei*
dir*esti*	far*esti*	dar*esti*	prender*esti*	partir*esti*
dir*ebbe*	far*ebbe*	dar*ebbe*	prender*ebbe*	partir*ebbe*
dir*emmo*	far*emmo*	dar*emmo*	prender*emmo*	partir*emmo*
dir*este*	far*este*	dar*este*	prender*este*	partir*este*
dir*ebbero*	far*ebbero*	dar*ebbero*	prender*ebbero*	partir*ebbero*

The stress falls on the penultimate syllable, except in the third person plural when it falls on the antepenultimate syllable (**ebbero**). *Note*: In the first person singular, the **-e-** of the **-ei** ending is a syllable.

A complication is that **-are** verbs make an additional change. The **a** in the infinitive ending becomes an **e**, so that they work like **-ere** verbs:

comprare	
compr*erei*	compr*eremmo*
compr*eresti*	compr*ereste*
compr*erebbe*	compr*erebbero*

Predictably, **essere** is irregular:

sarei	saremmo
saresti	sareste
sarebbe	sarebbero

A handful of other verbs, some of which you have already met and got used to, are irregular. They fall into three groups:

1 Verbs like **potere** which forms **potrei**: the **e** between the **t** and the **r** has disappeared. Other common verbs like this are:

dovere	→	**dovrei**	**vedere**	→	**vedrei**
andare	→	**andrei**	**sapere**	→	**saprei**
vivere	→	**vivrei**	**avere**	→	**avrei**

2 Other verbs, like **volere** which forms **vorrei**, not only have the shortened form but the first consonant changes and becomes the same as the second, giving **-rr-**. Common ones are: **rimanere** → **rimarrei**; **venire** → **verrei**. **bere** is a bit of an oddball and can be thought of as being in this group: **berrei**.

3 The verbs **dare**, **fare**, **stare**, make their conditional form thus:

dare	→	**darei**	**fare**	→	**farei**
stare	→	**starei**			

The conditional is used to:

• express what *you would do* if ...
• ask politely, make requests seem less assertive, make suggestions in a way that is more polite, even charming, as you have already seen:

> **Dovresti riposarti domani.**
> You ought to rest tomorrow.

> **Saresti molto gentile se ...**
> You would be very kind if you ...

> **Potresti aiutarmi?**
> Could you help me?

> **Dovrebbe essere a letto**
> (Unit 14, Dialogue 2)

Exercise 1

This is what Marco would do if he won a really big prize in a lottery. Write it in Italian.

> *Example*: He would go to Australia.
> *Answer*:   **Andrebbe in Australia.**

1 He would move house. (**cambiare casa**)
2 He would buy a house with a garden.
3 He would marry Anita. (**sposarsi con**)
4 They would learn to play golf.
5 He would not give up work. (**smettere di lavorare**)

Exercise 2

Well, what would you do if you won the big prize in a lottery? This is an open-ended exercise.

Using non . . . mai *'never, not ever'*

Here is another negative. As with **niente**, **mica**, **più**, you must have **non** before the verb:

> *Non* escono *mai* la sera. A loro non piace lasciare i bambini con una babysitter.
> They never go out in the evening. They don't like leaving the children with a babysitter.

> *Non* beve *mai* alcool.
> He/she never drinks alcohol.

> *Non* ho *mai* capito perché.
> I never understood/have never understood why.

Exercise 3

You are being asked whether you do certain things. They are things you would never dream of doing! Say so using **mai**.

1 Lei fuma?
2 Beve vodka?
3 Va spesso in discoteca?
4 Compra cibi surgelati (frozen food)?
5 Cammina per la strada a piedi nudi?

Other negative expressions

You have now met several negative expressions. The remaining ones are:

- **non ... ancora** 'not yet'

  > *Non* abbiamo *ancora* mangiato. Perché non viene a
  > mangiare con noi?
  > We haven't eaten yet. Why don't you come and eat
  > with us?

  > *Non* sono *ancora* pronto. Puoi aspettare?
  > I'm not ready yet. Can you wait?

  Note: **ancora** without **non** means 'still':

  > **E'** *ancora* **molto giovane.**   He's still very young.
  > **C'è** *ancora* **tempo.**   There's still time.

  or it can be used thus:

  > **Vuoi** *ancora* **dell'insalata?**
  > Do you want some more salad?

  > **C'è** *ancora* **del caffè?**
  > Is there still (any more) coffee?

- **non ... nessuno** 'no one', 'nobody', 'not ... anyone'

  > *Non* conosco *nessuno* a **Napoli.**
  > I don't know anyone in Naples.

  > *Non* abbiamo visto *nessuno.*
  > We didn't see anyone.

  It can also precede the verb, in which case **non** is not used:

  > *Nessuno* **fa le lasagne al forno come mia madre.**
  > No one makes lasagne like my mother.

  nessuno can also be used with a noun, i.e. as an adjective. It
  then behaves like **un**. When there is a verb and **nessuno** comes
  after it, **non** must precede it:

  > *Non* si vende in *nessun* negozio in questo paese.
  > It's not sold in any shop in this village.

- **nè ... nè** 'neither ... nor', 'not ... either ... or'

  > *Non* conosco *nè* la signora Biondi *nè* suo marito.
  > I know neither Mrs Biondi nor her husband/ I don't know
  > either Mrs Biondi or her husband.

  > *Nè* Mario *nè* Carla possono venire.
  > Neither Mario nor Carla can come.

Notice in the second case, since **nè ... nè** precede the verb, **non** is not necessary. This is always the case when the negative expression precedes the verb.

Most negatives can be used alone:

- **Sei andato negli Stati Uniti? –** *Mai.*
- Have you been to the United States? – Never.

- **Chi ti ha aiutato a fare tutto il lavoro? –** *Nessuno.*
- Who helped you do all the work? – No one.

- **Che cosa hai imparato alla conferenza? –** *Niente.* **Non ho capito!**
- What did you learn at the lecture? – Nothing. I didn't understand!

Reminder: When used with the **passato prossimo**, **niente**, **nulla** and **nessuno** go *after* the past participle. The other negatives go *before* the past participle.

Non **ho mangiato** *niente.*
Non **ho visto** *nessuno.*

But:

Non **ho   mai   visto il presidente.**
       più
       ancora

With **nè** the negative word goes in front of what it is negating:

Non **ho** *nè* **mangiato** *nè* **bevuto.**
Non **ho mangiato** *nè* **carne** *nè* **pesce.**

Exercise 4

Say the opposite of the following.

1 Vado spesso al cinema.
2 Vedo molta gente nella piazza.
3 A Maria piace tanto la musica rock.
4 Carlo ha molti amici.
5 Mangio sempre al ristorante.
6 Il direttore beve molto.
7 Ho molto da fare.
8 E' già arrivato il professore.

Offering to do something, insisting on doing something

How does Edoardo offer to get the lottery tickets? **Vado io a prenderli**. One of the cases in which you use the pronoun **io** rather than omitting it, is when you are offering to do something. In English you would stress the 'I' with your voice. In Italian you put it after the verb:

> **Lo faccio io.**
> I'll do it.

> **Pago io.**
> I'm paying.

Dialogue 2

Se fossi in te

*Aldo, whose Sicilian holiday we heard about, is troubled. He has been asked by the company he works for to move to the US for two years to oversee a new development the company is planning. It is a promotion and a challenge he would love to accept. But his wife has her career and the children are in high school (**liceo**). Enrico spots him looking glum in the canteen and gets him talking.*

1 Is Patrizia, Aldo's wife, pleased at the prospect of two years in the US?
2 Why does Aldo think it may be difficult for Maria to go?
3 Enrico thinks it may offer exciting possibilities for Patrizia. In what way?
4 Why does Enrico think it's an opportunity for the children?

ENRICO: Bravo, congratulazioni. E' un'occasione meravigliosa. Patrizia dev'essere molto contenta.
ALDO: Magari! Non ho ancora avuto il coraggio di parlargliene. Se fosse casalinga ... Ma ha il suo lavoro che non lascerebbe mai.
ENRICO: Ah, capisco.
ALDO: Poi ci sono i ragazzi. Maria è all'ultimo anno di liceo. Ha la maturità quest'anno e dovrebbe iscriversi all' università in autunno.

ENRICO: Guarda, Aldo. Se fossi in te, ne parlerei subito con
          Patrizia. Tenerti tutto per te non risolve niente. E poi,
          chissà? Potrebbe essere un'opportunità anche per lei.
          Può darsi che possa avere un anno o due di aspettativa.
          Forse potrebbe lavorare anche negli Stati Uniti o magari
          fare un master. Lì sono all'avanguardia nel suo campo.
ALDO: Non avevo pensato a questo. E' vero. Se potesse
          aggiornarsi in un'università, ne avrebbe vantaggi per il
          suo lavoro. Ma i ragazzi, come potrei convincerli? Se
          avessero 4 o 5 anni, se facessero ancora le elementari.
          Ma hanno la loro vita, le loro amicizie. Alla loro età è
          difficile partire.
ENRICO: Ma Aldo, non lo sai? Due anni negli Stati Uniti e il loro
          inglese sarebbe perfetto. Oggi è tanto importante per
          un giovane conoscere bene l'inglese. E anche per loro
          ci sono possibilità nel campo degli studî.
ALDO: In effetti, hai ragione.
ENRICO: Se fossi in te, presenterei la cosa come una decisione
          collettiva da prendere insieme nell'interesse dell'intera
          famiglia.

Vocabulary notes

se fossi in te   'if I were you' (you can say **se fossi te**, but **in** is often
                     used; **fossi** is explained below, p. 224)
magari!   'if only she were!' (in this context; see below, p. 229)

maturità*	the high school leaving certificate in Italy
	(necessary to enrol in a university: see notes)
aggiornarsi	'to get up to date'
le elementari	'elementary' or 'primary school' (**classi** is understood)

The imperfect subjunctive: 'If I were you . . .'

When you express an idea needing the conditional in the main clause, you need the *imperfect subjunctive* in the 'if' clause. The idea you are expressing is that *if* something were the case, *then* certain things would follow. You are talking about the improbable or even impossible.

Se io fossi in te, direi tutto a Patrizia.
If I were you, I would tell Patrizia everything.

Se avessi tempo, lo farei volentieri ma oggi non posso.
If I had time I would happily do it but today I can't.

Se potesse, ci aiuterebbe.
If he/she could, he/she would help us.

The subjunctive and other moods/modes

Language learners tend to panic at the word *subjunctive*, but they should try not to. What follows is technical but is given to try to clarify what the subjunctive is. Italian grammarians classify verbs into **modi**. This is usually translated into English by the word 'mood' but 'mode' might convey the sense better since the word refers to the *manner* in which the speaker presents the action or state of the verb. The **modi** are:

(a) **Modi finiti**: these have tenses and different forms for each person.

1 The *indicative* (**indicativo**), the mood/mode for presenting facts, straightforward statements:

    Carlo *mangiava.*   Charles was eating.

2 The *imperative* (**imperativo**), the mood/mode for giving orders:

    ***Sta'* zitto!**   Be quiet!

---

* In a recent reform of the education system, the name of the examination was changed to **esame di stato**, but it is still often referred to by the old name **maturità**.

3 The *conditional* (**condizionale**), the mood/mode for actions that depend on a condition being fulfilled:

> **Se venisse, gli *parlerei*.**
> If he came, I would speak to him.

4 The *subjunctive* (**congiuntivo**), the mood/mode for expressing an element of subjectivity with regard to the action (for example, doubt about it, desire that it should take place etc.). In the case we have been dealing with the speaker is expressing lack of probability.

> **Se *fosse* casalinga, le cose sarebbero diverse.**
> If she were a housewife, things would be different.

(b) **Modi non finiti**: these do not have different forms according to the person.

1 The *infinitive* (**infinito**), this can be present or past:

> *Present*:
>
> > ***essere* o non *essere***
> > to be or not to be

> Past (for verbs using **avere** for the **passato prossimo**):
>
> > ***avere amato* e *avere perduto***
> > to have loved and lost

> Past (for verbs using **essere** for the **passato prossimo**):
>
> > ***essere andato***
> > to have gone

2 The *participle* (**participio**), the ending can be changed as if it were an adjective:

> *finito/a/i/e*   finished

3 The *gerund*:

> *andando* a **Roma**   going to Rome

The form of the imperfect subjunctive

The subjunctive has four tenses: present, imperfect, perfect and pluperfect. The form of the imperfect subjunctive is not difficult, and you can use it without knowing the above summary of modes, but for some learners it helps to get the full picture clear. Take the same root as for the imperfect indicative (see Unit 13). Any verb that has a special root for the imperfect (e.g. **fare**) will have the same special root in the imperfect subjunctive, with three exceptions (see below). The endings are as follows.

parlare	*decidere*	*partire*	*fare*
parl*assi*	**decid***essi*	**part***issi*	**fac***essi*
parl*assi*	**decid***essi*	**part***issi*	**fac***essi*
parl*asse*	**decid***esse*	**part***isse*	**fac***esse*
parl*assimo*	**decid***essimo*	**part***issimo*	**fac***essimo*
parl*aste*	**decid***este*	**part***iste*	**fac***este*
parl*assero*	**decid***essero*	**part***issero*	**fac***essero*

The stress in the first and third person plural, falls on the antepenultimate syllable.

The three irregular verbs are:

essere	*dare*	*stare*
fossi	**dessi**	**stessi**
fossi	**dessi**	**stessi**
fosse	**desse**	**stesse**
fossimo	**dessimo**	**stessimo**
foste	**deste**	**steste**
fossero	**dessero**	**stessero**

The stress occurs as with the regular verbs.

In Dialogue 2 you met the most common use of the imperfect subjunctive. There are those who say the subjunctive is dying in Italian but this usage is very much alive.

Exercise 5

How would you say in Italian:

1 If we went to Rome we would see Marco.
2 If he wrote to me I would answer.
3 If we had the money, we would help him.
4 If you won the lottery, Anna, what would you do? (**tu**)
5 If you won the lottery, Prof. Turco, what would you do?
6 If they knew, they would be pleased.

The pluperfect subjunctive and the past conditional

These are used to say what you would have done if ... Look at these sentences:

Se *avessi saputo,* **non** *avrei parlato* **così.**
If I had known, I would not have spoken in that way.

Se *fossimo partiti* **un quarto d'ora prima,** *saremmo arrivati* **in tempo.**
If we had set off a quarter of an hour before, we would have arrived in time.

The events have taken place, they are past, but *if only the clock could be put back* ... In order to express that idea, both tenses have been put into the past, using **avere** plus a past participle in the case of verbs that form their **passato prossimo** with **avere,** and **essere** for those that make it with **essere.** The names given to these tenses are:

Pluperfect subjunctive:
   avessi saputo, fossimo partiti

Past conditional:
   avrei parlato, saremmo arrivati

Note: In colloquial speech this idea can be expressed by two imperfect tenses:

Se mi diceva che era stanco, lo aiutavo.
If he had told me he was tired, I would have helped him.

Se non andavo alla festa di Giulia, non incontravo Tommaso.
If I hadn't gone to Giulia's party, I wouldn't have met Tommaso.

This way of avoiding the subjunctive is one that some Italians prefer to take – and you might too.

Exercise 6

Did you ever play the game of consequences? Here are some actions and their consequences. If one thing hadn't happened neither would the other. Or if someone had done something, something else would not have occurred. Can you say this?

Example: **Sono arrivata in ritardo. Mio marito si è arrabbiato.**
Answer: **Se non fossi arrivata in ritardo, mio marito non si
            sarebbe arrabbiato.**
            If I hadn't arrived late, my husband would not have
            got angry.

1 Non mi ha detto che era stanco. Non l'ho aiutato.
2 Ha bevuto tanto. Si è sentito male.
3 E' andato veloce. Ha avuto un incidente.
4 Sono andata alla festa da Giulia. Ho incontrato Tommaso.
5 Ho comprato un biglietto della lotteria. Ho vinto un
   premio.

Ways of saying 'perhaps'

While talking of the unlikely and what one would do if circumstances allowed, you often need to say 'perhaps, maybe'. Italian
has more than one word for this.

Using forse

forse is problem-free. It expresses doubt, uncertainty, hesitation or
possibility, including the idea of hope:

Forse viene domani.
He/she may be coming tomorrow, perhaps he/she'll come
tomorrow.

E' stato forse un errore.
Maybe it was a mistake.

Using può darsi

può is of course the third person singular of the verb **potere** 'to
be able'. You can also say **può essere**. Used by itself **può darsi** is
very common and does not present any problems; but to introduce
a clause it becomes **può darsi che** and needs to be followed by a
subjunctive:

Può darsi che *possa* avere un anno o due di aspettativa.
Maybe she'll be able to have a year or two's leave.

This form and use of the subjunctive will be dealt with in Unit 17.

Using magari

magari has two meanings. The tone of voice tells you which.

(a) 'Perhaps' (like **forse**):

> **Magari viene domani.**
> He may be coming tomorrow.

> **Magari è stato un errore.**
> Perhaps it was a mistake.

(b) 'Would that it were so', expressing strong desire or hope:

> **– Hai vinto?**   **– Magari!**
> – Did you win?   – I wish I had!

> **– Patrizia deve'essere contenta ...**
> **– Magari!**
> – Patrizia must be pleased ...
> – I wish she were!

In this use it can be used with the imperfect subjunctive:

> **Magari fosse vero!**
> Would to God it were true!

Expressing doubt: chissà?

This literally means 'who knows?' and can also be written **chi sa?**. It is also used to express doubt, uncertainty or vague hopefulness:

> **Ci rivediamo, ma chissà quando.**
> See you again, but goodness knows when.

Reading

Per le vie dei borghi d.o.c.

I paesini più belli d'Italia

1 **What are the two requisites to qualify for membership of the club?**
2 **The author is suggesting by implication that the readers will want to ... do what?**

C'è un nuovo club, molto esclusivo, i cui soci meritano di essere conosciuti. E' il "Club dei Borghi più belli d'Italia". L'idea di un marchio di qualità da applicare ai paesi è venuto all'Anci, l'Associazione Nazionale dei Comuni Italiani (il sito: www.anci.it). Il borgo doc deve avere un centro storico con massimo 2 mila abitanti (15 mila nell'intero comune) e, soprattutto, una notevole qualità urbanistica e architettonica, certificata dalla Sovrintendenza alle Belle Arti. Paesini dalle magiche atmosfere, quindi, in cui siano bandite brutture come le antenne paraboliche, le insegne al neon, gli infissi di alluminio e persino l'asfalto delle strade, sostituito dall'acciottolato originario. Ecco allora i nomi e la storia di alcuni "soci" poco conosciuti, per visitarli in un weekend da fiaba.

(Adapted from an article in *Vera* magazine, March 2003, by kind permission of the publishers)

Vocabulary notes

d.o.c. denomoninazione di origine controllata   Here borrowed from a quality mark applied to wines.

urbanistica   As a noun, **urbanistica** is the art of planning towns etc. so that they are rational and aesthetically pleasing: town planning. These towns are old of course.

architettonico   Relating to architecture.

Sovrintendenza alle Belle Arti   The body charged with the conservation of monuments, archeological sites etc.

bandite (f. pl)   'banished, prohibited'

antenne paraboliche   'satellite dishes'

infissi   'window frames'

soci (sing. **socio**)   'members'

Cultural point

The article mentions the National Association of Italian **Comuni.** At all levels of administration there are groupings that work together for their mutual interests, pooling resources and ideas. You may like to visit the ANCI website: www.anci.it. For the **borghi d.o.c.** you will find it easier to go straight to www.borghitalia.it, which gives you links to each individual member. Regions group in the **Conferenza dei Presidenti delle Regioni e delle Province Autonome** (www.regioni.it). This site has links to each region. Similarly www.comuni.it. There are a lot of comuni.

16 Progetti e previsioni – che sarà, sarà

Plans and predictions – what will be, will be

In this unit you will learn how to:

- Talk about what you intend to do: the future
- Understand business letters
- Say you can or can't manage something: **ce la faccio/non ce la faccio**
- Use **andarsene** 'to leave', **cavarsela** 'to get by'
- Say you said you would do something
- Make the past participle agree when necessary
- Use the present for talking about the future
- Another use of the future: say something is likely, probable
- Access the internet for Italian websites

Dialogue 1 🎧

Benissimo. Possiamo firmare

Angela Smith had come to Italy to talk about a new project, you may remember. Her company has bought robots for welding from Mr Rossi's company in the past and now plans to update its equipment over the next two years. Here she is with Mr Rossi. Everything has been discussed, the robots have been demonstrated and Angela is satisfied they will meet her firm's needs. She and Mr Rossi are confirming the agreement verbally before signing the contract for the first consignment.

1 How many robots is Angela ordering at this stage?
2 What discount has Mr Rossi's company offered?
3 What percentage of the total price will be withheld until one month from the date of installation?
4 Who will see to the installation?
5 What does Mr Rossi promise to do during his next visit to England?

ANGELA: Allora, siamo d'accordo. Prendiamo il modello Merlino X390B specifico per la saldatura.

ROSSI: Ne avete bisogno di quattro, vero?

ANGELA: Per ora, sì. Ci fate uno sconto del 15%?

ROSSI: Sì, è inteso. Il pagamento si farà come concordato, cioè: il 30% alla firma dell'ordine, il 60% alla consegna e il restante 10% a 30 giorni. La consegna si farà come promesso, cioè fra due mesi. Al momento della consegna verrà un nostro tecnico che provvederà all'installazione dei robot.

ANGELA: Benissimo. Possiamo firmare il contratto, così Le verso anche l'assegno.

ROSSI: La ringrazio. Sono sicuro che si troverà bene come sempre anche con questo nuovo modello.

ANGELA: Sicuramente. Spero che venga a vedere dove verranno installati. Così si renderà conto di come stiamo crescendo.

ROSSI: Grazie, mi farebbe piacere. Verrò senz'altro durante il mio prossimo viaggio in Inghilterra.

Vocabulary

firmare, una firma	to sign, a signature
la saldatura	welding
la consegna	delivery, handing over
Le verso l'assegno	I will pay you the cheque (**versare** is used in banking to mean 'pay in, remit')
spero che venga	I hope you will come (present subjunctive, see Unit 17)
si renderà conto di come stiamo crescendo	you will realize how we are growing
senz'altro	without fail, of course

Language points

Talking about what you intend to do: the future

Il pagamento si *farà* **come concordato.**
Payment will be made as agreed.

verrà **un nostro tecnico che** *provvederà* **all'installazione**
one of our technicians will come and he will take care of
the installation

Sono sicuro che *si troverà* **bene come sempre ...**
I am sure you will be pleased as always ...

si renderà **conto ...**
you will realize, understand ...

Verrò **senz'altro durante il mio prossimo viaggio.**
I'll come without fail during my next trip.

dove *verranno* **installati**
where they will be installed

venire is used in this last example to form the passive – see Unit 9.
  The future tense is formed on the same base as the conditional:
the infinitive minus the final **-e**. Here are the future forms of each
type of regular verb and of three irregular verbs. **essere** is unique;
avere and **venire** represent the two types of irregular verbs we
showed you when dealing with the conditional.

comprare	*prendere*	*partire*	*essere*	*avere*	*venire*
compre*rò*	**prende*rò***	**parti*rò***	*sarò*	**avrò**	**verrò**
compre*rai*	**prende*rai***	**parti*rai***	*sarai*	**avrai**	**verrai**
compre*rà*	**prende*rà***	**parti*rà***	*sarà*	**avrà**	**verrà**
compre*remo*	**prende*remo***	**parti*remo***	*saremo*	**avremo**	**verremo**
compre*rete*	**prende*rete***	**parti*rete***	*sarete*	**avrete**	**verrete**
compre*ranno*	**prende*ranno***	**parti*ranno***	*saranno*	**avranno**	**verranno**

Notes

1 As with the conditional, the vowel in the **-are** infinitive ending
   becomes **e**.

2 There is a one-letter difference in spelling between the first person plural of the future and the same part of the conditional. It reflects a difference of pronunciation:

Future		Conditional	
saremo	we shall/will be	**saremmo**	we should/would be
prenderemo	we shall/will take	**prenderemmo**	we should/would take
verremo	we shall/will come	**verremmo**	we should/would come

It is vital to distinguish the single **m** of the future from the double **m** of the conditional. Pronouncing one **m** or two changes the meaning.

Exercise 1

Translate these sentences into Italian. They concern the visit of Mr Rossi's technician to install Angela Smith's robots.

1 Our technician will arrive at East Midlands airport at 16.00 on 17 July.
2 He will start the installation on the 18th.
3 He will finish by (**entro**) the end of the month.
4 He will need a room in a hotel.
5 Will it be possible to meet him at the airport? (meet: use **prendere**)
6 Will you be able to give him a car for the period?
7 He will explain the robots to your technicians during the installation.

Exercise 2

You are tired. Someone is asking you whether you have done certain things or whether you are going to do them now. Promise to do each tomorrow.

Example: **Sei andato a fare la spesa?**
Answer: **Andrò domani a fare la spesa.**

1 Hai spedito le cartoline?
No, le _____ domani.

2 Vuoi finire questo lavoro oggi?
No, lo _____ domani.

3 Telefoni a Mario oggi?
No, gli _____ domani.

4 Vuoi ritirare oggi i biglietti per il nostro viaggio?
No, li _____ domani.

5 Mi puoi aiutare adesso a fare la traduzione?
No, ti _____ domani.

Business letters

Business letters are more difficult than those between friends. It is usual to address a firm or organization as **Spettabile**, usually abbreviated to **Spett.le,** and to put the address the letter is going to at the top. **Alla cortese attenzione di** indicates whose attention the letter is for. The subject of the letter is set out in the heading, preceded by the word **oggetto**. Often a stylized business Italian is still used. Here are two examples of the type of letter Mr Rossi's company (Robotica Milanese) writes and receives:

Spett.le Ace Motori. S.r.l.
Via Gramsci 121,
Collegno (TO)

Alla cortese attenzione dell'Ing. Mancuso
Cinisello Balsamo, 20/03/2004

Oggetto: NS. OFFERTA N. 2430/04

Con la presente, siamo lieti di sottoporVi la ns. migliore offerta per l'impianto di Vs. interesse.

Rimanendo a disposizione per qualunque chiarimento tecnico commerciale, porgiamo distinti saluti.

M. Rossi
Area Manager
Robotica Milanese S.p.A.

---

1 **Whose attention is this letter for?**
2 **Can you guess what 'ns.' and 'Vs.' mean?**
3 **What is the letter about?**

Note the addressee's name is put at the top right. And the place of writing is often stated with the date of the letter.

An incoming letter is shown below:

Spett.le Robotica Milanese,
Via Leonardo da Vinci 10,
Cinisello Balsamo (MI)

Bologna, 10/6/2004   Alla C. A. Ing. Tondelli

NS. Rif: 140/04/C

OGGETTO: RICHIESTA DI INTERVENTO

Come già comunicato telefonicamente in data odierna, con la presente richiediamo con urgenza il Vs. intervento tecnico su impianto robotizzato ARTU' da Voi vendutoci.

RingaziandoVi per la collaborazione, con l'occasione porgiamo distinti saluti.

N. Bortolotti
Meccanica Panigale S.p.A.

---

1 **What is the letter asking for?**
2 **Robotica Milanese will not be surprised to get this request. Why?**

Vocabulary

in data odierna   of today's date

Common abbreviations are

ns.	**nostro**	
Vs.	**Vostro**	
C.A.	**cortese attenzione**	
u.s.	**ultimo scorso**	last month
p.v.	**prossimo venturo**	next month
c.m.	**corrente mese**	this month
gg.	**giorni**	days
S.r.l.	**società a responsabilità limitata**	limited company
IVA	**imposta sul valore aggiunto**	VAT – value added tax

Openings

To a firm:	**Spett.le ditta/società**
To a man:	**Egregio dott. Manzini**
To a woman:	**Gentile dott.ssa Vasino**

Common closing salutations
Porgiamo distinti saluti.
Cogliamo l'occasione per porgerVi i nostri più distinti saluti.
RingraziandoVi anticipatamente, con l'occasione porgiamo distinti saluti.

Note the practice of capitalizing **Voi, Vi** and **Vostro**. It is regarded as a courtesy to the company, as with Lei to individuals.

Reading

These days, much business is done using emails, which are less formal than letters. Their very nature seems to mean writers do not bother to correct spelling, nor observe the conventions of letter-writing. Here, however, is an email couched in formal, elegant Italian. Zanichelli Editore is a publishing house specializing in dictionaries etc. This circular email from them offers to send recipients information about their new publications.

Can you guess the meaning of the following:

1 **invio automatico**
2 **opere di consultazione**
3 **L'iscrizione è assolutamente gratuita e non comporta alcun obbligo di acquisto**
4 **senza immagini o allegati**
5 **casella di posta elettronica**
6 **senza alcun costo o onere**

From: notiziario_Zanichelli@zanichelli.it
To: sophie.rolfe@virgin.net
Sent: 27 July 2004 20:00
Subject: 0 Invito all'iscrizione al Notiziario
           Dizionari e opere di consultazione Zanichelli

Gentile Lettore,
Le scriviamo per informarLa che Zanichelli editore ha
attivato un servizio di invio automatico di e-mail
allo scopo di segnalare tempestivamente le novità
editoriali riguardanti il settore Dizionari e opere di
consultazione.
Con la presente, Le proponiamo di iscriversi a questo
servizio. L'iscrizione è assolutamente gratuita e non
comporta alcun obbligo di acquisto.
Le e-mail che Le invieremo saranno di dimensione
ridotte, senza immagini o allegati e tali comunque da
non creare problemi di alcun genere alla Sua casella
di posta elettronica.
In qualsiasi momento Lei potrà decidere la
cancellazione del Suo nominativo dalla mailing list
senza alcun costo o onere.
Per iscriversi è sufficiente rispondere a questo
messaggio, indicando esplicitamente la propria volontà
di aderire.
Con i nostri migliori saluti.
Bernardo Cioni
Servizio Sviluppo
Zanichelli editore S.p.A.

Zanichelli editore S.p.A.
Sede: Via Irnerio 34, 40126 Bologna
Capitale euro 25.000.000 - Partita Iva 03978000374
Codice Fiscale e n. iscr. nel Registro delle Imprese
08536570156
R.E.A. n. 329604
http://www.zanichelli.it/dizionari

Vocabulary

O = Oggetto	as in business letters, in spite of being preceded by 'Subject'
in qualsiasi momento	at any time
la propria volontà	your (own) wish

Cultural point

You will notice that the email format uses English. Notice also **mailing list.** Zanichelli produces dictionaries, so note their precision in the use of the word **e-mail**, although, as has been said, many Italians use **mail.** The Italian term is in the passage but is not often used. The company address is given in the same format that would appear on headed paper. **Sede** means 'Head office'. **Partita IVA** is the VAT registration number and **Codice Fiscale** is the tax reference number. Individuals also have a **Codice Fiscale.**

Dialogue 2 🎧

Un invito

Angela's visit to her cousin proved to be the start of a friendship. Gabriella had promised to take Angela to spend a day at the farmhouse she and her husband are restoring in the country. On one of Angela's trips to Italy, Gabriella telephones her at her hotel in Turin.

1 How is Angela going to get to the farmhouse?
2 When must she be ready?

GABRIELLA:	Pronto. Angela? Ciao. Sono Gabriella. Come va?
ANGELA:	Gabriella, ciao! Che piacere! Io sto benissimo grazie. E tu?
GABRIELLA:	Anch'io, bene, grazie. Senti, questo fine settimana andiamo in campagna. Ti ricordi che abbiamo una vecchia cascina? Avevamo detto che ti avremmo portata a passare una giornata lì. Vuoi venire con noi questa volta?
ANGELA:	Sì, mi farebbe molto piacere. A che ora partite?

GABRIELLA: Ci piacerebbe partire presto. Se passiamo a pren-
derti all'albergo sabato alle otto, ce la fai?
ANGELA: Certo che ce la faccio. Sarò pronta alle otto.
GABRIELLA: Allora, arrivederci a sabato.

Vocabulary

avevamo detto   we had said (some time in the past)

Using ce la fai?

ce la fai? (from **farcela** 'to manage') is a widely used idiomatic
expression. The two object pronouns, **ce la**, do not refer to anything
specific and do not change.

ce la faccio	I am managing	**ce la facciamo**
ce la fai		**ce la fate**
ce la fa		**ce la fanno**

Ce la fai?	Can you manage (it)?
Non ce la faccio.	I can't manage (it).
Ce l'ho fatta.	I did it/I've done it.

Two other common expressions use combined pronouns. In these
the first pronoun is a reflexive pronoun and changes with the
subject of the sentence.

andarsene 'to go (away), to leave'

me ne vado	I'm going (away)	**ce ne andiamo**
te ne vai		**ve ne andate**
se ne va		**se ne vanno**

cavarsela 'to get by'

me la cavo	I get by	**ce la caviamo**
te la cavi		**ve la cavate**
se la cava		**se la cavano**

Saying you said you would . . .

Avevamo detto che ti avremmo portata . . .

avevamo detto is the imperfect of the auxiliary plus the past
participle, corresponding to the English 'we had said'. It puts the

saying further back in the past than **abbiamo detto** 'we said'. No problems here. But in Italian, when reporting words that were originally in the future (**ti porteremo** 'we will take you'), you use the *past conditional*, not the conditional. The past conditional is made using the conditional of **avere** or **essere**, according to the verb, plus the past participle. In the following examples the actual words are shown first and then a reported version:

> **Arriverò prima delle otto.**
> **Ha detto che sarebbe arrivato prima delle otto.**
> He said he would arrive before eight.

> **Ti aiuterò di sicuro.**
> **Mi ha risposto che mi avrebbe aiutato di sicuro.**
> He answered that he would certainly help me.

> **Andremo al mare domenica.**
> **Hanno detto che sarebbero andati al mare domenica.**
> They said they would go to the seaside on Sunday.

Making the past participle agree

> **Ti avremmo portata ...**

When used with **avere**, it is usual to make the past participle agree with a direct object pronoun preceding it. The agreement is also made with **ne**:

> **La mela? L'ho mangiata.**
> The apple? I've eaten it.

> – **Dove sono i bambini?**   – **Non lo so, non li ho visti.**
> – Where are the children?   – I don't know, I haven't seen
> them.

Exercise 3

Complete the past participle in the following sentences:

1 E' arrivata tua mamma? Non l'ho vist _____
2 Hai visto i miei occhiali? Li ho smarrit _____
3 E' buona questa torta. Ne hai mangiat _____
4 Hai assaggiat _____ anche il gelato?

smarrire   to mislay (**oggetti smarriti** 'lost property')
assaggiare   to taste, try (food, drink)

Don't forget that when the verb is conjugated with **essere** the participle agrees with the subject.

Anna è andata a comprare il pane.
Anna has gone to buy bread.

More about the future

When talking about the future the *present tense* is often used, as indeed it is in English:

Andiamo in campagna questo fine settimana.
We are going to the country this weekend.

Andate al cinema stasera?
Are you going to the cinema this evening?

Lo faccio subito.
I'll do it immediately.

It is not *wrong* to use the future in these cases. The future tends to emphasize intention or advance planning, so Angela says:

Sarò pronta.
I'll be ready.

Quest'estate andremo in California.
This summer we are going (i.e. we have plans to go) to California.

The future can be used when contrasting a *near future* with a more distant future:

Questa sera non usciamo; venerdi però andremo a teatro.
We aren't going out tonight; on Friday however we are going to the theatre.

The following expressions are often associated with the future:

entro giovedì	by Thursday
entro domani	by tomorrow
fra due ore	in two hours' time
fra due giorni	in two days' time
fra poco	in a little while
la settimana prossima	next week
l'anno prossimo	next year

lunedì prossimo	next Monday
domani	tomorrow
dopodomani	the day after tomorrow

A common use of the future is to suggest something is *possible*, implying it is likely but you can't confirm it as fact:

– **Dov'è Giorgio?**
– Where's Giorgio?

– **Sarà in ufficio.**
– He'll be in his office/he's likely to be in his office.

Anna è partita questa mattina. Sarà già a Roma.
Anna left this morning. She's probably already in Rome.

Following from this, you will notice the *past conditional* used in journalism, particularly when the journalist is reporting what is thought to have happened rather than a fact:

Il conducente della macchina si sarebbe addormentato al volante.
The driver of the car appears to have fallen asleep at the wheel.

Il ministro avrebbe promesso una nuova riunione con il sindacato per domani.
It seems the Minister promised a new meeting with the union tomorrow.

Cultural point

The internet

You will probably want to look for Italian internet sites. Useful search machines are:

• www.google.it
• www.altavista.it

The Italian Embassy in London has a very useful website (www.embitaly.org.uk), which includes a list of Italian search engines and portals (doubtless the work of a particular enthusiast): go to the site index. There are also links to many different websites holding a variety of information about Italy. When surfing (**navigare in internet**), you will find English terms widely used or adapted (e.g. **un programma antivirus**, **un sito**, **chat** (meaning 'chat room' as well as the system of exchanging chat), **newsgroup**). Official government sites and, even more so, local authority sites are worth visiting. Try, for instance, www.comune.torino.it or www.comune.roma.it.

17 Un vestito per un matrimonio

A dress for a wedding

In this unit you will learn about:

- Clothes
- Saying what you think, what you want, what you need etc.: the present subjunctive
- Small towns, off the beaten track, for you to seek out when you are in Italy
- Idiomatic expressions using **avere** + a noun: **avere fame** – to be hungry

Dialogue 1

Desidero che mi dia un consiglio

Angela has been invited to a wedding and she thinks it would be fun to buy an outfit in Italy to wear to it. However, she doesn't know the shops well and so she telephones signora Rossi to ask her advice. She starts by asking how signora Rossi is.

1 Who is getting married?
2 What type of outfit does Angela say she wants?

ANGELA: Mi scusi se La disturbo. La chiamo perché desidero che mi dia un consiglio.

SIG.RA R: Ma molto volentieri se posso.

ANGELA: Ecco: la figlia della mia cugina di Torino si sposa a settembre. Mi piacerebbe comprare un abito per la cerimonia in Italia ma non so dove si possa trovare un vestito adatto che non sia troppo impegnativo. Infatti, bisogna che sia elegante ma se possibile che si adatti anche ad importanti occasioni di lavoro. Dunque voglio che sia semplice e anche che abbia un buon taglio e un bel tessuto.

SIG.RA R: Non c'è nessun problema, anzi mi farebbe molto piacere accompagnarLa in qualche negozio. Penso che sia possibile trovare qualcosa che Le piaccia. E' libera domani?

Vocabulary notes

ecco 'well' (in this context). Here, Angela is indicating she is about to give an explanation, a common use of **ecco**.

vestito 'clothes, a dress, an outfit'. The word can be applied to clothes for men or women.

abito 'a dress' (for a woman), 'a suit' (for a man). Add **da uomo** or **da donna** when necessary.

impegnativo 'exacting, binding'. Angela doesn't want to buy something that will be suitable only for the wedding. There is also the idea that it should not cost too much. **un impegno** is 'a pledge'; but also 'an engagement'. **sono impegnato/a** means 'I have an engagement'.

tessuto 'fabric, material' (also **stoffa**)

Language points

Saying what you think, what you want, what you need: the present subjunctive

We explained in Unit 15 that the subjunctive is used when there is an element of subjectivity in the way the action is being presented. In Dialogue 1 above a number of present subjunctives occur. Be warned: they do not always translate neatly into a similar English structure.

Desidero che mi *dia* un consiglio.
I want you to give me some advice.

Bisogna che *sia* semplice ma che *si adatti* anche ad importanti occasioni di lavoro.
It needs to be elegant but it must adapt to important working occasions as well.

Voglio che *sia* semplice e che *abbia* un buon taglio ...
I want it to be simple and to have a good cut ...
(to be well cut) ...

Penso che *sia* possibile trovare qualcosa che Le *piaccia*.
I think it is possible to find something you will like.

Form

The form is not difficult. There are two types: (1) verbs in **-are**; and (2) the rest. In the singular, there is one form for all persons. For this reason the subject pronouns are often used with the subjunctive. The **-ire** group subdivides: verbs that have **-isc-** in the present indicative also have it in the present subjunctive. You will also notice one form that is the same as that of the present indicative for all verbs. Which is it? Also, as you look, think whether one of the parts reminds you of another mood you have met.

(io)	parl*i*	vend*a*	cap*isca*	part*a*
(tu)	parl*i*	vend*a*	cap*isca*	part*a*
(lui/lei)	parl*i*	vend*a*	cap*isca*	part*a*
(noi)	parl*iamo*	vend*iamo*	cap*iamo*	part*iamo*
(voi)	parl*iate*	vend*iate*	cap*iate*	part*iate*
(loro)	parl*ino*	vend*ano*	cap*iscano*	part*ano*

The stress in the third person plural is always, as in many other moods and tenses, on the antepenultimate syllable: **parlino**, **capiscano** etc.

Yes, the first person plural, the **noi** form, is the same as for the present indicative. And the singular form is the same as that of the formal imperative (**-are** verbs: **scusi**; other verbs: **senta**, **dica**). Verbs that are irregular in the formal imperative are also irregular in the subjunctive. Common irregular subjunctives are:

essere	*avere*	*andare*	*fare*	*dare*	*dire*	*venire*
sia	abbia	vada	faccia	dia	dica	venga
sia	abbia	vada	faccia	dia	dica	venga
sia	abbia	vada	faccia	dia	dica	venga
siamo	abbiamo	andiamo	facciamo	diamo	diciamo	veniamo
siate	abbiate	andiate	facciate	diate	diciate	veniate
siano	abbiano	vadano	facciano	diano	dicano	vengano

The *perfect subjunctive* is formed with **avere** or **essere** and the past participle:

Credo che *abbia* finito di piovere.
I think it has stopped raining.

Uses

When is the present subjunctive used? This is more difficult to grasp than the form and a comprehensive treatment is beyond the scope of this introductory book. The subjunctive is used mostly in subordinate clauses, and is usually preceded by **che**. The most frequent uses are the following:

(1)   After verbs expressing an *opinion*, or perhaps casting doubt: **penso che . . .**, **credo che . . .**; the negative in particular casts doubt: **non penso che . . .**, **non so se . . .** :

Penso che **sia possibile . . .**
I think it is possible . . .

Credo che **abbia finito . . .**
I think he/she has finished . . .
(I think so, but I am not sure)

Non so se **sia possible . . .**
I don't know whether it is possible . . .

Spero che **venga . . .**
I hope you'll come . . .

In the last case (from Unit 16, Dialogue 1) the use of the subjunctive implies doubt. **sperare** can also be used followed by the indicative, indicating the speaker thinks the event will take place.

Remember **secondo me**. It is a way of saying what you think without needing a subjunctive, or indeed a verb (see Unit 5, Dialogue 1).

(2)   After verbs expressing desire, will, regret, fear and some other emotions: the most common is **desire** 'wanting':

Desidero che **mi dia un consiglio.**
I want you to give me some advice.

Voglio che **sia semplice.**
I want it to be simple.

Note: If the same person is the subject of both verbs you can use the infinitive:

Desidero darLe un consiglio.
I want to give you some advice.
(*I want* and *I am giving* the advice.)

(3)   After a number of *impersonal verbs*: **occorre che, bisogna che, è necessario che, è possibile che, può darsi che, sembra che, pare che, basta che, è meglio che** etc.:

Bisogna che *sia* elegante ma ... che si *adatti* anche ad importanti occasioni di lavoro.
It must be elegant but it must be suitable for important professional occasions too.

Può darsi che *possa* avere un anno o due di aspettativa.
(see Unit 15, Dialogue 2)
Maybe she'll be able to have a year or two's leave.

(4)   After a *relative pronoun* when the clause is referring to a type rather than the particular:

... qualcosa che Le *piaccia*
... something that you like

Ci vuole *un governo che sappia modernizzare il paese.*
What is needed is a government that knows how to modernize the country.

Note: If you are describing a particular government, not a type of government, you would say:

Abbiamo un governo che sa quello che fa.
We have a government that knows what it is doing.

(5)   The subjunctive is also used after a number of *conjunctions* including **benché** 'although', **poiché** 'since, as' (causal), **perché** 'so that' (not when meaning 'because'), **prima che** 'before':

Benché *abbia* ormai sessant'anni, è sempre molto giovane di spirito.
Although he (she) is now sixty, he (she) is very young in spirit.

Facciamolo prima che *cambi* idea.
Let's do it before he (she) changes his (her) mind.

All this is probably more than you can absorb in one reading. It also needs to be said that the present subjunctive belongs to fairly formal, careful speech and there is a tendency in spoken Italian to avoid it. The choice depends on the person speaking and how careful he wants his way of speaking to be. Many educated people, however, look down on someone who does not use the subjunctive: a few years ago, for example, a minister of education was the object of some mockery because of his failure to use it.

As you can see, the forms are very similar to the indicative so, as a foreign speaker of Italian, you should not worry unduly. It is not necessary to master all the intricate details in the relatively early stages of language learning. The use of the subjunctive learned in Unit 15 will probably prove more useful to you. At this stage, you should be noting subjunctives as you meet them so that, with practice, you will gradually understand them and be better able to get them right. Nevertheless, here is some practice for you.

Exercise 1

In the following exchanges the second speaker is uncertain about the facts. Can you supply the correct form of the verb to convey this uncertainty.

Example: – **Devo andare in banca.**
– **Non credo che (essere) _____ aperta**
a quest'ora.
Sono già le diciassette. (sia)

1 – Aldo dice che Giorgio viene alla festa domani. E' vero?
– Non penso che (venire) _____. Non sta molto bene.

2 – E' partita Anna?
– Non credo che (essere partita) _____. Mi ha telefonato
questa mattina.

3 – Invece di andare a New York, perché non andiamo a
Sydney?
– Non credo che si (potere) _____ cambiare la destinazione
adesso. Il viaggio è tutto prenotato.

4 – Giorgio arriva stasera, vero?
– Non penso che (arrivare) _____ stasera. Arriverà forse
domani.

5 – Luisa ha comprato una nuova macchina?
   – Non penso che ne (avere comprata) _____ una. Però la sta
   cercando.

6 – Aldo è andato in Francia questo fine settimana?
   – Non credo che (essere andato) _____. Voleva andare ma ha
   avuto dei problemi.

Exercise 2

Your holiday villa has a maid – what bliss! Tell her what you want
her to do this morning.

   Voglio che _____.

1 fare i letti
2 pulire la cucina
3 lavare questi vestiti
4 stirare la biancheria lavata ieri
5 preparare il pranzo per l'una

Exercise 3

You are shopping for various things. How would you say:

   'I'd like . . .'?

1 a blouse that is easy to iron
2 a sweater that can be washed in the machine
3 a handbag in which there is space for a book

Exercise 4

You're talking politics with a friend. Explain what you think are
the qualities needed in a prime minister: in Italy, **Presidente del
Consiglio (dei Ministri)**.

   Bisogna che (1 capire) _____ i problemi della gente comune.
   Nello stesso tempo è necessario che (2 avere) _____ una
   visione larga del suo lavoro. Ci vuole una persona che
   (3 sapere) _____ resistere alle pressioni. Naturalmente
   occorre che (4 essere) _____ molto paziente. Sarà possibile
   trovare una persona adatta?

Dialogue 2 ⌒

Alla boutique

Signora Rossi and Angela go to a shop where signora Rossi has often bought clothes for important occasions. She introduces Angela to the owner and explains what Angela is looking for.

1 **Why does the owner of the shop ask when the wedding is?**
2 **Angela likes the first outfit she tries on but there is a small problem.**
3 **Why is Angela pleased with her shopping expedition?**

NEGOZIANTE: Buongiorno signora Smith. Sono sicuro che c'è quello che cerca. In che mese è il matrimonio?

ANGELA: Ai primi di settembre.

NEGOZIANTE: Allora andrebbe bene un vestito di seta. A settembre non farà freddo. Venga a vedere qui. Che misura ha?

ANGELA: 44, penso.

NEGOZIANTE: Ci sono tailleur come questi. C'è anche la camicetta ma naturalmente in un'altra occasione la può sostituire. Oppure potrebbe prendere un vestito con giacca, come questi.

ANGELA: Posso provare questo?

Shortly Angela appears from the changing room wearing the outfit.

SIG.RA R: Che bello! Veramente Le sta molto bene questo colore.

ANGELA: Mi piace molto. E' proprio quello che volevo. Ma non è un po' larga la gonna?

NEGOZIANTE: Sì, ha ragione ma gliela possiamo stringere legger-mente. Ma non vuole provare un altro vestito? Guardi questo abito a fiori, lo provi. Può darsi che Le piaccia di più.

ANGELA: No, veramente mi piace molto questo. Se mi potete stringere la gonna senza che si noti, lo prendo.

The purchase concluded, Angela and signora Rossi go for a coffee in a nearby bar.

SIG.RA R: Il vestito che ha comprato è proprio bello ma come
               mai non ha voluto provarne ancora uno o due?

ANGELA: Mi è subito piaciuto quello e così abbiamo
               risparmiato tempo. Mi ero presa tutta la mattinata
               libera. Che ne dice, signora Rossi? Andiamo a
               visitare un museo?

SIG.RA R: Che bella idea! Ma diamoci del tu. E' più facile.

Vocabulary notes

boutique 'shop'. French word, used to indicate a smart dress shop.

sono sicuro che ... 'I am sure that . . .'. Since the shop owner is sure,
   there is no subjunctive here.

ai primi di settembre 'in the first (few) days of September'

andrebbe bene un vestito di seta 'a silk dress would be very suitable'

tailleur 'suit'. French word: jacket and skirt or coat and dress, for
   women only.

le sta bene 'it suits you'. **stare bene** and **andare bene** mean the
   same.

non è un po' larga la gonna? 'isn't the skirt a little big?' (lit. 'wide')

stringere 'to take in' (of clothes). **stringere** means 'to make tight, to
   squeeze'; **stringere la mano a qualcuno** is 'to shake hands'.

senza che si noti 'without it showing'. **senza che** requires a
   subjunctive.

abbiamo risparmiato tempo 'we've saved time'

che ne dice? 'what do you say about it?' That is, 'do you like the idea?'.

diamoci del tu 'let's use "tu"'. In English: 'let's use first names'. When you use 'tu' you also use first names.

Using avere *+ noun*

ha ragione 'you're right'

You met this in Unit 5 and again in Unit 15. A number of common ideas, which in English are expressed using 'to be' and an adjective, in Italian are conveyed by **avere** and a noun:

avere ragione	to be right	**avere torto**	to be wrong
avere caldo	to be hot	**avere freddo**	to be cold
avere fame	to be hungry	**avere sete**	to be thirsty
avere fretta	to be in a hurry	**avere bisogno di**	to need
avere sonno	to be sleepy	**avere 17 anni**	to be 17

Ho fame, andiamo a mangiare. C'è un ristorante qui vicino?
I'm hungry, let's go and eat. Is there a restaurant near here?

Mi scusi, ho fretta. Devo partire con il treno delle undici. Devo scappare.
Forgive me, I'm in a hurry. I have to catch the eleven o'clock train. I must fly.

Ho bisogno di un nuovo vestito.
I need a new dress/suit.

Vocabulary

Il vestiario

biancheria	underwear	**giacca**	jacket
(personale)		**pantaloni**	trousers
impermeabile	raincoat	**cappello**	hat
camicia	shirt (man's)	**gonna**	skirt
camicetta	blouse	**calze** (sing.	stockings
golf	cardigan,	**calza)**	
	knitted jacket	**calzini**	socks
cappotto	overcoat	**collant**	tights

tailleur	(women's) suit	**vestito**	(man's suit), (women's) dress
(di) lana	wool	**largo**	wide, loose
(di) seta	silk	**stretto**	narrow, tight
(di) cotone	cotton	**corto**	short
stare/andare bene a (qualcuno)		to suit (someone)	

Cultural point

As we saw, the influence of Paris, which used to be the fashion capital of the world, is still alive in words such as **tailleur** and **boutique**. However, you will probably know that it is the designers of Milan who now outshine those of Paris in the world of fashion. It is, of course, a sphere where imaginations are more than usually lively in the use of words as well as in design. Foreign words have a particular glamour. Reading the fashion pages you will find writers appear to try to avoid the standard words. It will add to your fun when you read – and you may well find English words being used, which of course sound exotic in Italian!

Exercise 5

We are now at the end of our course. You have studied the main structures of Italian grammar, been introduced to many of the situations you are likely to find yourself in in Italy and met a very large number of words. The second set of dialogues above contained many of the grammar points you have studied. Can you pick out examples of the following:

1 The conditional?
2 The imperfect?
3 The perfect (**passato prossimo**)?
4 The future?
5 The imperative?
6 Personal pronouns, direct and indirect object?
7 Combined pronouns?
8 Relative pronouns?

And what should you do next, especially if you didn't pick them out correctly? Yes, revise those points. Revision, combined with speaking, reading and hearing as much Italian as you can, will help you gradually to become more and more at ease with the language.

You are now ready to visit Italy and try out your Italian. Be prepared for surprises and disappointments, but also for fun and moments to treasure.

Readings

I borghi d.o.c.

And in readiness for that visit, here is information on three of the borghi d.o.c. (see Unit 15), which you may want to put on your itinerary.

1 **Why might you not be surprised to meet people dressed in thirteenth-century costume in Apricale?**
2 **Why can't cars go into Apricale?**

Apricale: Le auto? Non ci passano

Se passeggiando per le strade di Apricale inconstraste persone vestite come nel '200, forse non ci fareste caso. Raccolto intorno

Apricale. From the town's website www.apricale.org.
Courtesy the Mayor of Apricale.

alla piazzetta centrale, questo borgo tutto di pietra nella provincia di Imperia è situato su quella che era la via dell'olio, a 13 chilometri dal mare. E sulle strade lastricate, quasi delle mulattiere, . . . dovevano trovarsi a loro agio gli asinelli di un tempo, con le loro giare ricolme di olio. Non certo le auto . . . Le mura medievali, l'arco acuto e il castello con il giardino pensile sono ancora perfettamente conservati e, tra i muri, molti artisti hanno trovato lo spazio per bellissimi affreschi . . .

(Adapted from an article in *Vera* magazine, March 2003, by kind permission of the publishers)

Vocabulary notes

giare (f. pl.) 'jars'. These are usually terracotta and are used as containers and as measures of quantity for oil.

giardino pensile 'hanging garden'. This would usually be supported by arches and typically would be overlooking a valley.

le mura, i muri **muro** 'wall' has a plural **muri** for most meanings of the word. **Le mura** means the fortifications of a town, i.e. a set of walls designed for defensive purposes.

Dozza: come una galleria d'arte

1 What is the curious national competition that takes place in Dozza?

Sono quasi cento i muri dipinti di questo borgo dell'Emilia Romagna, trasformato in una vera e propria galleria d'arte all'aperto. . . . Il borgo fortificato, con le case addossate le une alle altre, termina nel punto più elevato con la Rocca di Caterina. Le vie di Dozza . . . sono teatro del curioso concorso Nazionale del Muro Dipinto. Il risultato sono opere d'arte che hanno dato un nuovo volto al paese, integrandosi perfettamente con l'atmosfera soave del borgo.

Vocabulary notes

le case addossate le une alle altre 'the houses built back to back with each other'

rocca (see **castello**) 'fortress, castle'

un nuovo volto 'a new face'

Note: In its cellars, the **Rocca** houses the **Enoteca Regionale**, the regional wine museum/showroom.

Castel di Tora: sul lago di Turano (Lazio)

1 Why are there many archeological remains in the area of Castel di Tora?
2 Antuni is another small town – what picture do you get of it.
3 And of the area separating it from a third, Collalto Sabino.

". . . un presepe che galleggia sulle acque del lago di Turano". Con questa immagine evocativa l'opuscolo dell'Anci presenta Castel di Tora, grazioso borgo a un'ora di distanza da Roma. Il paese fu fondato sulle rovine dell'antica città romana di Thiora, in una zona ancora ricca di testimonianze archeologiche. Da vedere sono la Fontana del Tritone, la cinta muraria e la torre del Castello del '200. Poco distante dal centro, su una penisola che si protende a picco nelle acque del lago, da non perdere il caratteristico borgo di Antuni . . . Solo 14 . . . sono i chilometri che separano Castel di Tora da Collalto Sabino. Altro borgo del club, che tra castelli diroccati e rifugi dei briganti domina l'intera vallata.

Vocabulary notes

un presepe 'a crib'. The writer is probably thinking of the crib in the sense of model of the stable where Christ was born.
cinta muraria 'the circle of walls, fortifications'
da non perdere 'not to be missed'
a picco 'with a sharp drop below'
castelli diroccati 'crumbling castles'
rifugi dei briganti 'the brigands' hideouts'. A feature of life particularly in southern Italy in the nineteenth century; **un rifugio** is a shelter.

These three extracts are taken from the article 'Per le vie dei borghi d.o.c.' in *Vera* magazine, March 2003, also used in Unit 15.

To find out more, visit the website www.borghitalia.it where you can find out about these little towns, region by region, and the aims etc. of the club that promotes them.

Buon viaggio e buona fortuna!

Grammar summary

When grammar points are dealt with in a single unit, the reader is referred to that unit. This section contains summaries of points that are scattered over two or more units.

Nouns and articles

Definite article	Indefinite article	Noun		Definite article	Noun	
Masculine singular				*Masculine plural*		
il	un	{	vino	i	{	vini
			padre			padri
l'	un	{	albergo	gli	{	alberghi
			ambiente			ambienti
lo	uno	{	spuntino	gli	{	spuntini
			zio			zii
			studente			studenti
Feminine singular				*Feminine plural*		
la	una	{	casa	le	{	case
			madre			madri
			stella			stelle
l'	un'	{	azienda	le	{	aziende
			estate			estati

Note: The indefinite article does not have a plural. The partitive article would convey the idea with a plural noun ('some') and can also be used with a single non-count noun, e.g. **pane** 'bread'. The form is **di** + definite article, see 'Prepositions with the definite article' below (p. 261).

Adjectives

In Italian, adjectives must *agree with* (match) the noun they describe in gender (m. or f.) and number (sing. or pl.). There are two main types: (1) those with a masculine singular ending in **-o**; and (2) those with a singular ending (both m. and f.) in **-e**.

	Masculine		Feminine	
	Singular	*Plural*	*Singular*	*Plural*
Type 1	**ross***o*	**ross***i*	**ross***a*	**ross***e*
Type 2	**verd***e*	**verd***i*	**verd***e*	**verd***i*

Adverbs

See Unit 8.

Prepositions with the definite article

See Unit 6. Some common short prepositions combine with the definite article. Here is the complete table.

	a	*di*	*da*	*su*	*in*	
il	**al**	**del**	**dal**	**sul**	**nel**	**libro**
l' (m. and f.)	**all'**	**dell'**	**dall'**	**sull'**	**nell'**	{ **albergo** **azienda**
lo	**allo**	**dello**	**dallo**	**sullo**	**nello**	**studio**
la	**alla**	**della**	**dalla**	**sulla**	**nella**	**casa**
i	**ai**	**dei**	**dai**	**sui**	**nei**	**negozi**
gli	**agli**	**degli**	**dagli**	**sugli**	**negli**	{ **alberghi** **studi**
le	**alle**	**delle**	**dalle**	**sulle**	**nelle**	{ **case** **aziende**

In older Italian, **con** and **per** were combined with the definite article, giving **col** and **pel** etc. This is unusual today, although in speaking **con** is combined with the definite article by some speakers. Learners need not worry about this. In the case of **al**, **del** etc. where there is a double consonant in the spelling it is because a double consonant is pronounced.

Pronouns

This is a summary of the information on personal pronouns given in Units 1, 5, 6, 8 and 9.

Subject		Direct object (unstressed)		Indirect object (unstressed)		Reflexive	Stressed	
io	I	**mi**	me	**mi**	to me	**mi** (to) myself	**me**	me
tu	you	**ti**	you	**ti**	to you	**ti** (to) yourself	**te**	you
lui	he	**lo**	him	**gli**	to him	**si** (to) himself	**lui**	him
lei	she	**la**	her	**le**	to her	**si** (to) herself	**lei**	her
Lei*	you	**La***	you	**Le***	to you	**Si*** (to) yourself	**Lei***	you
noi	we	**ci**	us	**ci**	to us	**ci** (to) ourselves	**noi**	us
voi	you	**vi**	you	**vi**	to you	**vi** (to) your- selves	**voi**	you
loro they (m.)		**li**	them	**gli**	to them	**si** (to) them- selves	**loro**	them
loro they (f.)		**le**	them	**gli**	to them	**si** (to) them- selves	**loro**	them

* formal form

Note: There exist the subject forms **egli/ella** 'he/she'; and also **esso/essa** 'it' and **essi/esse** 'they/them', which are usually used when referring to objects or concepts (not people). All belong to formal writing rather than speech.

Stressed or strong pronouns

me, **te**, **lui**, **lei**, **Lei** (formal 'you'), **noi**, **voi**, **loro** are used:

1 After a preposition:

> **Sta parlando di te.**
> He's talking about you.

Venite con me.
Come with me.

2 For emphasis:

Ama me, non te.
He loves me, not you.

Negatives

This is a summary of the information given in Units 3, 13, 14 and 15.

1 Simple negative, **non** placed before the verb:

Non **sono italiano.**
I am not Italian.

2 Stronger negative:

non ... mica	non ... per niente
non ... affatto	non ... per nulla

3 Other negative expressions:

non ... ancora	not yet
non ... mai	never, not ever
non ... niente ⎫ non ... nulla ⎭	nothing, not anything
non ... nessuno	no one, not ... anyone
non ... più	no longer, not any more
non ... nemmeno ⎫ non ... neanche ⎬ non ... neppure ⎭	not even
nè ... nè	neither ... nor, not ... either ... or

There must be a negative word before the verb. Most of the expressions in (3) above may be placed at the beginning of the sentence, in which case the **non** is not necessary:

Nessuno **sa dov'è andato.**
No one knows where he has gone.

With a compound tense, **niente**, **nulla**, **nessuno** and **nè ... nè** come after the past participle:

Non **ho capito** *niente.*
I didn't understand anything.

Non **ho visto** *nessuno.*
I didn't see anyone.

Non **ha detto** *nè* **sì** *nè* **no.**
He didn't say yes or no.

But:

Non **ha** *mai* **lavorato tanto.**
He has never worked so much.

Non **ha** *ancora* **deciso.**
He hasn't made his mind up yet.

Non **ha** *nemmeno* **finito di mangiare.**
He hasn't even finished eating.

Most of the negatives can be used without a verb or can stand alone:

– Ti piace?	*– Affatto.*
– Do you like it (him)?	– Not at all.
– Chi hai visto?	*– Nessuno.*
– Who did you see?	– No one.

– Hai visto Gianni e Paolo?
– Did you see Gianni and Paolo?

– Nè **l'uno** *nè* **l'altro**.
– Neither the one nor the other.

Interrogatives

These are words (pronouns or adjectives) for asking questions:

Che,[1] **che cosa, cosa?**	What?
Quale (+ vowel: **qual** with no apostrophe)/**quali?**	Which?
Chi?	Who?
Come?[1]	How?
Come mai	Why (but introduces a note of surprise into the question)
Dove?	Where?

Quando?	When?
Quanto? [1]	How much?
Perché? [2]	Why?

Note:

1 **come**, **quanto**, (plus verb) and **che** (plus noun or adjective), can also be used as exclamatives:

Come sei elegante!	How smart you are!
Quanto sei elegante!	How smart you are!
Che bello!	How lovely!
Che paura!	What a fright!
Che fortuna!	What luck!

2 **perché** also means 'because'.

Relative pronouns

- **che** 'who, whom, which' can refer to a person or an object and can be the subject or the object of the clause it introduces. See Unit 4 for a detailed treatment.

- **cui**, not **che**, is used after a preposition:

    La signora con cui ho parlato è stata molto gentile.
    The lady who I talked with was very nice.

- **il cui**, **la cui**, **i cui**, **le cui** all mean 'whose'; the article must be the one that would go with the object possessed:

    Il signor Rossi, la cui figlia vuole studiare negli Stati Uniti ...
    Mr Rossi, whose daughter wants to study in the United States ...

    L'autore, i cui libri hanno un enorme successo, ha accettato il nostro invito.
    The author whose books are having a great success has accepted our invitation.

- **il quale**, **la quale**, **i quali**, **le quali** – 'who, which' can replace **che** or **cui** and are especially useful to avoid ambiguity:

    La figlia di mio cugino, la quale lavora in Francia, ...
    My cousin's daughter, who works in France, ...

la quale makes it clear that it is the daughter, not the cousin, who works in France.

- **chi** 'he who, some … others' is used in proverbs and sayings and sentences such as those below:

  Chi va piano, va sano e va lontano.
  He who goes slowly, goes safely and a long way.

  C'è chi pensa che …
  There are those who think …

  Erano molto allegri: chi cantava, chi ballava, chi rideva …
  They were very happy: some were singing, some dancing, some laughing …

- **ciò che, quello che** 'what' refers to ideas, rather than specific nouns:

  So quello che bisogna fare.
  I know what it is necessary to do.

  Dimmi ciò che pensi.
  Tell me what you think.

- **tutto ciò che**, **tutto quello che** mean 'everything that/which':

  So tutto ciò che è successo.
  I know everything that happened.

Possessives

These ('my, your' etc.) are dealt with fully in Unit 10.

Demonstratives

- **questo** 'this, this one' has regular forms in **-o**, **-a**, **-i**, **-e**. See Unit 5.
- **quello** 'that, that one' has a regular form when it is a pronoun. When used as an adjective before the noun, its endings are those of the definite article: **quel**, **quell'**, **quello**, **quei**, **quegli**, **quella**, **quelle**. See Unit 5.
- **ciò** means 'that'. It refers to ideas or phrases, not specific people or objects. It is mostly used with **che** as a relative pronoun:

Trovo interessante *ciò che* dice.
I find what (that which) he says interesting.

But it will be found without **che**:

***Ciò* vuol dire che non hai capito.**
That means you haven't understood.

Indefinites

Reference list of indefinite adjectives (adj.) and pronouns (pr.):

uno (pr.) one, someone (used in the same way as impersonal **si**)

qualcuno (pr.) someone;

ogni (a.) every, each (+ sing.)

tutti i .../tutte le ... (adj.) every, each, all (+ pl.)

tutti/e (pr.) everyone (used without a noun and followed by plural verb)

tutti e due/tutte e due (pr.) both (*Note*: Used as an adjective the article is needed: **Tutte e due le sorelle** 'Both sisters')

ognuno (pr.) each person, everyone (sing. only)

ciascuno/a (pr.), **ciascun/a** (adj.) each, each one (sing. only)

qualcosa, qualche cosa (pr.) something

qualche (adj.) some (+ sing. noun) (refers to a few, not a large number)

alcuni/e (adj. and pr.) some (pl.)[1]

alcun/a (adj. sing.) can be used with **non** to form a negative: **Non ho alcun'idea** 'I don't have any idea'

altro/a/i/e (adj. and pr.) other, another[2]

qualsiasi, qualunque (adj.) any, whatever

chiunque (pr.) anyone (it doesn't matter who)

molto, molti/e (pr.); **molto/a/i/e** (adj.) much, many

poco, pochi (pr.); **poco/a/hi/he** (adj.) few, little

un poco, un po' a little (a bit)

troppo (adj. and pr.) too much

tanto (adj. and pr.) so much

parecchio (adj. and pr.) some, several, a good many, a good deal

tale/i (adj.) such

un tale (pr.) is used to convey 'someone or other'

certe persone some (people)

Note:

1 The partitive, **del**, also conveys 'some' but the amount is more open; **qualche** and **alcuni** mean 'a few'.

2 (a) **Ho comprato altri due libri** 'I bought two other/more books' (**altri tre, altri quattro** etc.); (b) **Certe persone pensano questo, altri no** 'Some people think this, others not'; **Ecco i pomodori. Altro?** 'Here are the tomatoes. Anything else?'

(See also the section on 'Negatives', p. 263.)

Verbs

Non-finite moods

See Unit 15.

The infinitive

Present

There are three main types, ending in (1) **-are**, (2) **-ere** or (3) **-ire**. For reflexive verbs the reflexive pronoun is attached to the infinitive: **divertirsi** 'to enjoy oneself'. In a sentence the reflexive pronoun must be the appropriate one for the subject of the verb preceding the infinitive:

> **Vogl*iamo* divertir*ci*.**
> *We* want to enjoy *ourselves*.

Note: (a) In group (2), some of the infinitives have the stress on the **e** of **-ere**, while others have the stress on the preceding syllable, e.g. **tem*e*re** but **v*e*ndere**. The verbs do not differ in form or stress at any other point of the conjugation. (b) Some verbs have infinitives that have become contracted over the centuries, e.g. **bere, produrre, porre**. In some tenses they function from the older infinitive, e.g. **bevere, producere, ponere**.

Past or perfect infinitive

Formed using **avere** or **essere,** according to which of these the verb is conjugated with (see 'Compound tenses', p. 273), and the past participle (see p. 125 and below).

avere mangiato	to have eaten
essere arrivato	to have arrived

Note: With reflexive verbs the appropriate reflexive pronoun is attached to the infinitive:

Sono contento di essermi divertito.
I am happy to have enjoyed myself.

The gerund

See Unit 11.

The past participle

See Unit 8.

Common *irregular* forms are:

-ere *verbs*

chiudere	**chiuso**	**spendere**	**speso**
decidere	**deciso**	**prendere**	**preso**
includere	**incluso**	**uccidere**	**ucciso**
rimanere	**rimasto**	**scrivere**	**scritto**
leggere	**letto**	**chiedere**	**chiesto**
vedere	**visto** *or* **veduto**	**rispondere**	**risposto**
perdere	**perso** *or* **perduto**	**mettere**	**messo**
nascere	**nato**		

-ire *verbs*

aprire	**aperto**	**coprire**	**coperto**
offrire	**offerto**		

Irregular verbs

essere	**stato**	**venire**	**venuto**
fare	**fatto**	**dire**	**detto**

stare	**stato**	**morire**	**morto**
dare	**dato**		

Note: These have a *regular* past participle:

avere	**avuto**	**potere**	**potuto**
volere	**voluto**	**dovere**	**dovuto**
andare	**andato**	**uscire**	**uscito**
sapere	**saputo**		

Finite moods

See Unit 15.

The indicative – simple tenses

Present

This is a summary of information given in Units 1 to 5.

Regular verbs

Note: Verbs in **-ire** divide into: (1) those that have an extra syllable, **-isc-**, in some parts of the present tense; and (2) those that form their present tense exactly like verbs in the **-ere** group.

-are	*-ere*	*-ire (1)*	*-ire (2)*
parlo	**vendo**	**capisco**	**parto**
parli	**vendi**	**capisci**	**parti**
parla	**vende**	**capisce**	**parte**
parliamo	**vendiamo**	**capiamo**	**partiamo**
parlate	**vendete**	**capite**	**partite**
parlano	**vendono**	**capiscono**	**partono**

In the third person plural of all these verbs the stress falls on the antepenultimate syllable.

Spelling

(1)   Verbs ending in **-care**, **-gare**, **-ciare**, **-giare**, **-sciare**. The sound does not change and the spelling is adapted to show this. The first two types (**-care**, **-gare**) insert an **h** before an **i** in the ending;

the others (**-ciare**, **-giare**, **-sciare**) omit the **i** of the stem before **i** or **e**. This is also true in other tenses.

cerco, cerchi, cerca, cerchiamo, cercate, cercano

pago, paghi, paga, paghiamo, pagate, pagano

comincio, cominci, comincia, cominciamo, cominciate, cominciano

mangio, mangi, mangia, mangiamo, mangiate, mangiano

lascio, lasci, lascia, lasciamo, lasciate, lasciano

(2) Verbs ending in **-cere**, **-ggere**. With verbs in the **-ere** group the opposite happens – the spelling does not change because the sound does:

vincere: **vinco, vinci, vince, vinciamo, vincete, vincono**

leggere: **leggo, leggi, legge, leggiamo, leggete, leggono**

Imperfect

For a table of regular forms see Unit 13. A few verbs are irregular and they are fully dealt with in Unit 13.

Future

For a table of regular forms see Unit 16. The following verbs are *irregular* in the future tense:

(a) *essere*: **sarò**, **sarai**, **sarà**, **saremo**, **sarete**, **saranno**

(b) verbs that lose the vowel of their infinitive: the endings follow the regular pattern:

> *andare*: **andrò**, **andrai**, **andrà**, **andremo**, **andrete**, **andranno**
> *avere*: **avrò**; *dovere*: **dovrò**; *sapere*: **saprò**
> *vedere*: **vedrò**; *vivere*: **vivrò**

(c) verbs that lose the vowel and also have the final vowel of the stem of the infinitive changed to become the same as the second, giving -**rr**-:

> *rimanere*: **rimarrò**
> *venire*: **verrò**
> *volere*: **vorrò**

(d) *bere*: **berrò**

(e) *dare*: **darò**; *fare*: **farò**; *stare*: **starò**

The first and third person singular are stressed on the final vowel, which is written with an accent to indicate this.

Past definite

This tense has not been presented in the text, but its use is explained briefly in Unit 13.

parl*ai*	**vend***ei* (***etti***)	**cap***ii*
parl*asti*	**vend***esti*	**cap***isti*
parl*ò*	**vend***è* (***ette***)	**cap***ì*
parl*ammo*	**vend***emmo*	**cap***immo*
parl*aste*	**vend***este*	**cap***iste*
parl*arono*	**vend***erono* (***ettero***)	**cap***irono*

Note:

(a) The stress falls on the penultimate syllable except in the third person singular, where the accented vowel is stressed, and the third person plural where the stress falls on the antepenultimate syllable.

(b) In the **-ere** group of verbs, as well as in some irregular verbs, there are alternative forms for the first and third person singular and third person plural. (These forms are given in brackets.) Many verbs in this group are irregular in this tense. They are irregular in the first and third person singular and the third person plural, but regular in the other parts. Therefore if you know the first and second person singular you can form the remaining parts. **bere**, **dire**, **fare** form the **passato remoto** from their older infinitives. Below are some examples:

avere:	**ebbi, avesti, ebbe, avemmo, aveste, ebbero**
dire:	**dissi, dicesti, disse, dicemmo, diceste, dissero**
fare:	**feci, facesti, fece, facemmo, faceste, fecero**
vedere:	**vidi, vedesti, vide, vedemmo, vedeste, videro**

Given the first and second person the others may be formed on these models.

bere:	**bevvi (bevetti), bevesti**
chiedere:	**chiesi, chiedesti**
chiudere:	**chiusi, chiudesti**
conoscere:	**conobbi, conoscesti**
decidere:	**decisi, decidesti**

leggere:	**lessi, leggesti**
mettere:	**misi, mettesti**
nascere:	**nacqui, nascesti**
prendere:	**presi, prendesti**
rimanere:	**rimasi, rimanesti**
rispondere:	**risposi, rispondesti**
sapere:	**seppi, sapesti**
scendere:	**scesi, scendesti**
uccidere:	**uccisi, uccidesti**

Also irregular are:

essere:	**fui, fosti, fu, fummo, foste, furono**
dare:	**diedi (detti), desti**
venire:	**venni, venisti**
volere:	**volli, volesti**
stare:	**stetti, stesti**
vivere:	**vissi, vivesti**

The indicative – compound tenses

Present perfect

See also Units 10, 11, 15 and 16. This is formed with the present tense of **avere** or **essere** and the past participle.

(A) Verbs conjugated with **essere** include:

1 verbs of motion: **andare, venire, arrivare, partire, entrare, uscire, salire, scendere, tornare, passare da**;
2 verbs indicating a change of state: **ingrassare, dimagrire, diventare, divenire, aumentare, diminuire, migliorare**;
3 **essere, stare, nascere, morire, piacere**;
4 verbs used reflexively;
5 verbs used impersonally, e.g. **è sembrato** 'it seemed';
6 verbs relating to weather conditions can be conjugated with **essere**, but they will also be found with **avere**: **è nevicato** and **ha nevicato**.

The past participle must agree with the subject:

sono andato/a	**siamo andati/e**
sei andato/a	**siete andati/e**
è andato/a	**sono andati/e**

mi sono divertito/a	**ci siamo divertiti/e**
ti sei divertito/a	**vi siete divertiti/e**
si è divertito/a	**si sono divertiti/e**

(B)   All other verbs are conjugated with **avere**:

ho finito	**abbiamo finito**
hai finito	**avete finito**
ha finito	**hanno finito**

The past participle does not agree with the subject. If there is a direct object pronoun preceding the verb, it agrees with that: **I biscotti? Li ho finiti.**

Other compound tenses can be formed with **essere** or **avere** according to the verb.

Pluperfect

The imperfect of **avere** or **essere** plus the past participle:

avevo finito	I had finished
ero andato/a	I had gone

Future perfect

The future of **avere** or **essere** plus the past participle:

avrò finito	I shall have finished
sarò andato/a	I shall have gone

The conditional

See Unit 15.

Conditional perfect

The conditional perfect is formed with the conditional of **avere** or **essere** and the past participle (see Notes).

avrei parlato	I would have spoken
sarei andato/a	I would have gone, etc.

The imperative

This is a summary of the information given in Unit 6. There is no first person singular for the imperative; and the third person plural is rarely used since the formal plural, **loro**, is rarely used. The plural 'you' is normally **voi**. As in the present indicative, the **-ire** group subdivides. An example of each type is given.

parl*a*	vend*i*	cap*isci*	part*i*
parl*i*	vend*a*	cap*isca*	part*a*
parl*iamo*	vend*iamo*	cap*iamo*	part*iamo*
parl*ate*	vend*ete*	cap*ite*	part*ite*
parl*ino*	vend*ano*	cap*iscano*	part*ano*

The stress is regular except that in the third person plural form it falls on the antepenultimate syllable.

The subjunctive

1 *Present*: see Unit 17.
2 *Perfect subjunctive*: this is formed using the present subjunctive of **avere** or **essere** and the past participle:

   abbia parlato   **sia andato/a**

3 *Imperfect*: see Unit 15.
4 *Pluperfect*: this is formed with the imperfect subjunctive of **avere** or **essere** and the past participle:

   avessi parlato   **fossi andato/a**

The passive

All the verbs above are *active*. Those that can take a direct object can be made passive using **essere** and the past participle, or sometimes **venire** or **andare** and the past participle (see Units 8 and 9).

Present:	**Il lavoro è fatto a mano.** The work is done by hand.
Perfect:	**Il lavoro è stato fatto a mano.** The work has been/was done by hand.
Imperfect:	**Il lavoro era fatto a mano.** The work was being done/used to be done by hand.
Future:	**Il lavoro sarà fatto a mano.** The work will be done by hand.
Future perfect:	**Il lavoro sarà stato fatto a mano.** The work will have been done by hand.

Conditional:	**Il lavoro sarebbe fatto a mano.** The work would be done by hand.
Conditional perfect:	**Il lavoro sarebbe stato fatto a mano.** The work would have been done by hand.
Present subjunctive:	**Occorre che il lavoro sia fatto a mano.** The work must be done by hand.
Imperfect subjunctive:	**Voleva che il lavoro fosse fatto a mano.** He wanted the work to be done by hand.

Verbs and other expressions followed by an infinitive

To express certain ideas, we frequently need to use a verb, an adjective, or a noun followed by a verb. In this case this following verb is in the infinitive. The precise structure necessary will depend on the first word.

- No preposition is required after **dovere**, **potere**, **volere**, **lasciare**, **piacere**, **preferire**, **sapere**, **vedere**; **basta**, **bisogna**, **facile**, **difficile**, **possibile**, **impossibile**, **necessario**; **bene**, **meglio**. For example:

  Mi piace ballare.
  I like dancing/to dance.

  Basta telefonare.
  All you need to do is telephone.
  (lit. 'It is enough to telephone')

  E' difficile sapere che cosa fare.
  It's difficult to know what to do.

- The preposition **a** is required after a number of verbs, including **andare**, **abituarsi**, **cominciare**, **imparare**, **provare**, **venire**; and after certain adjectives including **abituato**, **pronto**. For example:

  Vado a sciare domenica.
  I am going skiing on Sunday.

  Comincia a piovere.
  It's beginning to rain.

  Sei pronto a fare il bagno?
  Are you ready to bathe/have a bath?

• The preposition **di** is required after many verbs, including **credere**, **decidere**, **dimenticare**, **ricordarsi**; after adjectives such as **contento**, **felice**; and after nouns, where it is usually used with **avere**, e.g. **avere paura di**, **avere bisogno di**. For example:

Credo di farcela.
I believe I can manage it.

Ha deciso di partire domani.
He has decided to leave tomorrow.

Sono contento di sapere che stai meglio.
I am pleased to know you are better.

Ho paura di fare un errore.
I am afraid of making a mistake.

Students are advised to consult a good dictionary when in doubt.

Key to exercises

Unit 1

Al bar

Aranciata – this is a fizzy orange drink; Coca-Cola.

Prima colazione

1 Maria has a bun; Piera has a pastry. 2 Maria drinks a white coffee, Piera black.

Exercise 1

un vino rosso, **un** gelato, **una** birra, **un** caffè, **un'** acqua minerale, **una** spremuta, **un** succo di frutta, **un** tè, **un** vino bianco, **un'** aranciata

Exercise 2

1 un cappuccino 2 un'aranciata 3 una spremuta di arancia 4 una birra

Exercise 3

(1) 7, (2) 9, (3) 400, (4) 803, (5) 2.500, (6) 1.300, (7) 10.000, (8) 6.100 (9) 55, (10) 79

Exercise 4

1 Tre euro settantun centesimi 2 Due euro dieci centesimi 3 Venti euro 4 Trenta euro 5 Un euro sessanta centesimi; each coffee: ottanta centesimi 6 Dieci euro cinquantotto centesimi

Un appuntamento con il signor Rossi

1 To wait a moment and to sit down 2 S'accomodi

Un incontro per la strada

Because the teacher has to go, presumably he's hurrying some-where.

Exercise 5

Avv. Bruni: Buongiorno, signor Rossi, come va? Sig.Rossi: Bene grazie. E Lei? Avv. Bruni. Bene. Devo andare. ArrivederLa. Sig. Rossi: ArrivederLa (Buongiorno).

Exercise 6

In **Al bar**: 1 Prego. lit. I beg, request. 2 Va bene. lit. It goes well. It's fine, OK. In **Prima colazione**: 3 Desidera? lit. You desire? i.e. What would you like? In **Un appuntamento con il signor Rossi**: 4 Sono Angela Smith. I am Angela Smith. 5 Come va? How are you? In **Un incontro per la strada**: 6 Ha un raffreddore. He has a cold. 7 Mi dispiace. lit. it is displeasing to me. I'm sorry. 8 Sta bene. He's well. 9 Lavora molto. He's working a lot. 10 Devo andare. I have to go.

Bar famosi

1 In 1720. 2 Sparkling white wine and peach juice. 3 Yes. The food is very good, but the bill would be substantial. 4 Arrigo Cipriani.

Exercise 7

You should find it easy to make the list and the unit gives you help with all the meanings.

Unit 2

Sono americano, e lei?

1 In Boston. 2 In Rome. 3 His mother is Italian, from Siracusa in Sicily. 4 His brother lives in Los Angeles and he finds the US friendly and interesting. 5 Yes. He likes Bologna: it is friendly and interesting.

Exercise 1

1 Sean Connery è scozzese (britannico) 2 Michael Schumacher è tedesco 3 Kofi Annan è ghanese 4 Tiger Woods è americano 5 Arnold Schwarzenegger è austriaco 6 Meryl Streep è americana 7 Roma è una città italiana 8 New York è una città americana 9 Rio de Janeiro è una città brasiliana 10 Toronto è una città canadese 11 Sydney è una città australiana 12 Tokio è una città giapponese

Exercise 2

Chiara studia. Lucia canta. Paolo fuma. Luigí balla. Anna telefona. Marco lavora.
If you were doing them you would say: 1 Canto 2 Fumo 3 Lavoro 4 Telefono 5 Ballo 6 Studio

Exercise 3

1 Mi chiamo Charlie Hardcastle. 2 Sono sudafricano. 3 Abito a Johannesburg. 4 Parlo inglese e francese. 5 Mia madre è francese, di Bordeaux. 6 Bordeaux è una città simpatica.

Exercise 4

1 Mi piace lavorare 2 Mi piace New York 3 Mi piace cantare 4 Mi piace Roma 5 Mi piace parlare italiano 6 Mi piace Luciano Pavarotti

Exercise 5

1 Devo telefonare 2 Devo lavorare 3 Devo venire 4 Devo studiare

Mi chiamo Paolo Bianchi

1 His name is Paolo Bianchi. 2 From Milan. 3 In Milan. 4 In a hospital in Milan. 5 He is tall and fair-haired. 6 Yes. 7 He likes playing tennis and he also likes classical music.

Exercise 6

1 sono 2 sono 3 abito (or lavoro) 4 lavoro 5 sono

Exercise 7

Mi chiamo Giorgio. Abito a Napoli. Mia madre abita a Roma con mio fratello. Sono medico in un ospedale a Napoli. Mi piace il mio lavoro. Sono sportivo e mi piace giocare a golf e a tennis. Mi scusi, devo scappare. Mi dispiace. Arrivederci.

Mi chiamo Luisa Lucchini

1 History and geography. 2 Yes, she likes tennis and golf. 3 Because it is a big, lively city, interesting and stimulating. *You may also have said:* She likes opera and in Milan there is La Scala opera house.

Exercise 8

Possible combinations are: una birra: bionda, australiana; una signora, una madre, una signorina: romana, bionda, australiana, vivace, interessante; un signore, un marito, un fratello, un professore: alto, simpatico, interessante, americano, sportivo, vivace, sposato;un vino: bianco, americano, vivace, interessante, simpatico; un lavoro, un paese: interessante, simpatico; una città: interessante, australiana.

Suo marito, come si chiama?

1 He is a good pianist. 2 No, he is Scottish. 3 He works in a bank. (He is an accountant or financial adviser.) 4 No. He's mad about do-it-yourself. 5 In Toronto, Canada, presumably, since that is where Bill works.

Exercise 9

1 Sono australiana. Sono alta e bionda. Sono sposata. Lavoro a Sydney. 2 Sono canadese. Sono sposato. Mia moglie è inglese. Abito a Milano. 3 Sono italiano, sono siciliano, di Palermo. Mi chiamo Salvatore. Abito a Bologna. Lavoro in una banca. Sono sposato e mia moglie è scozzese. E' insegnante. 4 E' australiana, alta e bionda, sposata e lavora a Sydney. 5 E' canadese. E' sposato. Sua moglie è inglese. Abita a Milano. 6 E' italiano, siciliano, di Palermo. Si chiama Salvatore. Abita a Bologna e lavora in una banca. E' sposato e sua moglie è scozzese. Lei è insegnante.

Unit 3

A Perugia

1 It's the town hall 2 Along Corso Vannucci, the main street 3 To see the view over the valley towards Assisi

Exercise 1

You should have found the following. In Dialogue 1: Lei è americano? E Lei? Lei è in Italia per lavoro? E lei? E' a Bologna per lavoro? In Dialogue 2: E suo marito, come si chiama? Che lavoro fa? (twice) E come passa il suo tempo libero? E' sportivo, ama lo sport?

Exercise 2

1 il 2 il 3 la 4 la 5 il

C'è una banca qui vicino?

1 He asks whether there is a bank nearby 2 Because he thinks the bank is shut at that time

Exercise 3

1 C'è un ristorante qui vicino? 2 C'è una farmacia qui vicino? 3 C'è un albergo qui vicino? 4 C'è una fermata dell'autobus qui vicino? 5 C'è un supermercato qui vicino?

Scusi, dov'è il consolato americano?

The passer-by doesn't know where it is and suggests the tourist asks at the town tourist office.

Exercise 4

1 V (vero), 2 V, 3 F (falso), 4 F, 5 V. Only you can answer 6 to 12.

Exercise 5

1 No, non lavoro qui 2 No, non abito in questa città 3 No, non sono qui in vacanza 4 No, non sono americano/a 5 No, non parlo francese

Exercise 6

1 La Mole Antonelliana (the symbol of the city of Turin, in the way the Leaning Tower is for Pisa). 2 Piazza San Carlo (a lovely square). 3 Il Duomo (where the Turin Shroud is kept).

Exercise 7

Open

Exercise 8

1 vedo 2 Dipende 3 chiedere; abito 4 Prenda 5 Chiedo 6 abita 7 piace 8 chiama 9 lavora 10 vedi; prendi

A Roma

1 It used to be the residence of the Venetian ambassadors. (Venice was an independent republic until 1797. Rome was, until 1870, the capital of a state whose head was the Pope.) 2 Because it is a monument to the first king of the united Italy, Victor Emmanuel II, who was the figurehead and rallying point of the movement for unification. 3 It was the religious centre. 4 Because it runs through the area of the imperial forums/fora. 5 Between Piazza Venezia and Piazza del Popolo.

Unit 4

Devo andare a Torino

1 Relatively slow, taking over 2 hours for the journey 2 Faster, taking only an hour 20 minutes 3 30 euro by Eurostar, second class, return 4 40 euro

Exercise 1

1 diciotto 2 diciassette 3 dodici 4 diciannove 5 sedici

Exercise 2

1 milleduecentoquindici 2 millequattrocentonovantadue 3 mille-settecentoottantanove 4 milleottocentoquindici 5 milleottocento-quarantotto 6 millenovecentodiciotto 7 millenovecentoquarantasei 8 duemilacinque

Exercise 3

1 Sono le quattro e un quarto 2 Sono le due e mezzo 3 E' mezzogiorno meno cinque (or you may have thought it was nearly midnight: E' mezzanotte meno cinque) 4 Sono le tre e dieci 5 Sono le due meno un quarto

Exercise 4

Open

Exercise 5

1 e, 2 f, 3 d, 4 c, 5 a, 6 g, 7 b, 8 h
You would say: 1 Ballo … 2 Visito … 3 Prendo … 4 Guardo … 5 Leggo … 6 Scrivo … 7 Parto …

Exercise 6

1 E' 2 Abita 3 lavora 4 deve 5 parte 6 arriva 7 torna 8 finisce 9 dorme 10 preferisce 11 decide (lui)

Vorrei andare in Piazza Castello

1 No. 2 She has to get off behind the cathedral. She then has to take a little street which will take her into Piazza Castello. 3 The 15.

Come si fa a prendere l'autobus?

1 From a tobacconist, a newsagent, in a bar, or wherever there is a sign saying tickets are sold there. (Sometimes there is a ticket machine at the bus stop.) 2 In cities, generally one pays the same price for all journeys regardless of distance. 3 Because you are in touch with people and you avoid parking problems.

L'aeroporto

1 Because English is much used in airports (and in the air). 2 When the flight is going to an English-speaking country.

Unit 5

Vorrei una guida

1 A small, pocket one. 2 No. The shop has only one sort at the moment.

Exercise 1

1 F (falso), 2 V (vero), 3 V, 4 F, 5 F

Exercise 2

Alberto is a very polite (well brought up) boy. At the moment he is at high school. He is a very good student. He likes reading and often goes to bookshops to look at and buy books.

Exercise 3

1 b, 2 d, 3 a, 4 e, 5 c

Exercise 4

1 Vorrei andare a Roma. 2 Mi dispiace, non posso andare a Roma. 3 Potrei vedere il libro? 4 Puoi (formal può) giocare a tennis domani? Mi dispiace, non posso. Devo andare a Milano. 5 Non voglio partire domani. 6 Si può partire per Roma stasera? Mi dispiace, non si può. 7 Vorrei una birra. 8 Si può pagare con la carta di credito? 9 Si può vedere l'Etna da qui?

Cinque cartoline per favore

1 Ten, five small and five large 2 The USA

Exercise 5

1 No, tre caffè. 2 . . . quattro aranciate. 3 . . . cinque birre. 4 . . . sei acque minerali. 5 . . . sette spremute di arancia. 6 . . . otto cappuccini.

Exercise 6

1 L'albergo 2 La città 3 I ragazzi 4 Le cartoline 5 I francobolli 6 Lo studente 7 Gli uffici 8 Il monumento 9 Gli scontrini 10 Le città

Exercise 7

1 Quell'albergo 2 Quella città 3 Quei ragazzi 4 Quelle cartoline 5 Quei francobolli 6 Quello studente 7 Quegli uffici 8 Quel monumento 9 Quegli scontrini 10 Quelle città

Exercise 8

1 Preferiamo 2 Arriviamo 3 Comprano 4 Capite 5 Partono 6 Prendono

Exercise 9

(a) 1 andiamo 2 guardiamo 3 leggiamo 4 invitiamo 5 vogliamo
(b) 1 lavorano 2 cominciano 3 tornano 4 mangiano 5 Finiscono
6 vogliono 7 devono

Il mercato in Italia

1 Because each little town and each district in the big towns has
one at least once a week. 2 Because people come in from the
surrounding areas to meet each other.

Unit 6

Vorrei parlare con il signor Rossi

1 Next week, when she will be in Italy. She suggests Wednesday
at 9 a.m. 2 He invites Angela to have dinner with him and his wife.

Exercise 1

1 il mese prossimo 2 il mese scorso 3 l'anno prossimo 4 l'anno
scorso 5 ogni anno 6 domani mattina 7 ieri pomeriggio

Exercise 2

1 Il primo maggio 2 Il venticinque dicembre 3 Il quattordici luglio
4 L'undici giugno 5 Il venticinque aprile 6 Il venti settembre

Exercise 3

(1) 115; (2) 118 – or perhaps 113, general emergency number;
(3) 113; (4) 112; (5) 1.96.96

Andiamo al cinema

1 Monday and Wednesday 2 At Marisa's house

Exercise 4

. . . Biblioteca sulla salute e sullo sport . . . La possibilità nella bella
stagione di allenarsi all' aperto . . . dal lunedì al venerdì dalle ore
9.00 alle ore 21.15, il sabato dalle ore 10.00 alle ore 12.30
    . . . pranzo *nel* corso *dell'* intervallo . . . che segue *allo* shop-
ping, . . . prima *dello* spettacolo . . . sala *del* centro, . . . l'altra *nella*
città . . .

Exercise 5

More logical order: 5, 2, 4, 6, 1, 3 (or perhaps: 3, 1)

Exercise 6

1 Si sveglia. 2 Si alza. 3 Fa la doccia. 4 Si veste. 5 Si pettina.
6 Fa colazione. 7 Si prepara ad andare a lavorare.

Exercise 7

1 d, 2 h, 3 g, 4 e, 5 a, 6 c, 7 b, 8 f

Exercise 8

1 prendi 2 gira 3 va' 4 andare 5 gira 6 sta' 7 girare 8 rallenta
9 prendi 10 cerca 11 facciamo

Exercise 9

1 Mi dica 2 Mi dia 3 Abbia pazienza 4 Mi scusi 5 Si accomodi
6 Aspetti

Exercise 10

Your text message will read something like this:

Volo in ritardo di 2 ore. Per favore, telefona all'albergo per
informare che arrivo tardi.

You may have omitted some vowels and perhaps the
punctuation:

Volo in rtrdo 2 ore. Per fav tlfona albergo infrmre arrvo tardi.

La domenica in Italia

1 Because, while many adults do not work, the children are at
school in the morning. 2 Having relations to lunch; going for a
walk – in the park, through the streets of the town, or in the
country; going to the cinema; watching a football match, or listening
to the radio commentary while out walking with the family; skiing.
3 To the sea or to the country.

Unit 7

All'albergo (1)

1 Two double rooms. 2 They should have bathrooms and be quiet.
They don't mind whether the beds are double or single. 3 She asks
to see the rooms.

Exercise 1

1 due giorni 2 due settimane 3 due mesi interessanti 4 due nuovi
progetti 5 due banche 6 due giornali 7 due cappuccini 8 due birre
9 i nuovi film 10 gli spettacoli 11 i giornali interessanti 12 i super-
mercati francesi 13 le nuove gallerie 14 le strade che vanno in città
15 gli adulti responsabili 16 i vini rossi

All'albergo (2)

1 Taxes and service are included; breakfast is not. 2 Behind the
hotel, at the end of the courtyard.

Exercise 2

The order should be: 8, 1, 10, 2, 13 (or 8, 2, 13, 1, 10), 4, 14, 3, 5,
9, 7, 12, 15, 6, 11

Vorrei un po' di frutta

1 They are very sweet, good for juicing. 2 She wants bananas,
grapefruit and apples. 3 98 centesimi or 1 euro (½ kilo at 1 euro
96 centesimi a kilo).

Exercise 3

Quanto costano: le albicocche? le ciliegie? i limoni? i meloni?
le pesche? le prugne? le arance? le fragole? le mele? le pere?
i pompelmi? le susine? but Quanto costa l'uva?

Ho bisogno di formaggio

1 300 grammes. 2 Ham, cured ham, not cooked.

Exercise 4

– Trentadue euro novanta centesimi al chilo il prosciutto nostrano.
– Trentacinque euro sessanta centesimi al chilo il prosciutto di

Parma. – Quattro euro trenta centesimi il pecorino. – Tre euro trenta centesimi il prosciutto. – Sette euro sessanta centesimi in tutto.

Exercise 5

Vorrei 1 dei limoni, 2 dei francobolli, 3 del caffè, 4 del formaggio, 5 dell'uva, 6 dell'acqua minerale, 7 delle arance, 8 delle pesche, 9 del pane

Ci sono altri colori?

1 For his wife. 2 A green one. 3 Because his sister likes to wear her sweaters big.

Exercise 6

1 (a) compri (b) compro (c) comprate (d) compriamo 2 (a) leggo (b) legge (c) leggono 3 (a) preferisco (b) preferisce 4 (a) parlano (b) parlo (c) parla (d) parli 5 (a) vivono (b) viviamo

Il mio primo computer

1 It is about buying a computer for a child who has just started school. In Italy this will be a six-year-old, although recently the rising sixes have started to be admitted to school. 2 Buying a computer for a child is compared to buying a car to go shopping in. A Cinquecento is a small Fiat and would be adequate for the purpose.

Unit 8

Un po' di geografia

1 F (falso). 2 F – they are to be found in the Alps. 3 F – quite the opposite: three-quarters is mountain or hill. 4 V (vero). 5 F – they both have a long history of industrial development. 6 F – the Apennines are. 7 F – it is still active. 8 F. 9 V.

Exercise 1

1 Il fax deve essere spedito questa mattina. 2 La riunione può essere organizzata per lunedì. 3 L'albergo può essere prenotato per telefono. 4 La prenotazione può essere confermata per fax. 5 I biglietti devono essere ritirati a mezzogiorno. 6 Roma può essere informata via fax. 7 Il taxi può essere chiamato fra dieci minuti.

Fare il ponte nel Bel Paese

1 Because Andrea knows Italy well. 2 Spending too much time in the car. 3 He likes small, quiet places, she likes cities. 4 Verona. 5 Asolo.

Exercise 2

1 Bellissimo. 2 Simpaticissima. 3 Tranquillissimo. 4 Elegantissime. 5 Piacevolissimo.

Exercise 3

1 automaticamente 2 allegramente 3 velocemente 4 lentamente 5 bene 6 regolarmente

Exercise 4

1 Mi piace Roma. 2 Mi piacciono le montagne. 3 Mi piace visitare monumenti storici. 4 Mi piacciono le isole piccolissime. 5 Mi piacciono questi spaghetti.

Exercise 5

(a) 1 Ti piacciono i vini italiani? 2 Ti piace Venezia? 3 Ti piace studiare l'italiano? (b) 1 Le piacciono i vini italiani? 2 Le piace Venezia? 3 Le piace studiare l'italiano? (c) 1 Vi piacciono i vini italiani? 2 Vi piace Venezia ? 3 Vi piace studiare l'italiano?

Exercise 6

(a) 1 I should like to see the Campidoglio. 2 I should like to ride in a gondola in Venice. 3 I should like to throw a coin into the Trevi Fountain. 4 I should like to be at a Formula 1 race in Imola. 5 I should like to ski on the slopes of Mount Etna. 6 I should like to go to Pompei and Herculaneum. 7 I should like to see Stromboli, the volcano in the Aeolian Islands. (b) The choice is yours!

Exercise 7

1 C'è il lampadario etrusco. C'è also for numbers 2, 4, 6. Ci sono for numbers 3, 5, 7.

Translations: 1 The Etruscan lamp in the Museum of the Etruscan Academy. 2 Gino Severini's mosaics of the stations of the cross. 3 The picturesque streets in the upper (high) part of the town.

4 The view over the Val di Chiana (the Chiana Valley). 5 The works by the painter Luca Signorelli. 6 The Medici fortress. 7 The paintings by Fra Angelico in the Diocesan Museum.

Nord–Sud

1 It is poorer than the north. 2 A different history, different customs, a different climate, different terrain, the longer history of industrialization in the north, and being further away from the economic centre of Europe. 3 The ancient Greek monuments to be found there, fascinating towns and villages, the beautiful land-scape and coastline and the human warmth of the people are some of the attractions.

Unit 9

Al ristorante

1 Because it is light. 2 He says it is 'excellent, very good'. 3 Lombardy.

Exercise 1

1 Sì, mi piacciono, le prendo. 2 Sì, mi piace, la prendo. 3 Sì, mi piacciono, li prendo.

Exercise 2

Dov'è la lettera di Mary? Non la trovo. E la rivista? Non la vedo. Dove sono i francobolli per le cartoline? Non li trovo. Vedi la penna? Non la trovo. E questo conto. Non lo capisco. Aiuto!

Exercise 3

1 mi scrive … la leggo 2 ci conosce … Ci dà 3 Le passo 4 ti va bene 5 La vedo 6 (informal, singular, tu): ti porta … Ti lascia; (formal, singular, Lei): La porta … La lascia; (plural, voi): vi porta … Vi lascia

Exercise 4

1 Il signor Galli mi conosce bene. Lo vedo ogni settimana. Mi tele-fona spesso. 2 Conosci il signor e la signora Fabrizi? Ti piacciono? Li vedo ogni domenica. Gli parlo al telefono quasi ogni giorno. 3 Ti scrivo una lettera. Ti mando le foto di Gianni.

La cucina italiana

1 Because cooking is still very different from one region to another. 2 Because they grow it there. 3 Fruit and vegetables. 4 Because it is not produced there, there are no olives. 5 Butter, from the cows raised there.

Una ricetta

1 One for pasta – or at least, she implies that by saying she likes pasta. 2 Oil, garlic, broccoli, macaroni and parmesan cheese. 3 Chilli; you can also add anchovies or sardines, sultanas and pine nuts.

Unit 10

Vacanze in Sicilia

1 Because he has just come back from holiday. 2 Because he normally takes his holiday in August. 3 A holiday in Sicily; because there is so much to see, the countryside is wonderful, the sea spectacular and the food and wine are good. 4 He and his wife are going to the Gargano peninsula in July. 5 Marco is going to study English in Ireland and Maria is going on a sailing course in France.

Exercise 1

1 Sono stato (assuming you are a man; for a woman: Sono stata) 2 Sono andato/a 3 Sei andato/a 4 Sono andato/a 5 Siamo partiti 6 sono rimasti

Exercise 2

1 è arrivata 2 è andato 3 sono andati 4 è stato 5 siamo arrivati 6 sono venute

Exercise 3

1 il fratello 2 il nipote/il nipotino 3 la nipote 4 la figlia 5 il cognato 6 la zia 7 la moglie 8 lo zio 9 la sorella 10 il marito

Exercise 4

If you have followed Carlo's model you can't have gone wrong.

Exercise 5

1 Sono i tuoi genitori? 2 E' la tua macchina? 3 Sono le tue sorelle? 4 Sono i tuoi figli? 5 E' il tuo ufficio? 6 E' tua moglie?

To the hotel acquaintance you would say: 1 Sono i Suoi genitori?
2 E' la Sua macchina? 3 Sono le Sue sorelle? 4 Sono i Suoi figli?
5 E' il Suo ufficio? 6 E' Sua moglie?

Exercise 6

Only you can answer this but don't forget you must use **avere** and
you must either use **anni** or **ne**:

Ho quarant'anni/Ne ho quaranta

Il tempo

1 Yes, today. But not yesterday. 2 The weather is about to change.
They hope the change will bring snow.

Exercise 7

1 Cloudy 2 Rough 3 Snow 4 Rain 5 (Thunder)storms

Il clima italiano

1 Fog. 2 Because it is hot and humid. 3 The Adriatic Coast tends
to be colder, the Tyrrhenian milder. 4 The south.

Unit 11

Un giallo

1 Her family. 2 To the market. 3 To put the perishable food she
had bought in the fridge. 4 A white Volvo parked outside the
house, with two men in it. 5 As she came out of the door, they
turned away so that she did not see their faces. 6 Because they are
on holiday abroad.

Exercise 1

Sabato mattina *abbiamo fatto* la spesa e *abbiamo comprato* un
vestito nuovo per me. Il pomeriggio *siamo andati* a una mostra interessante e poi la sera *siamo stati* a cena da vecchi amici. Domenica
abbiamo fatto una gita con amici... *Siamo andati* in mare e *abbiamo
pranzato* sulla barca con loro. *Abbiamo* anche *fatto* il bagno e *preso*
il sole. Poi *abbiamo cenato* in un ristorante sul porto.

Exercise 2

1 E' uscita 2 E' salita 3 E' andata 4 E' uscita 5 E' andata 6 Si è seduta 7 Ha ordinato 8 E' stata raggiunta 9 E' uscita 10 E' salita 11 E' andata 12 ha lasciato

Exercise 3

1 Non ho comprato niente. 2 Non ho letto niente. 3 Non ho finito niente/Non ho scritto niente. 4 Non ho mangiato niente. 5 Non ho fatto niente.

La lettera di un'amica

1 Piero's marriage, the birth of her grandson and her own retirement. 2 Because it was her birthday and it was also the day her grandson was born. 3 She works as a consultant and as a writer and she looks after her grandson while her daughter is working. Her elderly parents also need help. 4 He has also retired and they were not used to being together so much. (This second point is implied rather than said.) Their house is big and each has a study of his/her own.

Exercise 4

(a) 1 Andando al lavoro, Sergio compra il giornale. 2 Essendo di Firenze, compra La Nazione. 3 Prendendo un espresso al bar, legge il giornale. (b) 1 Avendo una casa in campagna, i miei amici passano spesso il fine settimana lì. 2 Essendo grande il loro giardino, hanno sempre del lavoro da fare. 3 Avendo un orto, hanno sempre frutta e verdura fresca a tavola.

Exercise 5

1 Suona il pianoforte da ventiquattro anni. (He has played/been playing the piano for twenty-four years.) 2 Lavora ... da quattro anni. (He has been working as an engineer for four years.) 3 Conosce Antonio da quattordici anni. (He has known Antonio for fourteen years.) 4 Studia il francese da un po' più di un anno/da sedici mesi. (He has been studying French for a little more than a year/for sixteen months.) 5 Esce con Alessia da tre anni. (He has been going out with Alessia for three years.) 6 Abita a Milano da undici anni. (He has been living in Milan for eleven years.)

Exercise 6

Open

Unit 12

La cugina italiana

1 The daughter of Angela's aunt, that is of Angela's mother's elder sister, who married an Italian and who died some year's ago. 2 Because her mother had asked her to do so. 3 This is the first time she has done so. 4 A residential area on the outskirts of Turin.

Exercise 1

1 sposato 2 nel 3 maggiore 4 è nato 5 1985 6 figli 7 nata 8 è morto 9 minore 10 sposato

Ecco il mio appartamento

1 It faces west and gets the setting sun. 2 It's big enough for people to eat there. 3 Yes. (When asked if a door leads to a second bathroom she replies: Unfortunately not.) 4 Behind the building, in the courtyard. 5 A cellar.

Exercise 2

1 Ci abita da due anni. 2 Ci vado se ho tempo. 3 Ci sono stato due anni fa. 4 Ci traslocano a maggio.

Exercise 3

1 Ne abbiamo quattro. 2 Ne abbiamo tre. 3 Ne abbiamo sette in tutto. 4 Ne abbiamo uno (solo). 5 Ne abbiamo due – uno davanti e uno dietro (*or* Ne abbiamo uno davanti e uno dietro).

Answer for your own home using these structures.

Exercise 4

1 Ce ne sono tre. 2 Ce ne sono due. 3 Ce ne sono quattro. 4 Ce ne sono due. 5 Sì, ce n'è una (piccola).

Exercise 5

1 Vogliamo tornare l'anno prossimo ma non alla stessa villa. 2 L'anno prossimo vogliamo (vorremmo) un panorama sulla valle. 3 L'anno prossimo i nostri amici, i Simpson, vengono con noi, così abbiamo bisogno di quattro camere. 4 Preferiamo avere due stanze al pian terreno. 5 Vorremmo due o più bagni l'anno prossimo. 6 Soprattutto vogliamo una casa tranquilla (silenziosa), lontana dalla strada. Questa casa è (è stata) troppo rumorosa.

Exercise 6

Open

Dove vivono gli Italiani

1 Increasingly builders put in two, although sometimes the second one has a shower but no bathtub. 2 The dining room. 3 People want to get away from big cities, to the outskirts, to smaller towns or even to the country. 4 Often it is their grandparents' house. 5 They went to work in factories. 6 The fact that most families now have a car.

Unit 13

Nel 1967

1 Blocks of flats 2 Countryside, fields, a farm with animals 3 A farmhouse 4 It wasn't made up; it was just mud 5 By tram or by coach 6 Because they use robots instead

Exercise 1

1 era 2 faceva 3 aveva 4 avevano 5 erano 6 portava 7 andava 8 aveva 9 Sembrava 10 aveva 11 era

Exercise 2

Open

Exercise 3

1 erano 2 era 3 abitavamo 4 lavorava 5 guardavamo 6 avevamo 7 faceva 8 Eravamo 9 aveva 10 mangiavamo 11 portava 12 faceva 13 eravamo 14 ci divertivamo 15 Eravamo

Exercise 4

Open

Exercise 5

1 Leggevo 2 Ci parlavamo 3 ci guardavamo 4 Ero 5 Aspettavo 6 faceva 7 Aiutavo

Exercise 6

1 Sta facendo la doccia. 2 Sta facendo una besciamella. 3 Sta leggendo un racconto alla piccola Anna. 4 E' fuori. Sta facendo la spesa. 5 Sta dormendo.

L'Italia 1945–1995

1 Democracy. 2 Television, washing machines, plastic, motor cars, computers. 3 Electricity, drinking water and (flush) lavatory. 4 They left Italy to look for work in the Americas or in Europe. 5 People spoke dialects, Italian was not widely used. 6 The ethic of saving and of sacrifice. Today she sees (conspicuous) consumption and hedonism, the pursuit of (personal) happiness. 7 The political system has not developed in parallel to the standard of living.

Unit 14

Una distorsione alla caviglia

1 A bit better. 2 They didn't go to the cinema. Elena sprained her ankle and they went to the casualty department of the hospital. 3 Putting her foot to the ground.

Exercise 1

1 Viene spesso a trovarci. 2 Mi piacerebbe invitarlo a cena. 3 No, devo scrivergli oggi./Gli devo scrivere oggi. 4 Posso aiutarLa?/La posso aiutare? 5 No, spero di andarci quest'anno.

Exercise 2

1 Eccoli 2 Eccolo 3 Eccomi 4 Eccole

Exercise 3

(a) 1 Si diverta 2 Mi faccia un favore 3 Mi dia la chiave, per favore 4 Gli dica di venire domani (b) 1 Divertiti 2 Fammi un favore 3 Dammi la chiave, per piacere 4 Digli di venire domani

Exercise 4

1 Te lo faccio domani 2 Glielo spiego 3 Ce lo portano domani 4 Si, me ne ha parlato sabato

Dal medico

1 Sore throat, headache and stomach ache, lack of appetite and a feeling of extreme tiredness. 2 Influenza. 3 Some pastilles and a syrup as well as bed rest, lots to drink (water, weak tea etc., no alcohol).

Exercise 5

1 Una volta, sì, fumavo, ma ora non fumo più. 2 Una volta, sì, bevevo molto, ma ora non bevo più. 3 Una volta, sì, mangiavo carne rossa, ma ora non ne mangio più. 4 Una volta, sì, dormivo male, ma ora non dormo più male, dormo bene.

Exercise 6

1 Non lo vedo più. (I don't see him any more.) 2 Non mi scrive più. (He doesn't write to me any more.) 3 Non lo aiuto più. (I don't help him any more.) 4 Non ci telefoniamo più. (We don't telephone each other any more.)

Unit 15

La lotteria

1 Rarely. 2 He would buy a new car and he would take his friends on a world tour. 3 She would buy a house by the sea, install a grand piano, take piano lessons and spend her days playing the piano. She would also invite her friends to one long party.

Exercise 1

1 Cambierebbe casa 2 Comprerebbe una casa con giardino 3 Si sposerebbe con Anita 4 Imparerebbero a giocare a golf 5 Non smetterebbe di lavorare

Exercise 2

Open

Exercise 3

1 Non fumo mai 2 Non bevo mai vodka 3 Non vado mai in discoteca 4 Non compro mai cibi surgelati 5 Non cammino mai a piedi nudi (Do you remember: Neanche per sogno!, Unit 14)

Exercise 4

1 Non vado mai al cinema 2 Non vedo nessuno nella piazza 3 A Maria non piace affatto la musica rock 4 Carlo non ha nessun amico 5 Non mangio mai al ristorante 6 Il direttore non beve niente (Or: Il direttore non beve affatto/mica) 7 Non ho niente da fare 8 Non è ancora arrivato il professore

Se fossi in te

1 She doesn't know about it – Aldo hasn't dared tell her. 2 Because she is in her last year of high school and will be going to university in the autumn. 3 She might be able to get leave from her job and either work in the US or do some further study. They are in the lead in her field in the US. 4 Their English would benefit and good English is so important nowadays. They might also find interesting possibilities for their studies.

Exercise 5

1 Se andassimo a Roma, vedremmo Marco. 2 Se mi scrivesse, risponderei. 3 Se avessimo i soldi, lo aiuteremmo. 4 Se vincessi la lotteria, Anna, che cosa faresti? 5 Se vincesse la lotteria, Prof. Turco, che cosa farebbe? 6 Se sapessero, sarebbero contenti.

Exercise 6

1 Se mi avesse detto che era stanco, l'avrei aiutato. 2 Se non avesse bevuto tanto, non si sarebbe sentito male. 3 Se non fosse andato così veloce, non avrebbe avuto l'incidente. 4 Se non fossi andata alla festa da Giulia, non avrei incontrato Tommaso. 5 Se non avessi comprato un biglietto della lotteria, non avrei vinto un premio.

I Borghi d.o.c.

1 The old heart of the town must not have more than 2.000 inhabitants and the comune overall must have no more than 15.000; and it should have an attractive layout and architecturally pleasing buildings. 2 The last line suggests readers may like to have a 'fabulous' weekend visiting (one or more).

Unit 16

Benissimo. Possiamo firmare

1 Four. 2 15%. 3 10%. 4 A technician from Mr Rossi's firm. 5 Visit Angela's firm to see the robots in place.

Exercise 1

1 Il nostro tecnico arriverà all'aeroporto East Midlands alle 16.00 del 17 luglio/il 17 luglio alle 16. 2 Comincerà l'installazione il 18. 3 Finirà entro la fine del mese. 4 Avrà bisogno di una camera in un albergo. 5 Sarà possibile prenderlo all'aeroporto? 6 Vi sarà possibile dargli una macchina per questo periodo? 7 Spiegherà i robots ai vostri tecnici durante l'installazione.

Exercise 2

1 spedirò 2 finirò 3 telefonerò 4 ritirerò 5 aiuterò

Business letters

First letter: 1 Ingegner Mancuso. 2 nostro, Vostro (the capital letter is a courtesy). 3 It accompanies a quotation.
Second letter: 1 Technical help. 2 Because Meccanica Panigale have already telephoned to ask for help. This is merely a confirmation.

A formal email

1 automatic despatch 2 reference works 3. Joining is absolutely free and there is no obligation to purchase 4 without images or attachments 5 electronic mailbox (casella postale is a PO box) 6 Without any cost or obligation.

Un invito

1 Gabriella and her husband will come and collect her from her hotel. 2 On Saturday morning at 8 a.m.

Exercise 3

1 vista 2 smarriti 3 mangiata? 4 assaggiato

Unit 17

Desidero che mi dia un consiglio

1 The daughter of Angela's cousin Gabriella. 2 It must be smart but it must be suitable for important professional occasions as well as the wedding. She wants something simple, well cut and made of beautiful fabric.

Exercise 1

1 venga 2 sia partita 3 possa 4 arrivi 5 abbia comprata 6 sia andato

Exercise 2

1 faccia i letti 2 pulisca la cucina 3 lavi questi vestiti 4 stiri la biancheria 5 prepari il pranzo

Exercise 3

Vorrei: 1 una camicetta che sia facile da stirare 2 una maglia che si possa lavare in (nella) lavatrice 3 una borsa in cui ci sia spazio (posto) per un libro

Exercise 4

1 capisca 2 abbia 3 sappia 4 sia

Alla boutique

1 Because he can then tell what fabric will be suitable 2 The skirt is a bit too big 3 She finds an outfit she likes and it doesn't take long to do so; she has the rest of the morning free to visit an art gallery (museum)

Exercise 5

1 andrebbe bene; potrebbe prendere 2 volevo (**Mi ero presa** is a pluperfect 'I had taken') 3 ha comprato; non ha voluto; abbiamo risparmiato 4 farà 5 Venga; andiamo; diamoci 6 la può sostituire (direct object); Le sta molto bene (indirect object); che le piaccia (indirect object); mi piace (indirect object); mi potete (indirect object); lo prendo (direct object); diamoci (indirect, reciprocal). You may also have picked: che ne dice? ('of it') 7 gliela possiamo stringere 8 quello che cerca; quello che volevo; qualcosa che le piaccia; il vestito che ha comprato

I borghi d.o.c.

Apricale: 1 It is not explicitly said, but the implication is that it is because you are in a little town that hasn't changed much since the thirteenth century. 2 The streets are designed for pack animals (and people) only and are too narrow for cars. (The author knows of someone who bought a house there; all the building materials he needed to make the changes he wanted were brought up on a donkey.)

Dozza: The national competition for painted walls. As the passage says, many houses have paintings on their (outside) walls. The competition takes place each year.

Castel di Tora: 1 Because the town is on the site of a Roman town. It is in fact not far north east of Rome. 2 It is on a promontory, which drops steeply into the lake. 3 It is an area of ruined castles and places where brigands used to hide.

Italian–English glossary

The translations given are those applicable in this book. Where gender is not clear, i.e. in the case of nouns not ending in **-o** or **-a**, or not accompanied by an adjective, it is indicated. For verbs in **-ire**, those that work like **capire** (i.e. have **-isc-** in certain tenses) are indicated with *. Parts of speech (noun, adverb etc.) are indicated only when there might be confusion. Words stressed on the antepenultimate syllable and those where the learner might be uncertain of stress (i.e. those ending in **-io**, **-ia**) have the vowel of the stressed syllable underlined.

Abbreviations: n. = noun; sing. = singular; pl. = plural; m. = masculine; f. = feminine; inv. = invariable; fam. = familiar, informal; adj. = adjective; adv. = adverb; pp. = past participle, prep. = preposition.

A

a, ad	to, at
abbandonare	to abandon
abbastanza	fairly
abbigliamento	clothing
abbinamento	matching, combination
abbonato	subscriber
abbondante	abundant
abbraccio	a hug; (at end of letter) love from
abitare	to live
abito	clothes, dress, suit, outfit (can be used for men's and women's)
abituarsi	to become accustomed to
abituato	used to, accustomed
accadere	to happen
accanto a	next to, beside
accettare	to accept
accidenti!	good heavens!
acciottolato	surface paved with cobbles
acciuga	anchovy
accogliere (pp. **accolto**)	to welcome, to receive

accomodarsi	to make oneself comfortable		refresher course
accompagnare	to accompany, to go with	**aggiungere** (pp. **aggiunto**)	to add
accordo	agreement	**aglio**	garlic
essere	to agree	**agnello**	lamb
d'accordo	agreed, OK	**agosto**	August
accorgersi	to realize, to notice	**agricoltura**	agriculture
		agrumi (m. pl.)	citrus fruits
aceto	vinegar	**aiutare**	to help
acqua	water	**aiuto**	help
acqua minerale	spring water	**albergatore, -trice**	hotelier
acqua minerale naturale	still spring water		
		albergo	hotel
acqua minerale gassata	carbonated spring water	**albero**	tree
		albicocca	apricot
acquistare	to purchase	**alcool** (m.)	alcohol
adattarsi	to adapt	**alcuni/e**	some
adatto/a	suitable (for)	**al di là di**	beyond
addirittura	even	**alimento**	food
addormentarsi	to fall asleep	**allegro/a**	happy
aderire	to join, belong to (e.g. a club)	**allenarsi**	to train
		allergia	allergy
		alloggio	lodging, dwelling, place to live in
adesso	now		
adriatico/a	Adriatic		
adulto/a	adult	**allora**	then, well then
aereo	aeroplane	**allungarsi**	to stretch
aerobica	aerobics	**almeno**	at least
aeroporto	airport	**alpino/a**	alpine
affari (m. pl.)	business	**altare** (m.)	altar
affatto	not at all	**alterazione** (f.)	modification of the characteristics of a substance
affetto	affection		
affettuoso/a	affectionate		
affollare	to crowd, to flock to		
		altitudine (f.)	altitude
affollato/a	crowded	**alto/a**	tall, high
affresco	fresco, painting done on to fresh plaster	**altopiano**	plateau
		altrimenti	otherwise
		altro/a	other, another, more
aggiornarsi	to get up to date, to do a	**alzarsi**	to get up

amare	to love	**anticipo**	advance
ambasciata	embassy	**antico/a**	old, ancient, antique
ambasciatore (m.)	ambassador	**antipasto**	hors d'oeuvre, starter
ambiente (m.)	environment, surroundings	**anzi**	on the contrary, indeed
America	America	**anziano/a** (n. and adj.)	elderly (adj.); elderly person (n.)
americano/a	American		
amica	friend (f.)		
amicizia	friendship	**aperitivo**	aperitif
amico	friend (m.)	**aperto**	open
amministratore delegato	managing director	**appartamento**	apartment, flat
ammirare	to admire	**appassionato/a**	very fond of, very keen on
amore (m.)	love	**appena**	just, scarcely, hardly
ampio/a	spacious		
anche	also, too		
ancora	still; again; more	**appena possibile**	as soon as possible
non ... ancora	not yet	**Appennini** (m. pl.)	the Apennines
andare	to go; to suit		
andare in pensione	to retire	**appetito**	appetite
		appuntamento	an appointment
andare via	to go away	**appunto**	precisely, exactly
andarsene	to go away, to leave		
		aprile (m.)	April
andata	outward journey	**aprire** (pp. **aperto**)	to open
andata e ritorno	a return ticket		
anfiteatro	amphitheatre	**arancia**	orange
angolo	corner	**aranciata**	orangeade
animale (m.)	animal	**arancione**	orange
animazione (f.)	animation	**architetto**	architect
annata	year (see Unit 14)	**architettura**	architecture
		arco	arch, arc
anniversario	anniversary	**aria**	air
anno	year	**arido**	arid
annoiarsi	to be bored, to get bored	**arma**	branch, corps, arm (of a service)
annunciare	to announce		
antenna	aerial	**arrabbiarsi**	to get angry
antenna parabolica	satellite dish	**arrivare**	to arrive
anticipatamente	in advance	**arrivederci**	goodbye

arrivederLa	goodbye (formal, to one person only)
arrivo	arrival
arrosto	roast
arte (f.)	art
articolo	article
ascensore (m.)	lift, elevator
ascoltare	to listen to
asfaltato/a	covered with asphalt
aspettare	to wait for
aspettativa	leave of absence
assaggiare	to taste, try (food, drink)
assegno	cheque
assenza	absence
assistere	to be present at
assolutamente	absolutely, at all costs
astrazione (f.)	abstraction, abstract idea
attenzione (f.)	attention
attimo	moment
attirare	attract
attività	activity
attore, -ttrice	actor, actress (m.)
attraversare	to cross
attraverso	across, through
attuale	current, present
attualmente	at the moment, at the present time
augurio	(good) wish
auguri (pl.)	best wishes
Australia	Australia
australiano/a	Australian
autenticamente	authentically
autoambulanza	ambulance
autobus (m.)	bus
automatico/a	automatic

automobile (f.)	motor, car
automobilista	motorist (m. or f.)
automobilistico/a	motor (as adj.), to do with the motor car
autostrada	motorway
autunno	autumn, fall
avanguardia	forefront, lead, vanguard
avanti!	come in!
avere	to have
avvenimento	event
avvocatessa	(female) lawyer (but see text)
avvocato	lawyer
azienda	business, firm
azienda per il turismo	tourist office
azzurro	blue, sky blue

B

bacio	kiss
bacin(o)	little kiss
badare	to take notice of, to look after
bagaglio	baggage, luggage
bagno	bath, bathroom
balcone (m.)	balcony
ballare	to dance
bambino	child, baby
banca	bank
bancarella	stall
banco	bank
bandire*	to ban
bar (m.)	bar, café
barca	boat
barca a vela	sailing boat
barista (m.)	barman
basare	to base

base (f.) basis
  a base di based on
basilica basilica
basilico basil
basso/a low
bastare to be enough, sufficient
battere to beat
battistero baptistry
bellezza beauty
bellico/a relating to war
bello/a lovely, beautiful
benché although
bene well
  benissimo very well (adv.)
benessere (m.) well-being, prosperity
benvenuto welcome
  dare il benvenuto to welcome
bere (pp. **bevuto**) to drink
bestiame (m.) cattle
biancheria linen
bianco/a white
biblioteca library
biglietteria ticket office
biglietto ticket
binario platform
biondo/a fair-haired
birra beer
bisognare to be necessary
  bisogna it is necessary
bisogno need
  avere bisogno di to need
bistecca steak
blocchetto little block
blu navy blue, dark blue
bocca mouth
  in bocca al lupo! good luck!
bollente boiling
bollire to boil
bollito stewed
bolognese in the style of Bologna
boom (m.) economic boom
borgo a small town
borsa bag
borsa da spesa shopping bag
bosco wood
bottiglia bottle
box (m.) garage (integrated into building of house)
braccio, (pl. **le braccia**) arm
Brasile (m.) Brazil
brasiliano/a Brazilian
bravo/a skilful, expert, good (at doing something)
breve short, brief
brioche (f.) bun
britannico/a British
broccoli (m.) broccoli
brutto/a ugly, bad (of weather), nasty
buonanotte goodnight
buonasera good evening
buongiorno good morning, good day
buono/a good
burro butter
busta envelope
buttare to throw

C

cabina telefonica telephone box
cadere to fall

caffè (m.) coffee (black); café, bar

calamaro squid

calcio football, soccer

calcistico/a related to football, soccer

caldo/a hot

calmo/a calm

calore (m.) warmth

calza stocking

calzino sock

cambiare to change

cambiare aria to have a change of scene

cambio change, exchange

camera room, bedroom

cameriere waiter

camicetta blouse

camicia shirt

camminare to walk

campagna country, countryside

campanile (m.) bell tower

campeggio campsite

campo field, (mil.) camp

Canada (m.) Canada

canadese Canadian

canale (m.) canal, channel

cancello gate

Cancro Cancer

candela candle

cantare to sing

cantina cellar

caotico/a chaotic

capace capable

capelli (m. pl.) hair

capire* to understand

capitale (f.) capital

cappello hat

cappotto overcoat

cappuccino white coffee

carabiniere (m.) carabiniere, member of the military force with police responsibilities

carattere (m.) character

caratteristico/a characteristic, typical (of a place)

carciofo globe artichoke

carie (f.) caries, tooth decay

carino/a pretty, cute, sweet

carne (f.) meat

caro/a expensive, dear; (n.) loved one

carota carrot

carta paper, card, menu

carta di credito credit card

carta d'identità identity card

carta telefonica phonecard

cartello sign, notice

cartolina postcard

casa house, home

casalinga housewife, homemaker

cascina farm, dairy, dairy farm

casetta little house, cottage

cassa cash desk, till; also soundbox, (loud)speaker

cassiere/a cashier

castello castle, palace

catena chain

cattedrale (f.) cathedral

cattivo/a — bad, naughty

cattolico/a — (Roman) Catholic

causa — cause

  a causa di — because of

cavarsela — to get by, to manage

caviglia — ankle

celeste — blue, light blue

cellulare (m.) — cellular, mobile telephone

cena — supper, evening meal

centimetro — centimetre

cento — a hundred

centrale — central, middle

centralino — exchange, switchboard

centro — centre

cercare — to look for, to seek, to try

cerimonia — ceremony

certo — certainly; yes, of course

certo/a — certain, some

  certe persone — some people

che — that, which, who, whom

che! — what!

che? che cosa? — what?

chi? — who?

chiacchierare — to chat, chatter

chiamare — to call

chiamarsi — to be called

chiarimento — clarification

chiaro/a — clear

chiave (f.) — key

chiedere — to ask
  (pp. **chiesto**)

chiesa — church

chilo — kilo

chilometro — kilometre

chissà (chi sa?) — I wonder, maybe, who knows?

chiudere — to close
  (pp. **chiuso**)

ciao — hello, hi (informal); goodbye (informal)

cibo — food

cielo — sky

ciliegia — cherry

cima — summit

Cina — China

cinema (m.) — cinema

cinese — Chinese

cinque — five

ciò — that

cioccolata — chocolate

cioè — that is, i.e.

cipolla — onion

circa — about, approximately

circondare — to surround

circostante — surrounding

città — city, town

cittadina — small town

civiltà — civilization

classe (f.) — class

classico/a — classic, classical

cliente (m. or f.) — customer, client

clima (m.) — climate

coda — tail, queue

cogliere — to pick, pluck
  (pp. **colto**)

cognato/a — brother/sister-in-law

colazione, prima colazione — breakfast

collaborazione (f.) — collaboration

collant (m.)   tights
     (a pair of)
collega (m. or f.;   colleague
   pl. **-ghi, -ghe**)
collettivo/a   collective
collina   hill
collo   neck
colore (m.)   colour
coltivare   to cultivate
colto/a   educated
come   like, as
come?   how? what?
cominciare   to begin
commerciale   commercial
   (adj.)
commercialista   accountant
   (m. or f.)
commesso/a   shop assistant
comodo/a   comfortable,
     convenient
compagnia   company
compleanno   birthday
complesso/a   complex
comportare   imply, involve
comprare   to buy
comprendere   to include,
   (pp. **compreso**)   comprise
computer (m.)   computer
comunale   municipal
comune   common
comune (m.)   municipality,
     town council
comunicare   to communicate
comunque   however,
     anyway
con   with
concordare   to reach an
     agreement
condizionale   conditional
   (m.)   (mood of
     verb)
conducente (m.)   driver

conferenza   lecture
confermare   to confirm
confessare   to confess
confessarsi   to make
     confession
     (to confess
     oneself)
confinante   having a
     shared border,
     neighbouring
congratulazioni   congratulations
   (f. pl.)
congresso   conference
conoscere (pp.   to know, to
   conosciuto)   be acquainted
     with, to get
     to know
consegna   delivery,
     consignment
consegnare   to deliver, to
     hand over
conservare   to conserve,
     to preserve
considerare   to consider
considerarsi   to consider
     oneself
consiglio   (piece of)
     advice
consistere   to consist
consolato   consulate
consulente   consultant
   (m. or f.)
consumo   consumption
contadino   peasant, farmer,
     country
     dweller
contatto   contact
contento/a   pleased, happy
continentale   continental (adj.)
continuare   to continue
continuo/a   continuous,
     continual

conto — bill, account
  per conto loro — on their own
contorno — vegetables served with the meat course
contratto — contract
contro — against
controllo — check, control
convincere — to convince
  (pp. **convinto**)
coperto — cover (in restaurant)
coppia — couple
coprire — to cover
  (pp. **coperto**)
coraggio — courage
coraggioso — brave
cordiale — cordial
coricarsi — to go to bed, to lie down
corpo — body
corrente (f.) — current
corridoio — corridor
corrispondere — to correspond
  (pp. **corrisposto**)
corso — boulevard, wide street; course
cortese — courteous, kind
cortesia — courtesy
  per cortesia — please
cortile (m.) — courtyard
corto/a — short
cosa — thing
così — thus, so, like this, in this way
così via — and so on
costa — coast
costare — to cost
costiero/a — coastal
costituire* — to constitute

costo — cost
  a tutti i costi — at all costs to
costruire* — construct, to build
costruttore, -ttrice — builder
costume (m.) — custom
cotoletta — cutlet
cotone (m.) — cotton
cotto — cooked, having undergone a cooking process (pp. **cuocere**)
credere — to believe, think
crescere — to grow
cronaca — news
cucina — kitchen, cooking
cugino/a — cousin
cui — which, whom
culturale — cultural
cuocere — to cook
  (pp. **cotto**)
cuoco/a — cook
cuore (m.) — heart
cura — treatment, care
curare — to take care of, to treat (medically)
cuscino — cushion

D

da — from, since, to/at the house of
dappertutto — everywhere
dare (pp. **dato**) — to give
data — date
dato — datum, pl. data
davanti (a) — in front of
davvero — really

debole	weak	**diritto**	right; law
decidere	to decide	**discoteca**	discotheque
(pp. **deciso**)		**disoccupazione**	unemployment
decimo/a	tenth	(f.)	
decisione (f.)	decision	**dispiacere**	to displease
delegazione (f.)	delegation	**mi dispiace**	I am sorry
delicato/a	delicate	**disporre**	to have at one's
democrazia	democracy	(pp. **disposto**)	disposal, to
denaro	money		arrange
densità	density	**disposizione** (f.)	disposition
dente (m.)	tooth	**a disposizione**	available
dentista (m. or f.)	dentist	**disposto/a**	arranged
dentro	inside, within	**distanza**	distance
descrivere	to describe	**distorsione** (f.)	sprain
(pp. **descritto**)		**disturbare**	to disturb,
desiderare	to want,		bother
	desire, wish	**ditta**	firm, company
destinazione (f.)	destination	**diventare**	to become
destro/a	right	**diverso/a**	different
di	of, from,	**divertente**	amusing,
diagonale	diagonal		enjoyable, fun
diagonalmente	diagonally	**divertimento**	amusement,
dialetto	dialect		entertainment
dicembre (m.)	December	**divertirsi**	to enjoy oneself
dieci	ten	**doccia**	shower
dietro (adv.)	behind	**documento**	document (used
differenza	difference		to mean proof
difficile	difficult		of identity)
difficoltà	difficulty	**dolce** (m.)	pudding
di fronte	opposite	**dolce** (adj.)	sweet
diffuso/a	widespread	**dolore** (m.)	pain
dimenticare	to forget	**domanda**	question
diminuire*	to decrease	**domani**	tomorrow
di nuovo	again	**domenica**	Sunday
diocesano/a	diocesan	**dominante**	dominant
dipendere	to depend	**dominare**	to dominate,
dipinto	painting		overlook
dire (pp. **detto**)	to say	**donna**	woman
diretto	direct,	**donna d'affari**	businesswoman
	directed	**dopo**	after
direttore (m.),	director	**dopodomani**	the day after
-ttrice (f.)			tomorrow

doppio/a — double
dormire — to sleep
dottore, dottoressa — doctor
dove — where
dovere — to have to, must
dritto/a (also) diritto/a — straight
ducale — belonging to a duke or (in Venice) doge
due — two
dunque — so, therefore
duomo — cathedral
durante — during
duro/a — hard

E

e, ed — and
eccetera, ecc. — et cetera, etc.
eccezionale — exceptional
ecco — here is/are; there is/are (pointing out); well then (starting to explain something)
economia — economy, economics
economico/a — economical economic
edonismo — hedonism, pursuit of happiness
educato/a — polite, well brought up
egregio/a — distinguished
  Egregio Signore — Dear Sir
elefante (m.) — elephant

elegante — elegant
elementare — elementary
elementari (le classi) — elementary school
elenco — list, directory
elettricità — electricity
elettronica — electronics
elettronico/a — electronic
eliminare — to eliminate
emergenza — emergency
emigrare — to emigrate
emotivamente — emotionally
emozione (f.) — emotion
entrarci — to be to do with
  non c'entra — he/it is nothing to do with it
entrare — to enter
entrata — entrance
entro — by (a point in or a period of time)
epoca — age, period, era
  all'epoca — at the time
errore (m.) — error, mistake
esame (m.) — examination
esattamente — exactly
esatto/a — exact
esclusivamente — exclusively
escursione (f.) — excursion
esempio — example
  ad esempio — for example
esercizio — exercise
esistere — to exist
esodo — exodus, mass departure
espresso — black coffee, express (train, letter)
essere (pp. stato) — to be
  essere in giro — to be going around
est (m.) — east

estate (f.)	summer	**fatica**	drudgery, effort,
estendersi	to extend		physically hard
estero/a	foreign		work
all'estero	abroad	**fatto**	fact
età	age	**fattoria**	farm
etica	ethic	**favore** (m.)	favour
etichetta	label, sticker	per favore	please
etrusco/a	Etruscan	**fax** (m.)	fax
ettaro	hectare	**febbraio**	February
etto	100 grammes	**febbre** (f.)	fever, high
Europa	Europe		temperature
evacuare	to evacuate	**fegato**	liver
evitare	to avoid	**felice**	happy
evoluzione (f.)	evolution	**ferie** (f. pl.)	holidays
		fermare	to stop
F		**fermata**	stop
		fermo/a	still, not moving
fa	ago	**feroce**	fierce
fabbrica	factory	**ferrovia**	railway
faccia	face	**festa**	party
facile	easy	**fiaba**	fable, fairy tale
fagiolino	French bean,	**fidanzato/a**	fiancé(e)
	green bean	**figlio/a**	son/daughter
fagiolo	bean	figlio unico	only son
fai-da-te	do-it-yourself	**film** (m.)	film
falso/a	false	**finale**	final
fame (f.)	hunger	**finalmente**	at last, finally
avere fame	to be hungry	**finanziamento**	financing
famiglia	family	**finanziario/a**	financial
familiari	family members,	**fine** (f.)	end
	relations	**fine settimana**	weekend
famoso/a	famous	(m. or f.)	
fango	mud	**finestra**	window
farcela	to succeed,	**finire***	to end, to finish
	to manage,	**fino a**	as far as, until
	to make it,	**fiore** (m.)	flower
	to cope	**fiorente**	flourishing
fare (pp. **fatto**)	to do,	**firma**	signature
	to make	**firmare**	to sign
fare il biglietto	to buy a	**fiscale**	fiscal, relating
	ticket		to tax
farmacia	chemist's	**fissare**	to fix, to arrange

fisso	fixed (as opposed to movable, portable)	**friggere**	to fry
		frigorifero, frigo	refrigerator, fridge
fiume (m.)	river	**frizzante**	sparkling (of wine)
fondo	bottom		
fontana	fountain	**fronte** (f.)	forehead
forma	shape, form	**di fronte a**	opposite
formaggio	cheese	**frontiera**	frontier
formale	formal	**frutta**	fruit
formare	to form	**fruttivendolo**	greengrocer, fruit seller
formula	formula		
fornire*	to provide	**fuggire**	to flee
forno	oven	**fumare**	to smoke
foro	forum	**fungo**	mushroom
forse	perhaps	**funzionare**	to work, function
forte	strong		
fortezza	fortress	**fuoco**	fire
fortuna	fortune, luck	**fuori**	outside
fortunato/a	fortunate, lucky	**furto**	theft, burglary
foto (f.)	photo	**futuro**	future
fra	between, among		
fra un mese	in a month's time	**G**	
fragola	strawberry	**gabinetto**	lavatory; surgery (of a doctor or dentist)
francese	French		
Francia	France	**galleria**	art gallery
francobollo	(postage) stamp	**Galles** (m.)	Wales
fratello	brother	**gallese**	Welsh
frattempo	meanwhile	**gamba**	leg
nel frattempo	in the meanwhile	**gara**	race, competition
frazione (f.)	outlying village	**garage** (m.)	garage
freddo/a	cold	**garanzia**	guarantee
frequentare	to frequent; to attend (school)	**gelateria**	ice cream parlour
		gelato	ice cream
frequente	frequent	**genealogico/a**	genealogical
fresco/a	fresh, cool	**albero genealogico**	family tree
fretta	haste		
avere fretta	to be in a hurry	**generalmente**	generally, usually

genere (m.) kind, sort
  in genere generally
genero son-in-law
genitori (m. pl.) parents
gennaio January
gente (f. sing.) people
gentile kind
  Gentile Dear Madam
  Signora
geografia geography
gerundio gerund
gestire* to manage
gettare to throw
getto a jet, a spout
getto ink-jet
  d'inchiostro
già already
giacca jacket
giallo/a yellow
giallo, n a detective story
Giappone (m.) Japan
giapponese Japanese
giardino garden
giara terracotta jar for
    storage of oil
ginnasio high school (the
    first two years
    of the classical
    liceo)
giocare to play (a game)
giornalaio/a newspaper seller
giornale (m.) newspaper
giornata day (see Unit 14)
giorno day
giovane young
giovedì (m.) Thursday
girare to turn, to go
    around, to
    circulate
giro circuit, circle,
    tour
  andare in giro to go around

gita excursion, trip,
    outing
gitante tripper, person
  (m. or f.) on an outing
giù down
giugno June
giungere arrive, reach
  (pp. **giunto**)
giusto/a right, correct,
    just
gnocchi (m. pl.) gnocchi,
    dumplings
godere to enjoy
gola throat
golf (m.) golf; cardigan
golfo gulf, bay
gondola gondola
gonna skirt
governo government
grammo gramme
grana a type of hard
    cheese (slightly
    granular in
    texture);
    parmesan
Gran Bretagna Great Britain
granché a lot (usually
    used in
    negative
    sentences)
grande big, large
grandine (f.) hail
grattare to scratch
gratuito/a free
grazie thanks, thank
    you
greco/a Greek
grigio/a grey
griglia grill
grosso/a big
guardare to look, to
    watch

Guardia di   tax police
   Finanza
guarire*   to cure, to heal,
     to get better
guerra   war
guida (f. even   guide, guidebook
   if male)
guidare   to guide; to drive
     (a vehicle)

I

idea   idea
identità   identity
ieri   yesterday
illustrato/a   illustrated
immaginare   to imagine
immagine (f.)   image
immensamente   immensely,
     enormously
imparare   to learn
impegnativo/a   exacting,
     demanding;
     (of price)
     high
impegnato/a   engaged, busy,
     committed
impegno   commitment,
     pledge
imperfetto   imperfect
imperiale   imperial
impermeabile   raincoat
   (m.)
impianto   plant,
     machinery,
     equipment
impiegato   employee
importante   important
importare   to matter, to be
     important
   non importa   it doesn't
     matter

impossibile   impossible
impresa   enterprise,
     business
inattivo/a   inactive,
     dormant
     (of volcano)
incantevole   enchanting,
     delightful,
     charming
incendio   fire
incertezza   uncertainty
incidente (m.)   accident
includere   to include
   (pp. **incluso**)
incontro   meeting
indicatore   indicator
indietro   back; (of clock,
     watch) slow
indirizzo   address
indiscutibile   unquestionable,
     undisputable
indomani   the next day
industria   industry
industriale   industrial
industrializza-   industrialization
   zione
in effetti   in fact
infatti   yes, indeed
infelice   unhappy
infermiere/a   nurse
infine   finally
infinito/a   infinite;
     innumerable
infinito (n.)   infinitive
infisso   window
     frame
influenza   influence;
     influenza
influire*   to influence
informare   to inform
informarsi   to inform
     oneself

informazione (m.)	information
ingegnere (m.)	engineer
Inghilterra	England
ingiallito/a	yellowed
inglese	English
iniziativa	initiative
inizio	start, beginning
innamorato/a	in love
inoltre	besides, furthermore, moreover
inquinamento	pollution
in realtà	in fact
insalata	salad
insegna	sign
insegnante (m. or f.)	teacher
inserire*	to insert, to settle, to fit in
insieme	together
insistere	to insist
insolitamente	unusually
insolito/a	unusual
insomma	in short
installare	to install
installazione (f.)	installation
intanto	meanwhile
intensamente	intensively, strongly
interamente	entirely
interessante	interesting
interessarsi	to be interested in
interesse (m.)	interest
interno	interior; (telephone) extension
interno/a	internal
intero/a	whole
interrogativo	question, problem
interrompere (pp. **interrotto**)	to interrupt
intervallo	interval, break
intervento	intervention
inteso	understood, agreed
intimità	intimacy
intorno (adv.)	around
intorno a (prep.)	round, around
intuizione (f.)	intuition
inutile	useless
invece	instead, on the other hand
inventare	to invent
inverno	winter
investigatore (m.)	investigator, detective
inviare	to send
invio	despatch, sending
invitare	to invite
invito	invitation
io	I
Irlanda	Ireland
irlandese	Irish
irrigare	to irrigate
iscriversi	to enrol
iscrizione (f.)	enrolment, joining (a club, a service)
isola	island
isolare	to isolate
istruito/a	educated
italiano/a	Italian

L

là	there
lago	lake
lamentarsi	to complain
lampadario	chandelier, candleholder

lana	wool
largo	wide
lasagne (f. pl.)	pasta in flat sheets
lasciare	to leave
latitudine (f.)	latitude
lato	side
latte (m.)	milk
lavanderia	utility room, laundry
lavarsi	to wash (oneself)
lavatrice (f.)	washing machine
lavorare	to work
lavoro	work, job
legge(f.)	law
leggere (*pp.* **letto**)	to read
leggero/a	light
legno	wood
lei	she, her
Lei	you (formal)
lentamente	slowly
lento/a	slow
leone (m.)	lion
lettera	letter
letto	bed
lettura	reading
lezione (f.)	lesson
lì	there
libero/a	free
libertà	freedom, liberty
libreria	bookshop
libro	book
liceo	high school
lieto/a	happy
limone (m.)	lemon
linea	line
lingua	tongue, language
linguaggio	language
lirico/a	lyric
musica lirica	opera

litro	litre
locale (m.)	room, establishment, premises
locale	local
lombardo/a	Lombard, of Lombardy
lontano/a (adj. and adv.)	far
lotteria	lottery
luglio	July
lui	he, him
luminoso/a	light
lunedì (m.)	Monday
lungo/a	long
lungo	along
luogo	place
lupo	wolf
in bocca al lupo!	good luck!

M

ma	but
macché	you're joking! what nonsense!
maccheroni (m. pl.)	maccheroni, macaroni (short pasta tubes)
macchina	car, automobile
macchinetta	little machine
macellaio	butcher
macerie (f. pl.)	rubble, ruins
madre (f.)	mother
madre-lingua (f.)	mother tongue
magari	perhaps; would that it were so!
maggio	May
maggiorana	marjoram

maggiore bigger, major
  fratello elder brother
  maggiore
maglia sweater
magnifico/a magnificent,
    wonderful,
    splendid
magro/a thin, lean,
    non-oily
    (of fish)
mai never
maiale (m.) pig, pork
malattia illness
male bad
  fare male to hurt
  meno male fortunately,
    luckily
malessere (m.) malaise,
    indisposition;
    bad condition
    financially
malsano/a unhealthy,
    morbid
maltempo bad weather
mamma mummy, mom
mancare to be missing
mangiare to eat
mano (f.) hand
  (pl. **mani**)
mantenere to maintain
manzo beef
marchio symbol or mark,
    indicating
    where a
    product comes
    from
mare (m.) sea
marito husband
marrone brown
marsala dessert wine
    from Marsala
    in Sicily

martedì (m.) Tuesday
marzo March
massa mass
  di massa for the masses
massimo/a greatest, biggest
master (m.) a master's
    degree,
    particularly
    MBA
matrimoniale matrimonial, (of
    bed) double
matrimonio wedding
mattinata morning (see
    Unit 14)
mattino/mattina morning
maturità maturity; high
    school diploma
medicina medicine
medico doctor
medievale mediaeval
medio/a medium(-sized),
    middle,
    average
meglio (adv.) better
mela apple
melanzana aubergine,
    eggplant
melone (m.) melon
membro member
memoria memory
meno less, minus
mentre while
meraviglia wonder, marvel
meraviglioso/a marvellous
mercato market
mercoledì (m.) Wednesday
merenda snack (in the
    afternoon, for
    children)
meridionale southern
meritare to deserve
mescolare to mix

mese (m.) — month
messaggio — message
Messico — Mexico
messicano/a — Mexican
meta — destination
metà — half
metro — metre
metterci — (of time) to take
mettere — to put
   (pp. **messo**)
mezzanotte (m.) — midnight
mezzo — half, middle
   in mezzo a — in the middle of
mezzogiorno — noon, midday; south; southern Italy
mica — not at all
migliorare — to improve
migliore, il/la — the best
migliore (adj.) — better
milione (m.) — million
milite ignoto — unknown soldier
mille (m.) — a thousand
millimetro — millimetre
minestra — soup; the pasta course
minimo/a — least
ministro — minister
minore — smaller, minor
   il/la minore — the smallest
minuto — minute
mio/a — my
miracolo — miracle
misero/a — poor, wretched, paltry
misteriosamente — mysteriously
mistero — mystery
misura — size
mite — mild
modello — model
modernizzare — to modernize

moderno/a — modern
modo — way; mood
   in ogni modo — anyway, in any case
modulo — form
moglie (f.) — wife
molto (adv.) — very, very much
molto/a (adj.) — many, much
momento — moment, time
mondiale (adj.) — world
   la seconda guerra mondiale — the Second World War
mondo — world
moneta — coin
montagna — mountain
monte (m.) — mount, mountain
monumento — monument
morbido/a — soft
morboso/a — morbid
morire — to die
   (pp. **morto**)
mosaico — mosaic
mosso/a — (of sea) rough
mostra — exhibition
mostrare — to show
motivo — reason
mucca — cow
multa — fine
municipio — town hall
muscolo — muscle
museo — museum, gallery
musica — music
musica lirica — opera

N

nascere (pp. **nato**) — to be born
nascita — birth
naso — nose
Natale (m.) — Christmas
naturale — natural

naturalmente	naturally, of course
nazionale	national
neanche	not even
nebbia	fog
necessario/a	necessary
negoziante (m.)	shopkeeper, tradesman
negozio	shop
nemmeno	not even
neozelandese	New Zealander, from New Zealand
neppure	not even
nero/a	black
nervi (m. pl.)	nerves
nessuno/a	none, not one
neve (f.)	snow
nevicare	to snow
nevralgia	neuralgia
niente	nothing
nipote (m. or f.)	nephew, niece; grandson, granddaughter
nipotino/a	little nephew/ niece; grandson/ granddaughter
no	no
noce (f.)	walnut
noi	we
nome (m.)	name
non	not
nonna	grandmother
nonno	grandfather
nono/a	ninth
nord (m.)	north
normale	normal
nostrano/a	local, locally produced
nostro/a	our
notare	to note, notice

notevole	notable, significant, considerable
notizia	piece of news
noto	known, well-known
notte (f.)	night
nove	nine
novembre (m.)	November
novità	innovation, novelty, newness
nudo/a	naked, bare
nulla	nothing
numero	number
numeroso/a	numerous, many
nuora	daughter-in-law
Nuova Zelanda	New Zealand
nuovo/a	new
di nuovo	again
nuvoloso/a	cloudy

O

o	or
obliterare	obliterate, punch (a ticket)
occasione (f.)	opportunity, bargain; occasion
occhio (pl. **occhi**)	eye
occidentale	western
occorrere	to be necessary
occorre	it is necessary
occupare	to occupy
occuparsi (di)	to look after, take care of
occupato/a	occupied, busy
odierno/a	of today
odori (m. pl.)	herbs
offerta	offer

offrire to offer
  (pp. **offerto**)
oggetto object, purpose;
  (at head of
  letter) re
oggi today
ogni every, each
ognuno/a everyone, each
  person
Olanda Holland (more
  correctly:
  Paesi Bassi)
olandese Dutch
olio oil
oliva olive
oltre beyond
opera work; opera
operaio/a workman,
  worker
opinione (f.) opinion
opportunità opportunity
oppure or, or else
ora (adv.) now
ora (n.) hour, time
orario timetable,
  schedule
orchestrina small orchestra
  (as in a café
  or restaurant)
ordinare to order
ordine (m.) order
orecchio ear
organizzare to organize
orientale eastern
ormai now
oro gold
orologio clock, watch
orto kitchen garden,
  vegetable
  garden
oscillazione (f.) oscillation
ospedale (m.) hospital

ospitalità hospitality
ottavo/a eighth
ottimo/a very good,
  excellent
otto eight
ottobre (m.) October
ovest (m.) west

P

pace (f.) peace
padano/a relating to the
  valley/plain of
  the river Po
padre (m.) father
paesaggio scenery,
  countryside
paese (m.) country; village
pagamento payment
pagare to pay
paio (m.; pl. pair
  paia, f.)
palazzo palace, large
  building, block
  of flats/
  apartments
palestra gymnasium
pane (m.) bread
panino bread roll
panna cream
panorama view (m. inv.)
pantaloni trousers
  (m. pl.)
parcheggiare to park
parcheggio a parking space,
  a car park
parco park
parecchio/a a lot, a good
  deal, (pl.)
  several
parente relation
  (m. or f.)

parere	to seem	**pazienza**	patience
(pp. **parso**)		**avere**	to be patient
pari a	equal to	**pazienza**	
parlare	to talk, to speak	**pazienza!**	never mind!
parmigiano	Parmesan cheese	**peccato (che**	what a pity
parola	word	**peccato)**	
parte (f.)	part, side	**pecora**	sheep, ewe
la maggior	the majority	**pecorino**	cheese made
parte			from ewe's
partenza	departure		milk
participio	participle	**pedonale**	reserved for
particolare	particular		pedestrians
particolarmente	particularly	**peggio** (adv.)	worse
partire	to set off, leave,	**peggiore** (adj.)	worse
	depart	**pelle** (f.)	leather, skin
partita	match (sport)	**pendente**	leaning, hanging
Pasqua	Easter	**pendice** (f.)	slope
passaporto	passport	**penisola**	peninsula
passare	to pass	**penna**	pen
passato	sieved or	**pensare**	to think
	liquidized soup	**pensiero**	thought
passato/a	past	**pensione** (f.)	pension
passato	near past	**pepe** (m.)	pepper
prossimo	(tense), past	**peperoncino**	chilli
	perfect	**peperone** (m.)	(green or red)
passato remoto	remote past		pepper
	(tense), past	**per**	for
	absolute, past	**per cortesia**	please
	historic	**per favore**	please
passeggiare	to go for a walk	**per piacere**	please
passeggiata	walk, stroll	**pera**	pear
passo	step	**perché**	why; because;
pasta	pastry, pasta		so that
	(spaghetti etc.)		(+ subjunctive)
pastiglia	pastille	**perciò**	therefore
pasto	meal	**percorso**	journey, distance
patata	potato		travelled
patria	native land,	**perdere**	to lose
	fatherland	(pp. **perduto**	
patrimonio	heritage	or **perso**)	
pausa	pause, break	**perfetto/a**	perfect
paziente	patient	**perfino** (adv.)	even

pericoloso/a   dangerous
periferia   suburbs, outskirts
periodo   period
permettere   to allow, permit
  (pp. **permesso**)
però   however, but
persona   person
personaggio   personage, character
personale   personnel (n.);
  (n. and adj.)   personal (adj.)
pesante   heavy
pesca   peach
pescatore (m.)   fisherman
pesce (m.)   fish
pessimo   very bad
pettinarsi   to comb, do one's hair
pezzo   piece
piacere (m.)   pleasure
  per piacere   please
piacere   to be pleasing
  mi piace   I like, it is pleasing to me
piacevole   pleasant, pleasing
piangere   to weep, to cry
  (pp. **pianto**)
piano (adv.)   slowly, carefully, softly
piano   floor
  al secondo piano   on the second floor
pianoforte (m.)   piano
  pianoforte a coda   grand piano
pianta   plan
pian terreno   ground floor
pianura   plain
piatto   dish, plate

piazza   square
piazzale (m.)   large square
piazzetta   little square
piccante   sharp tasting, piquant
piccolo/a   small, little
piede (m.)   foot
  a piedi   on foot
pieno/a   full
pilota   pilot
pinolo   pine nut
pioggia   rain
piovere   to rain
pipa   pipe
pisello   pea
pittore, -ttrice   painter
pittoresco/a   picturesque
più   more, most, plus
  non . . . più   no longer
piuttosto   rather
pizzeria   pizzeria, pizza restaurant
plastica   plastic
poco, un po'   a little bit
poi   next, then
poiché   since, as
polenta   maize flour porridge, polenta
politica   politics
politico/a   political
polizia   police
pollo   chicken
polmone (m.)   lung
polso   wrist
pomeriggio   afternoon
pomodoro   tomato
pompelmo   grapefruit
ponte (m.)   bridge
popolare   popular, belonging to the people

popolazione (f.)	population	**prefisso**	telephone area/
popolo	the people		country code
porcino	cèpe (type of	**pregare**	to pray, ask
	mushroom)	**prego**	go ahead; don't
porgere (saluti)	to offer		mention it
	(greetings) in a	**premio**	prize
	formal letter	**prendere**	to take, to have
porta	door; (in airport)	(pp. **preso**)	(coffee, beer,
	gate		etc.)
porta-finestra	French window	**prenotare**	to book, reserve
portare	carry, take,	**prenotazione** (m.)	booking
	bring, wear	**preoccuparsi**	to worry
portatile	portable; (of	**preparare**	to prepare
	computer)	**prepararsi**	to get (oneself)
	laptop		ready
portico	portico,	**presentare**	to present,
	arcade		introduce
posizione (f.)	position	**presente**	present; (in
possedere	to possess		formal letter)
possibile	possible		this letter
possibilità	possibility	**presidente**	presidente
posta	post, mail	**presidente del**	prime minister
posto	place; space,	**consiglio**	
	room	**pressione** (f.)	pressure
potabile	potable,	**presto** (adv.)	soon, early,
	drinkable		quickly
potente	powerful; as a	**preventivo/a**	preventive
	noun (m.)	**preventivo**	estimate, (price)
	power		quotation
potenza	power	**previsione** (f.)	forecast
potere	to be able to	**prezzemolo**	parsley
povero/a	poor	**prezzo**	price
pranzo	lunch, midday	**prigioniero/a**	prisoner
	meal	**prima (di)**	before
pratica	practice	(prep.)	
praticante	practising	**prima** (adv.)	before, earlier
pratico/a	practical	**prima colazione**	breakfast
prato	meadow, grassy	**primavera**	spring
	field	**primo/a**	first
preciso/a	precise	**primo**	(in meal) the
preferire*	to prefer		first (pasta)
preferito/a	favourite		course

principale principal
privato/a private
probabile probable
probabilmente probably
problema problem
  (m.; pl. **-i**)
prodotto product, produce
produrre to produce
  (pp. **prodotto**)
professionale professional
professore teacher
    (secondary
    school or
    university)
professoressa (female) teacher
profumo perfume, scent
progetto project, plan
promettere to promise
  (pp. **promesso**)
pronto hello (answering
    the telephone)
pronto/a ready
pronto soccorso accident and
    emergency
    (hospital),
    first aid
pronunciare to pronounce
proporre to propose
proprietario/a owner
proprio (adv.) really, right,
    precisely
proprio/a own
prosciutto ham
prosciutto cotto cooked ham
prosciutto crudo cured ham,
    Parma ham
proseguire to continue
prospero/a prosperous
prossimo/a next
provare to try
proverbio proverb
provincia province

provvedere to see to, to take
    care of, make
    provision for
prugna plum
pubblicità advertising,
    publicity
pubblico/a public
pulire* to clean
pulito/a clean
pullman (m.) motor coach
punto point
può darsi maybe, perhaps
pure by all means,
    also; even,
    yet
purtroppo unfortunately

Q

qua here
quadrato/a squared
qualche cosa, something
  qualcosa
qualche some
qualcuno/a someone
quale which
qualsiasi any (it doesn't
    matter which)
qualunque any (it doesn't
    matter which)
quando when
quanto/a how much,
    how many
quartiere (m.) district
quarto/a fourth
quarto quarter
quasi almost
quattro four
quello/a that, that one
questione (f.) question
questo/a this
qui here

quinto/a	fifth
quotidiano/a	daily

R

raccontare	to tell, relate
racconto	story
radio (f.)	radio
radiografia	X-ray
radiolina	little, portable radio
rafforzare	to strengthen
raffreddore (m.)	cold
ragazza	girl, girlfriend
ragazzo	boy, boyfriend
raggiungere (pp. **raggiunto**)	to reach, to join
ragione (f.)	reason
avere ragione	to be right
rallentare	to slow down, to reduce speed
rapidamente	fast, quickly
rapido	express, fast train
rapido/a	fast
raramente	rarely
re (m.)	king
reale	royal
realtà	reality
in realtà	in fact
recente	recent
reddito pro capite	per capita income
regalo	present
regione (f.)	region
regolare	regular
regolarità	regularity
regolarmente	regularly
relativamente	relatively
religioso/a	religious
rendersi conto	to realize
rene (m.)	kidney

residenza	residence
residenziale	residential
resistere	to resist
respirare	to breathe
responsabile	responsible
restante (m.)	remainder
restare	to remain
restauro	restoration
resti (m. pl.)	remains
restituire*	to give back
resto	remainder
riaprire	to reopen
ricchezza	wealth
ricco/a	rich
ricetta	recipe; prescription
ricevere	receive
ricevuta	receipt
richiamare	call back, call again
richiedere (pp. **richiesto**)	to request
richiesta	request
ricordare	to remember, recall
ricoverare	to admit to hospital
ridere (pp. **riso**)	to laugh
ridurre (pp. **ridotto**)	to reduce
riempire	to fill
riforma	reform
rilassarsi	to relax
rimandare	to send back
rimanere (pp. **rimasto**)	to remain
rincorrere	to run around looking for
ringraziare	to thank
riparare	to repair
riparazione (f.)	repair
riposante	restful

riposarsi	to rest
ripostiglio	boxroom, lumber-room
riprendersi (pp. **ripreso**)	to recover
risaia	rice field, paddy field
rischio	risk
rischioso/a	risky
riso	rice
risolvere (pp. **risolto**)	to resolve
Risorgimento	revival, Risorgimento
risparmiare	to save
risparmio	saving, thrift
rispondere (pp. **risposto**)	to answer
risposta	answer
ristorante (m.)	restaurant
ristoratore/trice	restorative
ritardo	lateness, delay
ritirare	to withdraw; to collect
ritorno	return
ritrovarsi	to meet
riunione (f.)	meeting
riuscire	to succeed
riva	shore, bank
rivedere	to see again
rivelare	to reveal
rivista	magazine
robot (m.)	robot
robotizzato/a	robotized, automated
romanico/a	romanesque
romano/a	Roman
romantico/a	romantic
rosa (inv.)	pink
rosmarino	rosemary
rosso/a	red
rudere (m.)	ruin
rumore (m.)	noise
rumoroso/a	noisy
rurale	rural
russo/a	Russian

S

sabato	Saturday
sacrificio	sacrifice
sala	hall, room
sala da ballo	dance hall
sala d'attesa	waiting room
sala operatoria	operating theatre
salario	salary
salato/a	salty, salted
saldatura	welding
sale (m.)	salt
saletta	small room
salire	to go up, to get on/into (vehicle)
salmone (m.)	salmon
salone (m.)	hall, large room
saltare	to jump
salutare	to say hello to, to greet
salute (f.)	health
saluto	greeting
distinti saluti	yours faithfully
salvia	sage
sandalo	sandal
sangue (m.)	blood
sanitario/a	related to health
sano/a	healthy
santo (**san, sant'**)	saint
sapere	to know
saporito/a	tasty
Sardegna	Sardinia

sardina	sardine	**scultura**	sculpture
sbagliare	to make a mistake	**scuola**	school
		scuro/a	dark
sbarrato	blocked, barricaded	**scusare**	to excuse
		scusarsi	to excuse oneself, to apologize
scala	staircase		
scaloppina	escalope		
scappare	to dash (away), to escape, to run away	**sdraiarsi**	to lie down
		se	if
		secolo	century
scarpa	shoe	**secondo**	second (in a meal) the main (fish/meat) course
scegliere (pp. **scelto**)	to choose		
scelta	choice		
scemo/a	silly	**secondo/a**	second
scendere (pp. **sceso**)	to go down, to come down, to get off, out of (vehicle)	**secondo me, te, lui ecc.**	according to me, you, him etc.
		sedersi	to sit
		segnalare	to point out, to make known
scheda	(index) card		
schiena	back	**segretario/a**	secretary
sci (m.)	skiing, ski	**segreteria telefonica**	telephone answering machine
sciare	to ski		
sciatore, sciatrice	skier		
		seguire	to follow
sciroppo	syrup, linctus	**sei**	six
scolare	to strain, drain	**semaforo**	traffic light
scontato/a	discounted, with a discount	**sembrare**	to seem
		seminterrato	basement, semi-basement
sconto	discount		
scontrino	till receipt, check	**semplice**	simple
		semplicemente	simply
scoperta	discovery	**semplificato**	simplified
scopo	aim	**sempre**	always
scoprire (pp. **scoperto**)	to discover, uncover	**sempre dritto**	straight on
		sensato	sensible
scorso/a	last	**sensibile**	sensitive
Scozia	Scotland	**senso**	sense, feeling, meaning
scozzese	Scottish		
scrittore, -ttrice	writer	**sentimentale**	sentimental, related to the feelings
scrivere (pp. **scritto**)	to write		

sentire	to feel, to hear, to listen	**signora**	Mrs, madam, lady
senza	without	**signore**	Mr, sir, gentleman, man
senz'altro	of course, without fail		
separare	to separate	**signorina**	Miss, young lady
sera	evening		
serata	evening (see Unit 14)	**silenzio**	silence
		simile	similar
sereno/a	cloudless, clear	**simpatico/a**	likeable, nice
serietà	seriousness, (for a shopkeeper, trustworthiness)	**sindacato**	trade union
		sindaco	mayor
		singolo/a	single
serie (f.) (pl. **le serie**)	division	**sinistra**	left
		sintomo	symptom
servire	to serve	**sistema** (m.; pl. **-i**)	system
servizio	service		
doppi servizi	two bathrooms	**smarrire***	to mislay, lose
servizio sanitario	health service	**smettere**	to stop
sesto/a	sixth	**soccorso**	help, aid, assistance
seta	silk		
sete (f.)	thirst	**sociale**	social
sette	seven	**società**	society, company
settembre (m.)	September	**socio**	member
settentrionale	northern	**soggiorno**	living room
settimana	week	**sogliola**	sole (fish)
settimo/a	seventh	**sognare**	to dream
settore (m.)	sector	**sogno**	dream
sgabello	stool	**neanche per sogno**	never in 1,000 years
si	(indef. pr.) one, people, they; (refl. pr.) himself, herself, themselves		
		soldi (m. pl.)	money
		sole (m.)	sun
		solito/a	usual
		di solito	usually
		solo (adv.)	only
sì	yes	**solo/a** (adj.)	alone, single, only one
siccome	since, for the reason that		
		soltanto (adv.)	only
Sicilia	Sicily	**soluzione** (f.)	solution
siciliano/a	Sicilian	**sondaggio**	sounding, survey, opinion poll
sicuro/a	safe, certain, sure, secure		
		sonno	sleep

sopra	above	**spettacolare**	spectacular
soprattutto	especially, above all	**spettacolo**	show
		spiaggia	beach
sorella	sister	**spiegare**	to explain
sorprendente	surprising	**spinaci** (m. pl.)	spinach
sorprendere	to surprise	**spirito**	spirit
(pp. **sorpreso**)		**spogliatoio**	changing room
sorridere	to smile		
sosta	pause, stop	**sporco/a**	dirty
sostituire*	to substitute, to put something in place of	**sport** (m.)	sport
		sportivo/a	sporting, fond of sports
sotto	under	**sposare**	to marry
sottoporre	to submit	**sposarsi**	to get married
(pp. **sottoposto**)		**sposato/a**	married
sottosviluppato/a	underdeveloped	**spostare**	to move, displace
spaghetti (m. pl.)	spaghetti		
Spagna	Spain	**spremuta**	freshly squeezed citrus fruit
spagnolo/a	Spanish		
spago	string	**spumante** (m.)	sparkling (of wine), champagne-type
spalla	shoulder		
spasso	recreation		
andare a spasso	to go for a walk		
		spuntino	snack
spazio	space	**squadra**	team
spazioso/a	spacious	**stabile**	stable (adj.)
spazzare	to sweep	**stadio**	stadium
speciale	special	**stagione** (f.)	season
specifico/a	specific	**stamattina**	this morning
spedire*	to send	**(questa mattina)**	
spendere	to spend		
(pp. **speso**)		**stampante** (f.)	printer (machine for printing)
speranza	hope		
sperare	to hope	**stanco/a**	tired
spesa	expense, shopping	**stanotte**	tonight, this
		(questa notte)	night, last night
fare la spesa	to go shopping		
spesso	often	**stanza**	room
spettabile	Messrs (formal way of addressing firm in letters)	**stare**	to stay, to remain; + infinitive to be about to

stasera (questa sera)	this evening	**sud** (m.)	south
stato	state	**Sud Africa**	South Africa
Stati Uniti (m. pl.)	United States	**sudafricano/a**	South African
		suggerimento	suggestion
stavolta (questa volta)	this time	**suggerire***	to suggest
		sugo	gravy, sauce, juice
stazione (f.)	station		
stella	star	**suo/a**	his, her, your
stesso/a	same	**suocero/a**	father-/mother-in-law
stile (m.)	style		
stimolante	stimulating	**suonare**	to play (a musical instrument); to ring
stimolare	to stimulate		
stivale (m.)	boot		
stomaco	stomach		
storia	history	**superficie** (f.)	surface
storico/a	historical	**supermercato**	supermarket
strada	street, road	**superscontato**	with a big discount
stradale	related to the roads		
		supplemento	supplement
incidente stradale	road accident	**surgelato/a**	(deep) frozen
		susina	plum
stradina	little street, lane	**sveglia**	alarm clock
		svegliarsi	to wake up
straniero/a	foreigner	**sviluppo**	development
strano/a	strange	**Svizzera**	Switzerland
stretto/a	narrow	**svizzero/a**	Swiss
stringere (pp. **stretto**)	to squeeze, take in (clothing)		
		T	
studente (m.)	student		
studentessa	female student	**tabaccaio/a**	tobacconist
studiare	to study	**tacchino**	turkey
studio (pl. **gli studî**)	study	**tagliatelle** (f. pl.)	pasta in flat ribbons
		taglio	cut
stufato	stew	**tailleur** (m.)	(woman's) suit
su	on, upon, up	**tanto/a**	so much, (pl.) so many, (+ adj.) so
subito	immediately, suddenly		
succedere (pp. **successo**)	to happen	**tardare**	to be late
		tardi	late
successo	success	**tariffa**	tariff, fare
succo	juice	**tartufo**	truffle

Italian	English	Italian	English
tasca	pocket	**testa**	head
tascabile	pocket (adj.)	**tifoso/a**	fan (sport)
tassa	tax	**tilt (in tilt)**	upside down, in confusion
tasso	rate, level		
tastiera	keyboard	**timo**	thyme
tavernetta	party room (in basement of modern house)	**tinello**	small dining room; kitchen-diner; scullery
tavola, tavolo	table	**tipico/a**	typical
tavola calda	snack bar	**toast** (m.)	toasted sandwich
tavolino	small table	**togliere**	to remove
taxi (also: **tassì**)	taxi	(pp. **tolto**)	
tè/the (m.)	tea	**tomba**	tomb
teatro	theatre	**tornare**	to return, to come back
tecnico	technician		
tecnico/a	technical	**torre** (f.)	tower
tedesco/a	German	**torta**	cake
telefonare	to telephone	**tortellini** (m. pl.)	pasta with meat stuffing
telefonata	telephone call		
telefonicamente	by telephone	**torto, avere**	to be wrong
telefonino	mobile telephone	**tra**	between, among
		traduzione (f.)	translation
telefono	telephone	**traffico**	traffic
teleselezione (f.)	direct dialling (long distance)	**tram** (m.)	tram
		tramonto	sunset
televisione (f.)	television	**tranquillo/a**	quiet
temperatura	temperature	**transizione** (f.)	transition
tempestiva-mente	in good time	**trappola**	trap
		traslocare	to move house
tempio	temple	**trattoria**	restaurant
tempo	time, weather	**travellers cheque** (m. inv.)	travellers' cheque
tempo libero	free, spare time		
temporale (m.)	storm		
tenere	to hold, to keep	**tre**	three
tennis (m.)	tennis	**treno**	train
terra	earth, land, ground	**triste**	sad
		troppo	too
terrazzo	terrace, balcony	**trota**	trout
terreno	land, ground	**trovare**	to find
territorio	territory	**andare a trovare**	to go and see (a person)
terzo/a	third		
tessuto	fabric, cloth	**trovarsi**	to be situated

tu	you (fam.)		**V**	
tuo/a	your		**va bene**	OK, good,
tuono	thunder			that's fine
turismo	tourism		**vacanza**	holiday
turista (m. or f.)	tourist		**valido/a**	valid
turistico/a	touristic		**valigia**	suitcase
tutto/a	all		**valle** (f.)	valley
TV, tivù (f.)	TV		**valuta**	currency
			vantaggio	advantage
U			**variare**	to vary
			vario/a	various
uccidere	to kill		**vasca (da bagno)**	bathtub
(pp. **ucciso**)			**vecchio/a**	old
ufficio	office		**vedere**	to see
ufficio postale	post office		(pp. **visto**	
ultimo/a	last (in a series)		or **veduto**)	
umano/a	human		**veicolo**	vehicle
umidità	damp, humidity		**vela**	sail, sailing
umido/a	damp, wet		**veloce**	fast
un, un', uno,	a, an, one		**velocemente**	rapidly
una			**vena**	vein
unico/a	unique, only		**vendere**	to sell
unificazione (f.)	unification		**vendita**	sale
università	university		**venditore, -trice**	seller
universitario/a	university		**venerdì** (m.)	Friday
uomo	man		**venire**	to come
(pl. **uomini**)			(pp. **venuto**)	
uomo d'affari	businessman		**venire fuori**	to come out
uovo (m.; pl.	egg		**vento**	wind
le uova f.)			**veramente**	actually, truly,
urbano/a	urban			really
vigile urbano	town		**verbo**	verb
	policeman		**verde**	green
urgenza	emergency		**verdura**	(green)
d'urgenza	urgently, as an			vegetable
	emergency		**verificare**	to check
usare	to use		**vero/a**	true
uscire	to go out		**versare**	to remit, to pay
uscita	exit			in, to pay
utile	useful			(a cheque)
uva	grapes		**verso**	towards; at
uva passa	raisins			about

vestiario   clothing,
                    wardrobe
vestirsi   to get dressed,
                    to dress
vestito   clothing, dress
via   street
via (adv.)   away with . . . ,
                    be off! go
                    away!
via aerea   by air mail
viaggiare   to travel
viaggiatore,   traveller
 -trice
viaggio   travel, journey
viale   avenue
vicino   near, close
 (adj. and adv.)
vicino/a (n.)   neighbour
vigile (urbano) policeman
vigile del fuoco fireman
vigore (m.)   vigour
 in vigore   in force
villaggio   village
vincere   to win
 (pp. **vinto**)
vino   wine
viola   violet
visione (f.)   vision
visita   visit, medical
                    examination
visitare   to visit (place);
                    to examine
                    (patient)
viso   face
vita   life

vitello   veal
vivace   lively
vivere   to live
 (pp. **vissuto**)
vivo/a   alive
vocabolario   vocabulary
voce (f.)   voice
voi   you (pl.)
volante   driving wheel
volare   to fly
volentieri   willingly, with
                    pleasure
volere   to want
volere bene   to be fond of,
 a qualcuno   love, someone
volere dire   to mean
volo   flight
volta   time, occasion
vostro/a   your
vulcanico/a   volcanic
vulcano   volcano
vuoto/a   empty

Z

zero   zero
zia   aunt
zio   uncle
zitto/a   quiet, silent
 sta' zitto   be quiet!
zona   zone, area
zucchero   sugar
zucchino   zucchino
                    baby marrow,
zuppiera   soup tureen

English–Italian glossary

This list is selective. Words included in the 'Vocabularies' in the various units are not usually given below. (The list of topics on p. 348 will help you find the appropriate 'Vocabularies'.) Many words that are similar in Italian will be located easily in the Italian–English glossary. The gender of nouns not ending in -o or -a has been included. The feminine of adjectives is given when it is different from the masculine.

A

a, an	un, una
a lot	parecchio, molto
above	sopra
to accept	accettare
accident	incidente (m.)
according to	secondo
across	attraverso
advance	anticipo
advice	consiglio
aeroplane	aereo
after	dopo
afternoon	pomeriggio
again	ancora, di nuovo
against	contro
age	età
ago	fa
agreement	accordo
airport	aeroporto
all	tutto/a
to allow	permettere
almost	quasi
alone	solo/a
along	lungo/a
already	già
also	anche
although	benchè
among	fra, tra
amusement	divertimento
amusing	divertente
answer	risposta
to answer	rispondere
any (it doesn't matter which)	qualsiasi
apartment, flat	appartamento
to apologize	scusare
appointment	appuntamento
arrival	arrivo
art gallery	museo, galleria d'arte
at	a
at least	almeno
to attend (school)	frequentare
average	medio/a

B

bad	cattivo/a
badly	male

bag	**borsa**	by ('by Sunday')	**entro**
bank	**banca**	by	**da, per**
to be	**essere**		
to be able to	**potere**	**C**	
to be bored	**annoiarsi**		
to be born	**nascere**	to call	**chiamare**
to be called	**chiamarsi**	car	**macchina, auto (-mobile)** (f.)
to be fond of	**volere bene a**		
beautiful	**bello/a**	car park	**parcheggio**
because	**perché**	cash desk	**cassa**
to become	**diventare**	cathedral	**duomo, cattedrale** (f.)
before	**prima (di)**		
to begin	**cominciare**	cellar	**cantina**
beginning	**inizio**	centre	**centro**
behind	**dietro (a/di)**	century	**secolo**
to believe	**credere**	to change	**cambiare**
besides	**inoltre**	change (after paying)	**resto**
better (adv.)	**meglio**		
better (adj.)	**migliore**	chemist's shop	**farmacia**
between	**fra, tra**	cheque	**assegno**
beyond	**oltre**	child	**bambino/a**
big	**grande, grosso/a**	to choose	**scegliere**
		city	**città**
bigger	**maggiore**	to clean	**pulire**
biggest	**massimo/a, più grande**	clean	**pulito/a**
		climate	**clima** (m.)
bill	**conto**	coin	**moneta**
birthday	**compleanno**	cold (adj.)	**freddo/a**
block of flats	**palazzo**	cold (n.)	**raffreddore** (m.)
book	**libro**	colour	**colore** (m.)
to book	**prenotare**	to come	**venire**
booking	**prenotazione** (f.)	comfortable	**comodo/a**
boy	**ragazzo**	comfortable, to make oneself	**accomodarsi**
brave	**coraggioso/a**		
bread	**pane** (m.)	common	**comune**
bread roll	**panino**	consulate	**consolato**
breakfast	**(prima) colazione** (f.)	to continue	**continuare**
		cooking	**cucina**
bus	**autobus** (m.)	cool	**fresco/a**
business	**affari** (pl.)	corner	**angolo**
but	**ma**	correct	**giusto/a**
to buy	**comprare**	to cost	**costare**

cotton	**cotone** (m.)
country	**paese** (m.)
currency	**valuta**
current	**attuale**

D

daily	**quotidiano/a**
damp	**umido/a**
date	**data**
day	**giorno, giornata**
dear	**caro/a**
to decide	**decidere**
to decrease	**diminuire**
to deliver	**consegnare**
to depart	**partire**
departure	**partenza**
dialling code	**prefisso**
to die	**morire**
difference	**differenza**
different	**diverso/a, differente**
difficult	**difficile**
directory	**elenco**
dirty	**sporco/a**
discount	**sconto**
to displease	**dispiacere**
to do	**fare**
doctor	**dottore, -essa; medico**
door	**porta**
double	**doppio/a**
down	**giù**
to drive	**guidare**
during	**durante**

E

each	**ogni**
early	**presto, in anticipo**
earth	**terra**

egg	**uovo** (m.; pl. **uova**, f.)
electricity	**elettricità, luce** (f.)
embassy	**ambasciata**
engaged (not free)	**occupato/a**
to enjoy oneself	**divertirsi**
entrance	**entrata**
envelope	**busta**
environment	**ambiente** (m.)
et cetera, etc.	**eccetera, ecc.**
even	**pure**
evening	**sera**
every	**ogni**
everyone	**ognuno, tutti**
everywhere	**dappertutto**
example	**esempio**
excellent	**ottimo/a**
to excuse	**scusare**
exit	**uscita**
expense	**spesa**
expensive	**caro/a**
to explain	**spiegare**

F

factory	**fabbrica**
fairly	**abbastanza**
to fall	**cadere**
family	**famiglia**
far	**lontano**
farmer	**contadino**
fast	**rapido/a, veloce**
field	**campo**
firm	**ditta**
first	**primo/a**
fish	**pesce** (m.)
flat (n.)	**appartamento**
flight	**volo**
follow	**seguire**
football	**calcio**

for	**per**	hand	**mano** (f.)
foreigner	**straniero/a**	happy	**felice, contento/a**
free	**libero/a**	to have	**avere**
French	**francese**	he	**lui**
fresh	**fresco/a**	to heal	**guarire**
friend	**amico/a**	health	**salute**
from	**da, di**	healthy	**sano/a**
fruit	**frutta**	heavy	**pesante**
full	**pieno**	hello (on telephone)	**pronto**

G

garden	**giardino**	to help	**aiutare**
generally	**in genere, generalmente**	help	**aiuto**
		here	**qua, qui**
to get by	**cavarsela**	here is, are	**ecco**
to get in/on (vehicle)	**salire su**	high	**alto/a**
		hill	**collina**
to get off/out of (vehicle)	**scendere da**	history	**storia**
		to hold	**tenere**
to get up	**alzarsi**	holiday	**vacanza**
girl	**ragazza**	hospital	**ospedale** (m.)
to give	**dare**	hot	**caldo/a**
to go	**andare**	hotel	**albergo**
to go down	**scendere**	hour	**ora**
to go out	**uscire**	house	**casa**
to go up	**salire**	how?	**come?**
gold	**oro**	how many?	**quanti?**
good wishes	**auguri**	how much?	**quanto?**
good heavens!	**accidenti!**	however	**comunque, però**
goodbye	**arrivederci, arrivederLa**	hunger	**fame (la)**

I

government	**governo**		
to greet	**salutare**	ice cream	**gelato**
greeting	**saluto**	if	**se**
to grow	**crescere**	illness	**malattia**
guide	**guida** (f.) (even if male)	immediately	**subito**
		impossible	**impossibile**
guidebook	**guida** (f.)	in	**a, in**
		in fact	**in effetti, in realtà**

H

half	**metà, mezzo**	in front of	**davanti a**
ham	**prosciutto**	in short	**insomma**

indeed	**infatti**
to injure	**ferire**
inside	**dentro**
instead	**invece**
interesting	**interessante**
to introduce	**presentare**

K

to kill	**uccidere**
kind	**gentile**
kitchen	**cucina**
to know	**sapere** (fact), **conoscere** (person/place)

L

language	**lingua**
last (most recent)	**scorso/a**
last (in series)	**ultimo/a**
lateness	**ritardo**
lavatory	**gabinetto, toilette** (f.)
to learn	**imparare**
leather	**pelle** (f.)
left	**sinistro/a**
less	**meno**
letter	**lettera**
lift	**ascensore** (m.)
light (n.)	**luce** (f.)
light (adj.)	**leggero/a**
like	**come**
to like	**piacere a** (see Units 2, 3 8)
to listen	**ascoltare**
little bit	**un poco, un po'**
to live	**abitare, vivere**
long	**lungo/a**
to look at	**guardare**
to look for	**cercare**

to lose	**perdere**
to love	**amare**
lovely	**bello/a**
luckily	**meno male**
lucky	**fortunato/a**
lunch	**pranzo**

M

magazine	**rivista**
to make	**fare**
to make a mistake	**sbagliare**
man	**uomo** (pl. **uomini**)
many	**molti**
market	**mercato**
married	**sposato/a**
match (sport)	**partita**
to matter	**importare**
to mean	**volere dire**
meanwhile	**intanto**
meat	**carne** (f.)
mild	**mite**
minute	**minuto**
Miss	**signorina**
money	**denaro** (sing.), **soldi** (pl.)
month	**mese**
more	**più**
motorway	**autostrada**
mountain	**montagna**
mouth	**bocca**
Mr	**signor(e)**
Mrs	**signora**
much	**molto/a**
museum	**museo**

N

| name | **nome** (m.) |
| near | **vicino/a** |

to need	**avere bisogno di**	
never	**mai**	
never mind!	**pazienza!**	
new	**nuovo/a**	
news	**notizia**	
newspaper	**giornale** (m.)	
next	**poi**	
next (in order)	**prossimo/a**	
next to	**accanto a**	
night	**notte** (f.)	
no	**no**	
no one	**nessuno/a**	
noise	**rumore** (m.)	
not at all	**mica**	
not even	**neanche,**	
	nemmeno,	
	neppure	
nothing	**niente**, **nulla**	
to notice	**notare**	
now	**adesso, ora**	
number	**numero**	

O

of	**di**
office	**ufficio**
often	**spesso**
old	**vecchio/a**
on	**su**
on the contrary	**anzi**
on the other hand	**invece**
only	**solo**
open	**aperto/a**
to open	**aprire**
opposite	**di fronte a**
to order	**ordinare**
other	**altro/a**
our	**nostro/a**
outside	**fuori**
own	**proprio/a**
to own	**possedere**

P

pain	**dolore** (m.)
pair	**paio** (m.; pl. **paia**, f.)
paper	**carta**
passport	**passaporto**
to pay	**pagare**
peace	**pace** (f.)
pen	**penna**
people	**gente** (f. sing.)
pepper	**pepe** (m.)
perhaps	**forse, può darsi, magari**
piece	**pezzo**
place	**posto, luogo**
plan	**pianta, progetto**
platform	**binario** (lit. track)
to play	**giocare**
to play (musical instrument)	**suonare**
please	**per favore, per piacere, per cortesia**
pleased	**contento/a**
poor	**povero/a**
possible	**possibile**
postcard	**cartolina**
to prefer	**preferire**
price	**prezzo**
project	**progetto**
to put	**mettere**

Q

question	**domanda**

R

rain	**pioggia**
to rain	**piovere**
rather	**piuttosto**

to read	**leggere**	skin	**pelle** (f.)
ready	**pronto/a**	to sleep	**dormire**
to realize	**rendersi conto di**	slow	**lento/a**
really	**davvero, proprio**	slowly	**piano,**
reason	**motivo, ragione**		**lentamente**
	(f.)	small	**piccolo/a**
receipt	**ricevuta**	to smoke	**fumare**
to receive	**ricevere**	so	**così, dunque**
region	**regione** (f.)	so many	**tanti**
to remain	**rimanere**	so much	**tanto/a**
to rest	**riposarsi**	so that	**perché**
restaurant	**ristorante** (m.)		(+ subjunctive)
to return	**tornare**	softly	**piano**
rich	**ricco/a**	some	**alcuni/e** (with
right (not left)	**destro/a**		pl.); **qualche**
right (*v.* duty)	**diritto**		(with sing.)
room	**stanza**	someone	**qualcuno/a**
		something	**qualche cosa,**

S

			qualcosa
same	**stesso/a**	space	**posto, spazio**
to say	**dire**	to speak	**parlare**
scarcely	**appena**	square	**piazza**; (adj.)
schedule	**orario**		**quadrato/a**
sea	**mare** (m.)	stamp	**francobollo**
to see	**vedere**	state	**stato**
to seem	**sembrare, parere**	station	**stazione** (f.)
to sell	**vendere**	still (not moving)	**fermo/a**
several	**parecchi**	still (adv.)	**ancora**
she	**lei**	stop (bus-)	**fermata**
shopping, to	**fare la spesa**	to stop	**fermare**
do the		straight	**dritto/a**
short	**breve, corto/a**	strange	**strano/a**
to show	**mostrare**	street	**strada, via**
silk	**seta**	sun	**sole** (m.)
similar	**simile**	supermarket	**supermercato**
since (reason)	**siccome, poichè**	supper	**cena**
since (time)	**da**	sweet (adj.)	**dolce**
sister	**sorella**		
to sit down	**accomodarsi,**		
	sedersi		

T

size	**misura**	to take	**prendere**
skilful	**bravo/a**	to take care of	**curare**

tall	**alto/a**	to try	**provare**
telephone	**telefono**	to turn	**girare**
to thank	**ringraziare**		
thank you	**grazie**	**U**	
that	**quello/a, ciò**		
that is, i.e.	**cioè**	ugly	**brutto/a**
theft	**furto**	under	**sotto**
then	**allora, poi**	to understand	**capire**
there	**là, lì**	unemployment	**disoccupazione**
therefore	**perciò**		(f.)
thing	**cosa**	unfortunately	**purtroppo**
this	**questo/a**	unhappy	**infelice,**
this evening	**stasera**		**scontento/a**
this morning	**stamattina**	up	**su**
through	**attraverso,**	to use	**usare**
	per	used to	**abituato/a a**
thus	**così**	useful	**utile**
ticket	**biglietto**	usual	**solito/a**
time	**ora** (by clock),		
	tempo, volta	**V**	
	(occasion)		
timetable	**orario**	very	**molto**
tired	**stanco/a**	village	**paese** (m.)
to	**a**		
today	**oggi**	**W**	
together	**insieme**		
tomorrow	**domani**	to wait for	**aspettare**
tongue	**lingua**	to wake up	**svegliarsi**
tonight	**stanotte**	walk	**passeggiata**
too	**troppo**	to walk	**camminare**
towards	**verso**	to want	**volere,**
town	**città**		**desiderare**
town hall	**municipio,**	war	**guerra**
	palazzo	to wash (oneself)	**lavarsi**
	comunale	washing	**lavatrice** (f.)
traffic light	**semaforo**	machine	
train	**treno**	water	**acqua**
travel	**viaggiare**	weak	**debole**
tree	**albero**	week	**settimana**
trip	**gita,**	to weep	**piangere**
	escursione (f.)	well (adv.)	**bene**
true	**vero/a**	what?	**che cosa?**

when?	**quando?**	to work (opposite: play)	**lavorare**
where?	**dove?**		
while	**mentre**		
who?	**chi?**	worker	**operaio**
why?	**perché?**	world	**mondo**
to win	**vincere**	worse	**peggiore**
wine	**vino**	to write	**scrivere**
wish	**augurio**		
with	**con**	**Y**	
with pleasure	**volentieri**		
woman	**donna**	year	**anno**
wool	**lana**	yesterday	**ieri**
word	**parola**	you (formal)	**Lei**
work	**lavoro**	you (fam.)	**tu**
to work (to function)	**funzionare**	young	**giovane**
		your	**vostro, tuo, Suo**

Index

The numbers given against each entry refer to the unit(s) where the relevant information is given.

Topics